How Many Miles to Babylon?

Filippo Pigafetta's map of Africa

How Many Miles to Babylon?

Travels and Adventures to Egypt and Beyond,
1300 to 1640

ANNE WOLFF

LIVERPOOL UNIVERSITY PRESS

First published 2003 by
Liverpool University Press
4 Cambridge Street
Liverpool L69 7ZU

British Library Cataloguing-in-Publication data
A British Library CIP record is available

ISBN 0-85323-658-5 cased
0-85323-668-2 limp

Typeset by XL Publishing Services, Tiverton
Printed and bound in the European Union by
Biddles Ltd, Guildford and King's Lynn

For Edwin

How many miles to Babylon?
Threescore miles and ten.
Can I get there by candle-light?
Yes, and back again.
If your heels are nimble and light,
You may get there by candle-light.
Songs for the Nursery (1805)

Contents

Preface

I think it is fair to say that one is always drawn to the country of one's birth and I am no exception. My father was a cotton merchant who operated in the markets of Cairo and Alexandria, selling cotton to the manufacturers of cloth in Manchester after World War I. Thus he followed in the footsteps of earlier traders who bought goods from Egypt to satisfy the European markets. Unlike many of his contemporaries, he learnt to speak and write Arabic during the five years he lived there.

Inspiration for *How Many Miles to Babylon?* ('Babylon' being the medieval European Christians' name for Cairo) came first from reading the volumes of the *Voyages en Egypte* published by L'Institut Français Archéologie Orientale du Caire. I would like to thank the director for his kind permission in allowing me to quote from these sixteenth-century chronicles. I would also like to thank the editors of the Studium Biblicanum Franciscanum in Jerusalem for allowing me to quote from their publications of the writings of the early Franciscan friars in Palestine, Egypt and beyond. My thanks go to the librarians of the Map Room at the Cambridge University Library, who undertook valuable research on my behalf, and to Helen Tookey, who with Andrew Kirk oversaw the editing of the text at Liverpool University Press. Paul and Janet Starkey of Durham University gave up their time to advise on Arabic spelling and provided helpful suggestions.

Above all, I owe a great debt to the late Professor John Morrison, formerly fellow of Trinity College, Cambridge and first President of Wolfson College, Cambridge, who read the manuscript chapter by chapter and sustained me with his encouragement.

Permissions

The publishers are grateful to the Syndics of the University of Cambridge for permission to reproduce illustrations from the *Atlas Historique de la Ville et des Ports d'Alexandrie* on page 62 and *Cairus Civitates Orbis Terrarum* on page 113; to Harper Collins Publishers for permission to reproduce a map from the *Times Atlas of World History* on page 16; and to La Casa Editrice Bonechi, Florence, for permission to reproduce two illustrations from David Roberts, *A Journey into Egypt* on pages 258 and 265. Every effort has been made to trace copyright holders and the publishers would be grateful to be informed of any errors or omissions.

List of Illustrations

Frontispiece
Filippo Pigafetta's map of Africa (*Description of Aegypt from Cair Downwards*, London, John Wolfe, 1597).

Chapter 6. Venetian Diplomacy and the Arrival of the Ottomans

Chapter 7. Exploring the Pyramids and Mummy Fields

Chapter 8. Pilgrims to the Monastery of St Catherine

List of Abbreviations

Glossary

amir: military commander, or more generally a military officer

bailo (Venetian *baily*): Venetian ambassador to Turkey

braccio: variable measure, average 66cm. From Italian for 'arm'; in this sense plural *braccia*, in some other senses plural *bracci* is used

bastinado: punishment by beating on the soles of the feet

bottes: meaning 'barrels', term formerly used for measuring ships' loads

hajj: annual Muslim pilgrimage to Mecca

ka'ba: venerated stone cuboid structure at the centre of the great mosque of Mecca

kiswa: veil of the outer covering of the *ka'ba*

madrasa (or *madrassa*): school of higher Islamic learning

mahmal: empty litter sent with the annual pilgrimage caravan to Mecca from Egypt

minbar: stepped rostrum in a mosque

qadi: Islamic judge

sakieh (or *sakkieh*): waterwheel used in irrigation

sanjac: ruler of a province under an Ottoman pasha

speos temple: cave temple

ushabti (or *shabti*) *figure*: funerary figurine placed with the dead in an ancient Egyptian tomb

Introduction

Babylon of Egypt. A strange muddle of a name used by medieval pilgrims visiting the lands of the Bible. The notion that there was a 'Babylon' in Egypt where Nebuchadnezzar cast Shadrach, Meshach and Abednego into the fiery furnace (Daniel 3.20) was often repeated in accounts by early travellers from Europe. There have been various reasons put forward for this quaint belief. It seemed that since the days of the exile from Babylon (597–538 BC) Jews had lived by the Nile on the site of what is now Old Cairo. Furthermore, Strabo (*Geography* 17.1.36) spoke of 'Babylon' as being a military fortress, established before the Romans by refugees from ancient Babylon. So the association persisted. In any case, in the medieval mind, Egypt was always a place of wonders, so fanciful tales were swallowed by the credulous together with all the rest of the magic and conjecture.

Although stories of crusaders who fought in Palestine and Syria are well documented, those of Europeans in Egypt and the Near East after AD 1300 up to the beginning of the seventeenth century are little known. And yet from available chronicles of that period, an overall picture of the manners and customs of the Egyptians, descriptions of the countryside and accounts of the fabulous city of Cairo, there emerge scenes of astonishing variety. An image of the antique land of Egypt in late medieval and early Renaissance times gradually unfolds in these accounts, and with the emergence of concrete facts, Nebuchadnezzar's 'Babylon' in Egypt gradually disappears into the realm of folklore.

However, the art of telling stories, whether they be fact or fiction, is not an easy one. Homer, writing in the eighth century BC, painted on a large canvas. His works, known to humanists in Italy from early

in the fourteenth century, were subsequently disseminated throughout
Europe. He told of the ten-year Trojan War by focusing it entirely
through a few characters; and by letting his characters speak, and by
describing what they did, he presented a memorable story. Unlike some
modern historians, he resisted the temptation to lace his account with
subjective opinion, and allowed his characters to speak for themselves
in order to gain the maximum effect. In attempting to describe Egypt
and beyond, territory little known throughout Europe from the end of
the thirteenth to the beginning of the seventeenth centuries, Homer's
method has much to commend it. But the canvas in question is far
more extensive and contains infinitely more characters who described
their adventures over a 300-year span. From the early printed sources
it is often difficult to choose one traveller's tale from another. Some
are repetitive and prosaic, but others are lively and vivid, enabling the
audience to relate to the writers' hopes and fears when finding themselves in a strange country so far from home. In this book, I hope that
by taking the reader along the routes they travelled (not necessarily in
chronological order), a panoramic view of medieval and Renaissance
Egypt is unfolded.

Trade had always taken place between Muslims and Europeans
(particularly by Italian city states) during the Crusades, but the volume
increased substantially after the Mamluks finally expelled the
Christian armies from the coastal strip of Palestine, and the capture of
Acre in 1291, a port that had been the last refuge of the Crusader king-
doms. A prominent Venetian trader, Marino Sanudo (or Sanuto) called
Torsellus (also known as 'the elder') had visited Palestine during
1285–86 to gain experience with the family trading company, when
he was only about 15 or 16 years old. Later, Marino used his knowledge to promote the idea of imposing economic sanctions against the
sultan of Egypt. His work, published in three books accompanied by
ten maps, was entitled *Secreta fidelium crucis super Terrae Sanctae
recuperatione*. Then as now, maps and topographical descriptions that
could be used for military information were available for secret intel-
ligence. From 1305, the Popes had moved to Avignon and it was there
in 1321 that Marino presented his work for the delectation of John
XXII.

With the expansion of commerce, it followed that the main body of travellers to Egypt were the merchants who established depots in the Near East, one of the most important of which was at the port of Alexandria. Out of the several European states that had set up trading stations there by the fourteenth century, the most prominent were Genoa (which had gained the upper hand over the Pisans), Venice, the Catalans and the French. Although numbers of foreign residents varied yearly, by 1480 as many as 80 Venetians resided in the city, though in 1483 a Dominican monk, Felix Fabri from Ulm, considered the Genoese colony to be the most important. He visited their hostelry and admired its beauty and vast dimensions.

By the end of the fourteenth century, Venice had become immensely wealthy: the maritime republic owned 3300 ships and employed 36,000 seamen. The Venetian golden ducat issued in 1284–85 was accepted and even preferred everywhere in the Levant. The Genoese, the Venetians' long-standing enemies and competitors, were hampered by the quarrels that continually erupted between the predominant ruling families. And in 1380, after the fierce battle off the port of Chioggia in the Venetian lagoon, their fleet was defeated by the Venetians under the command of the intrepid Admiral Vettor Pisani, recently released from jail (due to popular demand) by the Venetian senate. After this reverse, Genoa slowly declined into second place. In 1424 the Genoese had 63 large boats of more than 1000 *bottes* to their credit, but in 1473 this had declined to only 23. Up to the middle of the fifteenth century, Genoa was prominent in the slave trade at the cosmopolitan town of Caffa on the Black Sea, until menaced by the Turks, after which their traders tended to use Chios as a centre of operations. At Caffa, Italian merchants bought Tartars, Circassians and Russians either as prisoners of war or from punitive expeditions, as well as children sold by their parents to the agents of Egyptian sultans. This human merchandise was marketed together with black fox and ermine furs, Tartar hats made of wool and leather, and consignments of wax and honey.

The resilient Venetian traders swiftly came to enjoy many advantages over other states operating in the Levant. Such advantages stemmed from the legislation emanating from an all-powerful senate with a consuming interest in the promotion of corporate trade and wealth. In addition, there was the provision of strong, state-owned fleets of galleys manufactured with great speed to a common pattern in the arsenal, though the Republic kept a monopoly on all the most profitable sea routes. Commerce was furthered by a network of trading stations that had been set up along the Adriatic. In addition, Venice had acquired some strategic Greek islands and ports, which had fallen into their lap after their brutal desecration of Constantinople in 1203 during the fourth Crusade led by the aged Doge, Enrico Dandolo. These former Greek possessions were colonised by rich Venetian families, often absentee landlords. Marco Sanudo (father of Marino Sanudo), who had followed Enrico Dandolo on the fourth Crusade, acquired the island of Naxos and assumed the rather pretentious title of 'Duke'. In the sixteenth century, however, such acquisitions were increasingly contested by the Turks,

The Serenissima decreed that all Venetian trading companies must keep most careful records of transactions, so that proper taxes could be levied to pay for increased state ownership. Although the system of double-entry book-keeping had been employed by Genoese bankers from as early as 1340, followed soon after by those of Florence, the Venetians were not far behind in this respect. In any case, their account books show that they used a variety of mercantile accounting practices. It is through the study of such records that historians can obtain first-hand information about the large volume and type of lucrative trade transacted by Venetian merchants operating in Egypt and Syria. Further light was shed by Florentine merchants who took care to keep *libri di ricordanze*, recording their business affairs.

At the meeting place of the cosmopolitan markets of the Venetian Rialto, traders could exchange news with their fellow citizens as well as with merchants from elsewhere in Europe. They had ready access to the association of German and other north European merchants across the bridge, who had taken up residence at the imposing Fondaco dei Tedeschi, while at the nearby Fondaco dei Turchi came merchants from the Ottoman Turks. Around the Rialto, warehouses bulged with luxuries from every part of the world amid a babble of foreign tongues. Shakespeare's merchant Antonio rightly observed of Venice that 'the trade and profit of this city / Consists of all nations'. Furthermore, Venetians could confidently transact their business and make deals with the assurance that the courts of Venice would enforce them. In Egypt they made their purchases of spices, potash, sugar (the rose and violet sugars of Alexandria were a special delicacy), Eastern silks, textiles, Chinese porcelain, and jewels (particularly pearls), as well as goods from other Levantine ports. Their subsequent onward shipments of such goods to northern markets were planned as peaceful operations to be undertaken in agreement with the terms of commercial treaties made by the Republic, which ensured that special measures were taken for the protection of merchandise overseas. At the commercial centres of Ghent, Arras and Cambrai and the markets of Bruges, buyers came readily from England and northern France. The Hanseatic league of merchants (headed by Lübeck) imported Eastern luxuries, among them expensive velvets, damasks and pearls for the affluent in northern cities. Bulky commodities such as soap and grain were cheaper if sent by sea.

With the importation of spices it followed that there was an enormous improvement in the preservation of medieval food. Not only were spices considered healthy and wholesome, but they were also used to camouflage the doubtful tastes of flagging meat and fish long past their 'sell-by dates'. In daily use in Italian kitchens was a sauce known as *savore sanguino*, rich and red, often bought ready prepared from apothecaries' shops, consisting of pounded raisins, cinnamon; sandal and sumach (now used only for tanning and dyeing). Other sauces included *peverata*, a mixture of meat, fish, pepper, cinnamon and nutmeg, and *camellina*, a white sauce consisting of a blend of sugar, cinnamon, cloves, bread and vinegar. In England the 'grete pie' or 'torta' was thought incomplete if brought steaming to table without its additions of spices, liberally applied. Comfits made of cinnamon, nutmeg, ginger, aniseed and gangingal were copied from Eastern customs and handed round to guests. (Ganginal or galinga was a bitter Chinese root obtained in Alexandria used for its heating properties.) In Florence the apothecaries, who enjoyed the same status as doctors, kept their medicinal cures and spices in majolica and pewter jars of great elegance, to entice the housewives into their premises, which gave off intriguing aromas of strange Eastern perfumes.

Compared to modern times communications between countries were slow, there being only a meagre postal service between European centres of trade; the time taken for letters varied depending on whether it was winter or summer. In 1440, for example, the mail between Venice and Bruges from March to June took on average between 20 and 29 days. Otherwise couriers between the great merchant houses were employed to carry small parcels and letters. Generally the roads were deplorable as the old Roman highways had deteriorated into gravel and dirt (though there was some improvement in the latter half of the fourteenth century). Merchants preferred to travel in convoys: it took about 70 beasts to carry the equivalent of the contents of a 70-ton mechanised truck. A mounted convoy could be expected to travel about 20–25 miles per day.

Despite the slowness of transport, mobility and the ability to adapt to fluid conditions became a major factor affecting the prosperity of wealthy Venetian patrician companies. When the opportunity arose, they could switch their capital swiftly at will, first into Western goods, then into the Levantine markets, depending on the political and commercial position at any propitious moment. The German cotton buyers from Ulm, Frankfurt and Augsburg, the cotton sellers of Syria and the purveyors of English wool were unable to adapt themselves as quickly as the Venetians, whose strategic geographical position was so much to their advantage. Business was also aided by terms laid down by the Senate concerning Venetian navigation, such that the great family partnerships and companies, as well as the smaller traders, enjoyed rights and privileges from state-regulated voyages. The normal arrangements were to despatch two armadas a year, consisting of the great oared and armed galleys to Alexandria and the Levant, one in spring and the second in the autumn. These were known as the *muda*, a term that embraced several meanings: sometimes it appertained to the actual fleet, sometimes to a specific time after which ships were forbidden to load and occasionally to a season's business. Merchants limited risk by means of insurance against storms, natural hazards and even piracy – in consequence, merchandise transported in the armed galleys of Venice attracted lower premiums. Of all the territories beyond the Adriatic, the countries ruled over by the Mamluks were the greatest markets for Venetian exports of Flemish and English woollens, saffron, brocade, satin and velvet, furs from Russia and the famed glass from Murano. Furthermore, in spite of the wars with the Turks in the sixteenth century, the prosecution of trade with the Ottoman Empire did not cease.

If the maritime power of Venice dominated the Eastern spice trade in the fourteenth and fifteenth centuries, the powerful Medici bankers in Florence were not slow in spreading their tentacles far and wide in efforts to seek out their share in the Eastern markets. In 1422 their influence and wealth enabled them to oversee the circulation of around two million florins. In the fifteenth century, having acquired the ports of Pisa and Leghorn, the Florentines launched armed galleys of their own to set sail to Egypt. Florence, Lucca and Milan became famed centres of the silk trade and their manufactures of cloth and garments swelled the exports to dress the opulent courtiers at the Mamluk courts.

The Mamluk sultans, who ruled like oriental despots over Egypt, Syria and Palestine, until their defeat by the Ottoman Turks in 1517, gathered in enormous revenues from the merchandise in transit from India and the Far East to Europe. Though they often maintained an intransigent attitude to European merchants, nevertheless the taxes derived from this lucrative trade helped to shore up their habitually depleted treasuries. They were also keen buyers of wood, iron and silver, commodities they lacked, for making arms, ships, coins and harnesses. Reversals in trading relations occurred, however, when either side became too greedy. One such quarrel arose in 1430 between Venice, together with other European states, and the Circassian sultan al-Ashraf Barsbay (ruled 1422–37), when the latter, on finding himself short of funds, decided to monopolise the sugar and spice trade. He ordained that the powerful, closely knit company of Arab dealers known as the *Karimi* merchants, who customarily handled the spices from India, the Yemen and south Arabia and sold them in the Egyptian markets, should sell their goods only to him. Centred in Egypt and the Yemen, the *karimis*, who had commenced trading in 1181, had spread their nets as far away as China, Asia, Samarkand, Ormuz and Senegal.

Acquiring great wealth, they had made enormous gifts to the sultans of Egypt, and had even loaned them vast sums to stave off the attacks of the Mongols. In spite of these benefits, Barsbay felt that it would be to his advantage if he were in sole control, so that he could subsequently charge a vastly increased sum not only to the Venetians, who were the largest buyers, but to other foreign states as well. No doubt taking advantage of an element of surprise and the fact that communications were slow, at first he succeeded in selling off the spices at inflated prices. Thus he felt encouraged to extend this practice to the Syrian cotton trade.

It was a short-sighted move to demote the *Karimis* from operating as influential merchants to the status of being merely employees. In retaliation, amid righteous indignation, the Venetian Senate forbade all exports to Egypt of coin, bullion and other materials needed by the country, and even though it was painful to them, the purchase of spices was suspended. After lengthy negotiations, political difficulties were resolved and trade revived, to the relief of all concerned. The large fleet of galleys that departed from Venice for Beirut and Alexandria in July 1433 transported a goodly company of 150 merchants and 460,000 ducats in cash. Together with the accompanying *cocce*, merchant round ships or cogs, with their cargoes of oil, honey and fruit, the total value of these exports came to approximately 1,000,000 ducats. To the Mamluk sultans, the extent of the power and wealth of Venice in the fifteenth century could not be ignored.

Besides the substantial numbers of merchant adventurers who chanced their fortunes on the seas, pilgrims came from far and wide to visit the sacred shrines and holy places of Palestine and Egypt. The church encouraged them to go, and granted them indulgences that were notched up at each shrine or location having a biblical reference. Clerics blessed those departing dressed in their pilgrim garb. Even if it took months to get there, the pilgrimage often became something of an adventure holiday, away from the daily routines, and enthusiastic descriptions of the pilgrims' journeys in the form of travelogues were produced for the edification for those back home. Their prescribed tour of Egypt and Sinai was laid out before them, something to be perused beforehand, a forerunner of the modern travel brochure.

There were also a few missionary journeys undertaken by a handful of monks and friars who, by necessity, were directed through Egypt to the court of the emperor in Abyssinia, which, although an ancient Christian country, was looked upon as being heretical and in need of correction by the church of Rome. The Muslims themselves were for the most part considered unteachable. Some of the missionaries' prolonged and hazardous adventures are included in this book among the accounts by mainstream travellers to Egypt, even though they might be regarded as something of a digression.

Following the rise of classical studies, which acted as a catalyst for humanists in the Italian Renaissance, a few educated sixteenth-century travellers, who had read of Egypt in the newly translated works of such authors as Herodotus, Theophrastus, Diodorus Siculus and Pliny and Strabo, came to the country to study the novel flora and fauna. Pierre Belon du Mans, a doctor from Paris, published various natural history studies on his return home, as did Prospero Alpini, a naturalist from Padua. Both made detailed sketches to illustrate their works.

To the general reader of travel literature, most of the earlier European chronicles up to the thirteenth century appear stilted, having a limited vocabulary, with the same words recurring with monotonous frequency. Some were written in medieval Latin, others in the emerging vernacular of a particular country. And however resourceful, however brave they were, not all travellers knew how to tell a good tale. As the Crusades were drawing to a close, there are two exceptions from the constrained chronicles of that epoch. Both of them were concocted with the help of a collaborator. *The Travels of Marco Polo*, which became known to the public at the end of the thirteenth century as *A Description of the World* (*Divisamont dou Monde*), would not have caught the imagination of the audience if Marco had not collaborated with Rustichello of Pisa, a well-known writer of romances. Their combined work became one of the world's best-known travel books, even though its veracity may be questionable in places.

Baron Jean de Joinville, author of the life of the sainted Louis IX of France (reigned 1226–70), dictated his work within the framework of a conversation when he was 80 years of age. In this form the telling of the story became less inhibited. Some crusader knights were in fact almost illiterate. His principal aim was to extol the virtues of his friend King Louis, and to report on the disastrous battle of al-Mansura near Damietta during the seventh Crusade on 5 February 1250. But Jean was one of the few travellers of that time whose curiosity led him to observe extraneous matters beyond the chronicle itself. He spoke about the composition of the Saracen army in Egypt, the royal body-guard (*halqa*) and the sultan's minstrels, whose chief instruments were horns, drums and a species of tambourine. He painted a graphic picture of the enemy encampment, enclosed within a wall of wooden trelliswork, the outer side of which was covered in blue canvas. He described the grisly assassination of the young sultan al-Mu'azzam Turan Shah by his amirs. He was interested in the customs of the native Bedouin, who wore great hairy mantles that covered their entire bodies. In bad weather the men sheltered their servants, wives and children in a kind of tent made with hoops of barrels tied to poles, somewhat like ladies' litters, over which they threw sheepskins cured with alum.

The growth of commerce, in the fourteenth and fifteenth centuries, gave rise to frequent diplomatic discussions between the Saracens (as the Europeans called the Muslims) and the Franks (as the Europeans were collectively known by the Muslims), so that language became of paramount importance. Already by the end of the thirteenth century, some European scholars were studying Arabic. Christians from many countries congregated in Spain to study together under Arabic-speaking and Jewish teachers, and translated books from Arabic into Latin. A great part of the legacy of Greece became known to the West in the Arabic translations available in Spain. Among the international students who congregated in that country were Gerard of Cremona, from Italy, Hermann the Dalmation from Germany, Adelard of Bath, and Michael Scot. The first translation of the Qur'an into Latin was undertaken by Robert of Chester and Hermann the Dalmation for Peter, the Abbot of Cluny. The Dominican friar William of Tyre, who was delegated by Pope Gregory X to accompany Marco Polo as a missionary to the court of Kubilai Khan, was an Arabic scholar of some renown. From the sixteenth century onwards, European printing presses were producing editions of Arabic books, and in 1539 there appeared the first Latin treatise on Arabic grammar. The illustrious Arab philosopher physician, Ibn Sina (Avicenna) (980–1037) compiled a vast medical encyclopaedia, which was translated into Latin by Gerard of Cremona in the thirteenth century. It remained the source book for European medical studies for many centuries after.

There seemed to be no obligations on the part of the Muslims, however, to learn Frankish languages. Perhaps they felt that there were far too many. And with some notable exceptions, most European visitors to Egypt did not speak Arabic. The Mamluk rulers were themselves Turkish-speaking, thus differing from the indigenous population. Business was almost always conducted on Egyptian soil through the dragomans, interpreters who were often renegade or local Christians employed in lucrative positions. In particular, when important European embassies were sent to the court of the sultan to negotiate trade agreements and matters of foreign policy, discourse invariably took place through an interpreter. One concern with Western relations touched on by the Muslims was indicated by *The Quintessence of Experiences*, a work by an anonymous Persian physician at the beginning of the sixteenth century, in which he wrote about a new disease that he described as 'the Armenian Sore' or 'the Frankish Pox'. He claimed that this originated in Europe, and later it became known throughout the Muslim world as the Frankish disease. It was clearly syphilis.

European traders mostly lived in isolated communities in the Muslim countries of the Near East, and in general did not interact much with the local people. Except for trade, dealings with the Christians were often regarded as being undesirable. Jews, so numerous in the customs service in Mamluk Egypt, and after 1517 under the Turkish occupation, were also employed at court and in diplomatic circles at a high level. Their vast commercial network in the Middle East and command of various European languages stood them in good stead. They were often disliked by Christian visitors to Egypt, who resented their seeming power and influence.

Travellers' accounts became more numerous in the sixteenth century, when Europeans flocked in greater numbers to Egypt and beyond, and with the further expansion of trade and missionary endeavour, there came the exploration of new territories in search of expanding markets. The first-hand descriptions of journeys undertaken were gradually enhanced by the development of language and vocabulary in the vernacular. Together with the study of classical writers and the implementation of new knowledge of hitherto unknown geographical regions, there came the dawn of travel literature, which gathered momentum in the centuries that followed. These early works (occasionally copied by others who found the way too hard themselves), sometimes enhanced by pictorial maps and woodcut illustrations, were read with mounting interest back home in Europe, some books running into several printed editions.

Up to the seventeenth century, although there was increasing interest in antiquities, no one sailed to Egypt merely for pleasure or with the sole desire to view the ancient structures. Travellers did not go there as did later antiquarians, expressly to dig the ground for the purpose of archaeological study, though if they chanced on a particular ancient artefact or mummy that took their fancy during their explorations, they did not hesitate to take it home.

Medieval travellers to Egypt from Europe only had a hazy idea of the history of the Mamluk sultans, though they would probably have known the name of the current ruler, and possibly those of his immediate predecessors. Modern readers however, have access to such Muslim chroniclers as al-Maqrizi (1346–1442), Ibn Taghribirdi (d. 1474) and the last historian of the Mamluk sultanate, Ibn Iyas (1448–1554), who witnessed and recorded the Ottoman conquest of Egypt in 1517. Some of the random facts gleaned by the disparate parade of European pilgrims and merchants can often be fitted into the context of late medieval Arab histories.

While the intrepid Europeans who flocked to the Near East at this period bequeathed a valuable picture of life in Egypt, hitherto little known, since the mid-twentieth century enthusiasm for the country, particularly for the mysterious pharaohs and the lure of their opulent golden treasures, has reached enormous proportions. Because of the organisation of mass travel, a flood of modern tourists, labelled and ticketed, engulf the major antiquities in ever-increasing tides. The urban Cairo, so imaginatively described by earlier travellers, many of whom found the city superior to their own, is swiftly being covered by a sea of anonymous concrete amid a polluted haze and the roar of traffic. But lone tourists with a modicum of imagination who wander away from prescribed itineraries can find glimpses of a medieval house, rescued from the bulldozer and lovingly restored. A vaulted ceiling in a bazaar is witness to its early origin, while the two ancient gates, the Bab al-Nasr and the Bab al-Futuh in the crenellated wall, marking the old northern boundary of Cairo, though in a shabby state, remain in use. To the south of the city in Old Cairo, some of the churches described by medieval pilgrims are still on view. Though the phenomenon of the Nile's summer rise is no longer remarkable and crocodiles and hippopotami do not impede the passage of steamers, the birds depicted on the tomb walls of pharaonic nobles and described by classical writers still hover over the reed beds lining the river banks. In spite of swift urban and suburban changes, the journey on the river remains much as described with such astonished delight by those earlier travellers.

Notes

Bottes (or barrels): a measure of ships' tonnage at least up to the fifteenth century.
Venetian trading networks: F.C. Lane, *Andrea Barbarigo, Merchant of Venice* contains a detailed account of the widespread trading activities of a family of Venetian merchants, whose tentacles spread throughout Europe and the Middle East (double-entry book-keeping, pp. 19–20; advantages of Venice as a trading centre, p. 46; organisation by Senate, pp. 47–51; dissemination of spices to northern Europe, pp. 54–56; quarrel concerning spice trade between Egypt and Venice, pp. 52–53; resumption of trade in 1433, pp. 76–77). **Baron Jean de Joinville (b. c. 1224–25):** Shaw (ed. and trans.), *Joinville and Villehardoun, Chronicles of the Crusades* (campaign in Egypt, pp. 201–64).

CHAPTER 1

The Mamluk Rulers of Egypt

Even if the sporadic fires of the Crusades had mostly subsided by the end of the thirteenth century, the glowing embers occasionally erupted when they were fanned into life by mutual hostility. Arab and European versions of the Crusades differed since opinions on both sides were rooted in ignorance and suspicion. 'Abd al-Rahman, known as Ibn Khaldun (1332–1406), the great Arab philosopher and historian, regarded the Franks as barbarians who lived without benefit of the sunlight of the Islamic world, the people dull of understanding and their tongues heavy. Born in Tunisia, Ibn Khaldun went to Cairo in 1382 and became chief judge. Though he had heard rumours that students were numerous in the country of Rome and the northern Mediterranean and that the arts and sciences flourished, he dismissed them by remarking merely that God knew best what went on in those parts. Muslims conceded that the Franks in general were brave warriors, but thought them crude and ignorant. The battles of Hattin near Tiberius, where Saladin defeated Reynald of Chatillon in 1186, and at 'Ayn Jalut, when the sultan al-Muzaffar Qutuz and his general, the dark-skinned al-Zāhir Baybars, outmanoeuvred the Mongols, are still very much alive in Arab memories today. On their side, medieval Christian travellers regarded with contempt such alien Muslim practices as circumcision, polygamy and the prohibitions against wine and pork.

The Mamluks were a military elite in a foreign land, nobodies from the Eurasian steppes. Nevertheless they gained respect because of their military prowess, which enabled them to defeat the Mongols and Christian invaders. Therefore when Europeans arrived in Egypt in the fourteenth century, they found the Mamluk slave sultans well established as rulers of Syria and Egypt in the Cairo citadel, a fortress conceived under Saladin, whose wise administration had left traces for posterity in the construction of citadels, highways and canals. Even the Franks had acknowledged his chivalry, piety and sense of justice, while Dante accorded him an honourable place in limbo. Saladin died on 4 March 1193 aged 56. At the end of his life, due to his failing strength, the sultan constantly wore a coat lined with the furs of Bortàs and a number of tunics and sat on a very soft cushion and a pile of carpets. Old age had made him 'as weak as a little bird just hatched' and his legs 'had so little flesh on them they were like little sticks'. He died so poor that when he was buried near the Great Ayyubid Mosque in Damascus, his friends were obliged to find money for his funeral.

Less than a hundred years after Saladin's death, Hulegu, the grandson of Genghis Khan, who had taken Syria and overrun Gaza, moved on and demanded Egypt's unconditional surrender. But in Cairo, the sultan al-Muzaffar Qutuz, who discarded any notions of chivalry as displayed by Saladin, summarily cut off the head of the Mongol envoy, and emulating methods used by the Mongols, sent off a large army to fight them. Having retaken Gaza, Qutuz pressed home his advantage, knowing that Hulegu had been obliged to return home with a large force, because of current succession problems.

It was Baybars, the ruthless Turkish slave and general of Qutuz, of towering stature, husky voice and pale blue eyes (his right having a prominent white spot), who was predominant in expelling the terrifying Mongols from Syria. In spite of the enemy's depleted forces it was no mean feat, as Mongol cavalry, unpredictable as a dust storm, could advance 70 miles a day and shoot their steel-tipped arrows with uncanny accuracy over 200 yards at full gallop. Only their stench, it was said, heralded their approach. After the battle of 'Ayn Jalut, al-Zahir Baybars treacherously murdered Qutuz on a hunting trip and was installed without dissent as sultan, reigning from 1260 to 1277 in Cairo. This victory in 1260, together with the success of the sultan al-Ashraf Khalil in expelling the Crusaders from Acre in 1291, provided a temporary respite. And in this more stable environment, the sultan al-Nasir Muhammad I in his third reign (1310–41) could turn to internal matters of government.

1.1 Territory ruled over by the Mamluks up to their conquest by the Ottoman
Empire in 1517

From 1250 to 1390, the Mamluk sultans consisted mostly of the Bahris, succeeded by the Burjis (or Circassians until 1517). The Bahris, named after their barracks (Bahr al-Nil) on al-Rawda island in the Nile, were formerly Qipchaqs, a Turkish tribe who were a mixture of Kurds and Mongols, based in southern Russia. The Burjis, named after their quarters in al-Burj in the Cairo citadel, originated mostly from the Caucasus. The Mamluk regime was unusual, being broadly speaking an autocratic government of former Christian or Mongol slaves who had been bought by merchants (such as the Genoese) when adolescents for existing Egyptian Mamluks. Once in the Cairo barracks, a large building four stories high in the precinct of the citadel, the boys were first converted to Islam under the strict discipline of their teachers and afterwards trained extensively in the martial arts as cavalry soldiers before being emancipated. An officer or amir received a grant of land in lieu of pay and on condition of maintaining a certain number of Mamluk soldiers, to whose upkeep he normally devoted about two thirds of his revenue. Theoretically the grants were not hereditary, though this was at times hard to enforce.

Emanuel Piloti (b. Crete 1371), a prosperous Venetian merchant who traded in the Levant between 1396 and c.1436, owned warehouses in Cairo and Alexandria. His career of over 40 years spanned the reigns of five Circassian Mamluk sultans. While he was in Cairo, Emanuel, who had gained the friendship of the sultan al-Nasir Faraj, observed the methods used to train the new recruits. On arrival the boys were divided into classes of 25, each class having its own room, the floor being strewn with reed mats for cleanliness instead of carpets, and put in the care of eunuchs who oversaw their education and welfare. For each group of pupils there was a master who came daily to teach them the Qur'an, to write and to say their prayers; when they became older they were taught the elements of Islamic theology. Finally when they reached adult age, they received instruction in the skills of arms and the arts of war. As soon as their education was complete they were led before the sultan and examined by masters as to their new religion. Emanuel watched the passing out ceremony in August at the time when Cairo was celebrating the Nile's inundation, when the young slaves were led into the grand parade-ground and

drilled 'in the manner of a dance' one after the other. Afterwards the
sultan, accompanied by three of the senior amirs, reviewed them and
distinguished those especially able by drawing them into the centre of
the ground. The following day, the ruler, sitting in his accustomed
place, presented the new recruits with a certificate inscribed with their
names and their salary of a prescribed number of ducats per month.
Besides this, each was given a horse and another for his servant as well
as promises of payments of food.

Once emancipated, the young Mamluks were given licence to leave
the citadel and seek rented lodgings in the city; three times a week they
were ordered back to the parade-ground to go through their military

1.2 Mamluk soldier in a *furusyya* exercise

exercises and partake in mock battles for the sultan's pleasure. An illustrated fourteenth-century Arab cavalry manual indicates that the military exercises quickly developed into organised contests including polo, played between the sultan and his amirs, and the gourd game. The latter entailed the throwing of a palm staff and shooting arrows from a moving horse at a gourd target, often of gold or silver and containing a pigeon, tied to the top of a high pole. The winner who pierced the gourd and released the pigeon not only could keep the gourd but was accorded a robe of honour as a gift from the sultan. The most expert performers were given the title of 'master', promoted and rewarded with the rent of twenty villages. Emanuel saw the crowd of 'young blackamoors' owned by their new masters going to the citadel with sacks to collect their daily rations of bread and meat, and barley for their horses, these provisions given to them in addition to their stipends.

In theory, the Mamluks of a particular master shared a close bond of loyalty to him and to each other, though there were often exceptions to this comfortable idyll. It was inevitable that Mamluk households became factions which supported their masters in the contest for high office, and in the ascent of the slippery pyramidal slope at the apex of which was the sultan's throne. When a master was deposed or died, it often happened that his supporters suffered from the malevolence of successive masters.

Military training exercises on horseback, which included lessons in the lance and the short Tartar bow, took place in the hippodromes under the citadel and by the Nile, where the sultan came to watch. In particular the formidable Baybars visited his hippodrome, the Maydan al-Kabk, by the citadel daily at noon, remaining until the evening prayer. He inspired the troops to such an extent that there was hardly an amir or Mamluk soldier who did not devote himself to improving his proficiency.

The sultan's Royal Mamluks bore the brunt of fighting and guarded his person. The most talented and ambitious of this group rose to become officers, amirs of ten, forty, one hundred or a thousand lances. When conferring a position on any man, such as a newly created Mamluk, a gift to a foreign ambassador or high official at court, the

1.3 Helmet of the sultan Barsbay

sultan used to clothe him according to rank. Often this gift was known as the robe of honour. A Saracen amir could usually be recognised by his hat, sword and distinctive coat, which was worn over his under-shirt and drawers. The coats of amirs of high standing had decorated sleeves, often adorned with expensive furs such as sable and ermine, and they also received from the sultan costly belts of precious metals, which were studded with precious gems or jade. The gold or silver belts accorded to the Mamluks of lesser rank were not so decorated. In later years, amirs wore cloaks having collars of different colours, sometimes lined with squirrel, and, if it rained, they donned cloaks of rough hairy material for protection. To mark the beginning of the summer season, there was a parade which took place between 11 May and 26 May, when the sultan by custom put on white garments, some-times adorned with a yellow silk sash, to inaugurate the polo season. With the coming of winter, between 6 November and 29 November,

1.4 Brigandine with the name of the sultan Jaqmaq

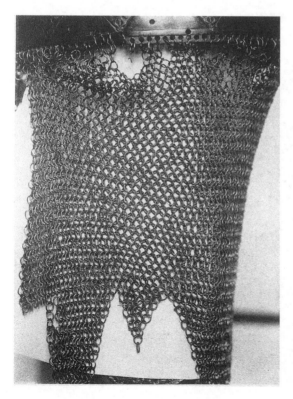

1.5 Neck guard of the sultan Muhammad b. Qalaûn

he discarded them for garments of wool and fur. The sultan's changes of clothes were emulated, but not always on the same dates, by his amirs in the army and the bureaucracy.

In 1323, a monk from Clonmel in Ireland watched the game of polo played in the parade ground by the citadel:

> Here is a certain flat and square space which is called *Mida*. In this spot at times the Sultan takes recreation with his Admirals [amirs] and the other officers of his army. The game they play resembles very closely that played by the shepherds in Christian lands with a ball and curved sticks, with this exception that the sultan and his nobles never strike the ball unless they are on horseback, and they never play in a military manner...

His further description of the scene resembles that of a modern-day football match:

1.6 Mamluk helmet

1.7 Parts of a belt

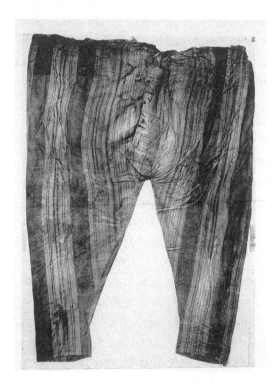

1.8 Mamluk trousers

On this spot is a large and lofty pavilion in which the wives of the Sultan and of the other nobles take their places, protected from the tremendous pressure of the spectators and watch the game especially the exploits of the Sultan; and whenever he should strike the ball, the spectators all cheer and praise him sounding countless trumpets and striking harsh kettle drums and cheering and raising such a din that they seem to hinder the motion of Arcturus, and to crash with the inhabitants of Sodom; and adding the noise of the horses and the colli-sions of the riders and the rush of spectators from other parts, one might almost believe that the foundations of the earth, with its columns and pillars were taking to flight and overthrowing the order of the universe.

Recurrent succession crises occurred in Cairo when a new sultan wished to ensure that his own Mamluks, or even one of his sons, took over the key positions after his death. Besides the adolescent freed slaves, there could be found other Mamluks from many nations; European travellers to Egypt met court officials in high positions (whom they called renegade Christians) who had been born in Italy, Germany, Hungary and elsewhere and forcibly brought to Cairo after being captured and made to abjure their Christian faith. To European visitors, they made imposing figures dressed in their long white linen garments and tall hats.

Abolishing all vestiges of self-administration in Egypt, the Mamluk elite substantially changed the existing urban government. Mamluk officials became inspectors of the markets who oversaw the fraterni-ties of craftsmen; theologians, engineers, physicians and traders lost their independence and were dependent on the regime. Every aspect of lucrative trade was controlled for tax purposes, and all departments were administered by armies of bureaucratic scribes. In order to preserve the high standards of this military society, new Mamluks were continuously imported. Ideally each successive sultan was chosen from among the most powerful amirs, though many were promoted with forceful deviousness via the harem. Some rulers tried to decree that their sons would succeed them, though this policy often ended in disaster and bloodshed. Without adequate military power to support

1.9 Admirals and councillors
of the sultan of Egypt

him and enough gold to pay his entourage, a sultan could expect to be
overthrown by a stronger candidate, a state of affairs which produced
a good deal of paranoia. During a complex 264-year period, no fewer
than 45 rulers gained the sultanate, sometimes amid gruesomely
bloody power struggles. Even so, several of the stronger and wiser
rulers succeeded in establishing periods of stability, so that during their
reigns there flourished the most remarkable flowering of Muslim
architecture and learning.

The Prophet Muhammad, who taught his disciples to perform
regular ablutions and to wash all parts of the body, considered rightly
like many wise men that intemperance was the source of evil maladies.
His tenets influenced the medical studies in Muslim Cairo, renowned
for their erudition, which reached their apogee in the twelfth century.
Prominent among several hospitals in the city which treated free those
of all classes and faiths as a utopian health service was the sultan
Qala'un's Maristan, which originally admitted lunatics but soon
opened as a general centre for those suffering all kinds of diseases,

something remarkable to the Franks. The hospitals were endowed with considerable funds, which allowed the doctors (many of whom were Jews) high salaries and the patients comfortable treatment. Each kind of illness was treated in special rooms and by particular physicians; as ophthalmia was endemic in Egypt there were departments for eye diseases. Patients suffering from insomnia had rooms apart, where musicians and storytellers lulled them to somnolence. Impoverished patients who were healed were given five pieces of gold, thus permitting them a respite before resuming hard labouring work. Besides the practice of medicine, the art of drugs was considered the most noble of sciences. Cohen al-'Attar, who composed in Cairo a manual of 25 chapters about medicinal plants in c.1259, counselled any pharmacist to watch his words and above all his writings, as in these his thoughts will be known. Side by side with human ailments was the study of veterinary medicine. A prominent zoologist known as al-Damiri (b. 1341 in Cairo) wrote a *Life of the Animals* in which he listed all known species of animal, their habits and food.

Besides Emanuel Piloti, other European merchants were received at the Mamluk courts. During the sultanate of al-Zahir Barquq (first reign 1382–89, second reign 1390–99), founder of the Burji-Circassian dynasty, Bertrando de Mignanelli, an Italian merchant, wrote a very fair biography of him in Latin, published in Italy in 1416. Although it was composed by a devout Christian, there was remarkably little religious bias. Bertrando took his source material from contemporary events as well as from personal connections with the leading amirs. Born into the nobility of Siena in 1370, Bertrando had settled in Damascus where he became a wealthy man, having found good luck in business and being accorded the greatest honour. Speaking Arabic as fluently as his native Italian, his services as a translator were in demand both by the powerful Barquq himself and by Christian visitors to the Mamluk court. Bertrando served as an intermediary for a legation sent to Barquq by Gian Galeazzo Visconti of Milan:

> At the time, the distinguished Duke of Milan sent to the Sultan his preacher, Master James of the Cross. He was visiting Damascus with some horses and dogs and other gifts for the Sultan, who welcomed

him in my presence happily and graciously. The Sultan in turn sent to the Duke some leopards which pleased him very much. He valued the Duke's friendship highly and sent a gracious letter in reply to him. At the Sultan's request I translated this letter from Arabic into our own Latin, just as I had previously translated the scribe's letter in Arabic.

The duke's purpose was to befriend the sultan, on the advice of Brother Gerard of Toulouse, a Franciscan from the monastery of Mount Sion in Jerusalem, who wished to get permission to rebuild the Church of the Nativity in Bethlehem. Although the repairs were to be undertaken at the duke's expense, permission was initially refused. But Bertrando persisted and eventually obtained it after many labours, expenses and discussions. Though the duke died, Bertrando kept the permission, hoping that some other donor could be found. On his death on 26 January 1455, aged 85, Bertrando's body was carried in grand procession to the tomb of his ancestors in the church of San Dominicos in Siena.

Bertrando related that as a boy 'in Circassia', Barquq was put in charge of feeding the swine; afterwards he was kidnapped by pirates and sold to a slave merchant. Bought by Yalbuga, the most powerful amir in Cairo, he was trained in arms at a school and given lessons in riding and handling arms. Since he had a good mind and retentive memory, Barquq easily outstripped his comrades in everything. Intensely ambitious, it appeared that he made use of every ruse and devious intrigue to further his own promotion. Quickly attaining high rank, he disposed of all who might threaten his path to power. Even his sworn brother Baraka, who had shared his ascent in the ranks of the Mamluk militia, was lured to Alexandria and murdered. By gaining ascendancy over the ruling boy sultan, Hajji, and marrying his mother Bagaded ('a good woman'), Barquq engineered his place on the throne on 26 November 1382. He had persuaded the boy to abdicate in his favour, having promised him that he would be treated better than in the past. 'This he gladly accepted, being of little sense and spirit, and hoping womanlike to find more pleasure in the meanest position than in his former state.' Not all Barquq's subjects agreed with his seizure of absolute power, even though he ruled for seven years peacefully, mildly and admirably. In 1389, he was deposed and went into hiding. But surviving further coups, he regained the throne and achieved a remarkable defeat over the menacing Tamerlane; other plots followed, but they were in vain and he ruled in peace till the end of his life, dying peacefully in 1399 in the city of Cairo. Altogether, at the age of over 60 years he had ruled over Egypt and Syria as grand amir, regent and sultan for 21 years and 57 days.

Although they found the regime imposed on them repressive, the population of Cairo revelled in showy military exercises and enter-tainments, and particularly in the procession of the *mahmal* (the decorated empty palanquin borne on a magnificent camel to denote Egyptian sovereignty), which accompanied the Mecca caravan. Three days before the procession started orders were issued to decorate the shops situated along the route. The *mahmal* procession started from the citadel, accompanied by lance exercises, and was led by the most important dignitaries of the court. The chosen lancers, forty in number, rode immediately behind, wearing iron cuirasses covered with coloured silk, while their horses were clad with steel caparisons and cheek straps as for war. The soldiers held lances, decorated with richly embroidered waving royal standards which were prominently displayed in battle. At other times, the riders were often accompanied by a few small boys, who stood on the horses, each twirling two lances. Alteratively the boys might perch on a wooden horse-shoe resting on the edge of two swords. Accompanied by the noise of naphtha fire-works and the sound of loud drums, many of the Royal Mamluks were dressed up in comical or frightening jester's garments. Known as 'the Devils', the riders indulged in various pranks at the expense of the gawping crowds, though the authorities forbade the carrying of arms and such japes after sunset.

The Arab cavalry manual depicts the horses as stocky, having shortish legs and a long neck and head. The tail was usually tied up in a knot. The saddle cloth, with elaborate floral and coloured designs, stretched back to the tail, coming to a sharp point on the thighs. The horsemen wore their black hair in a pigtail down their backs, over which was a yellow or brown cap around which was a white turban. They had colourful outer garments with collars, cuffs and hem trimmed with gold bands, belted at the waist, and underneath these wore long-sleeved shirts. The riders usually wore white boots, though sometimes brown or grey, with long spurs, and carried curved swords. There were at least two kinds of shield, made of hide or wood and metal. On occasions a rider would don an iron helmet and carry a shield and sword all emitting flames (the fire was produced by burning pieces of cloth dipped in saltpetre). This was a most spectacular entertainment for the Cairo crowds.

Other magnificent events took place such as a sultan's progress from the capital to war, or into the desert on hunting expeditions with falcons and leopards. When Qala'un went to the chase he was usually accompanied by one third of his army and uniquely among his amirs he employed a single rare eagle to denote his high status. The sultan al-Nasir Muhammad surrounded himself by a vast and formidable retinue mounted on horses, mules, asses and camels, which covered the desert like locusts for an area of almost five miles.

The Mamluk historian Ibn Taghribirdi (1409–70), the son of a high-ranking officer under the sultan Barquq and his son Faraj, watched his sister the Khwand al-Kubra Fatima, the chief wife of Faraj, take part in the impressive parade on Tuesday 22 March 1412, when the sultan rode from the citadel on his departure for Syria with the rest of the amirs and army, 'all magnificently armed and accoutered'. Ibn Taghribirdi chronicled the events of his lifetime in *The Events of the Times within the Passage of Days and Months*:

> In his vast battalion there were three hundred led horses of the finest in the Royal Stables, with gold saddles some of which were set with costly jewels; their saddlecloths were of satin with brocaded borders, and upon their croups were costly cloths of silk, some embroidered with gold. Some of the horses had brocade trappings ornamented with feathers and pearls, all the horses had bridles of gold and silver inlay with pendants of enamel or heavy gold. Behind the led horses there were three thousand others in droves; then a large number of carts drawn by oxen and bearing seige weapons, large naphtha projectile machines and immense naphtha guns and the like. The armoury followed on more than a thousand camels, carrying cuirasses, helmets,

1.10 Mamluk tents

coats of mail and vests of mail, arrows, spears, swords etc.; then the treasury in iron chests covered in coloured silk and containing more than 400,000 dinars. Finally came all the drummers and flautists; these were the Sultan's bought mamluks, wearing large caps and yellow Tartar cloaks, most of whom were approaching puberty and all remarkably handsome; they had studied the art of playing the drum and flute until they had become highly proficient. This was something not practised by any ruler before him. The Sultan's womenfolk then followed in seven litters, which had been covered with coloured satin except that of my sister, which was covered with brocade because she was the Grand Princess, mistress of the court. Behind them were thirty litters (formed with two chests or panniers, one on each side of a camel), covered with silk and cloth. Then the royal cuisine was set up, for the use of which shepherds had driven along 28,000 sheep, as well as many cows and buffaloes for the sake of their milk. The number of camels which were in the train of the Sultan amounted to 23,000, an extremely large number.

Faraj was depicted as a cruel man, even for the standard of the day when barbarous punishments were meted out according to a ruler's whims. Before his departure, he had summoned to the citadel his divorced wife Bint Suruq, of whom he was still fond, having learnt that she had formed a liaison he found distasteful with one of his amirs. As witnessed by Faraj's chief wife Fatima, after greeting Bint Suruq decked out in her best garments, the sultan struck her a blow with his dagger in the Hall of the Columns and severed her fingers stained with henna. She cried out and fled, but he followed her, cutting a piece of flesh from her shoulder. After more blows, he cut off her head and seized it by its braids, her magnificent ruby earrings still in her ears. During these happenings, the walls of the Hall and the forecourt became spattered with blood. When the luckless amir was summoned, Faraj unwrapped the head from its cloth, and asked him if he recognised it. When the man bowed his head, the sultan cut it off, wrapped both heads in a garment and ordered that they be buried in one grave.

According to Ibn Taghribirdi, when Faraj camped at Gaza en route for the Syrian campaign, he cut in two at the waist nineteen Zahiri Mamluks; and he was so drunk at the time that he did not know what he was doing. This was al-Malik al-Nasir Faraj's seventh expedition to Syria, but so much was the hatred he had engendered that men's hearts turned against him and he was deposed. After he had been besieged in the tower of the citadel at Damascus for several days, he was gruesomely attacked by five assassins, who after wounding him with daggers, felled and strangled him before eventually finishing him off by cutting his jugular vein and stripping off his clothes:

> Al-Malik al-Nasir Faraj was then dragged by the feet and thrown upon a high pile of refuse on the ground under the open sky; his body was naked except that his drawers covered his pudenda and part of his thighs and his eyes were open. Men passed by the body – emir and beggar, slave and freeman, for God had turned away their hearts from giving him burial or interment, and grooms and slaves and the rabble sported with his beard and his body.

Emanuel Piloti also witnessed the departure of his erstwhile patron. He was told that the caliph (whose office he likened to that of the Pope in Rome) considered that the sultan's death was merited because of his injustice to his people and the fact that he ate pork flesh and drank wine on Fridays.

Muslim attitudes towards Christian foreigners in their territories tended to be ambivalent, influenced by the view taken by the current ruler. Above all the sultans were swayed by advantages to be gained by trade, though if there had occurred any hostile action by the Franks, Europeans could expect harsh reprisals. These reprisals were often directed against the Franciscans who had come to Palestine, Syria and Egypt in 1219 during the lifetime of their founder. Brother Francis of Assisi had journeyed to the Middle East fired by missionary endeavour, believing (like other pious unworldly people) that his peace mission during the fifth Crusade could succeed in peace. Though the sultan al-Kamil in the enemy camp received the saint with the greatest kindness and offered him gifts (which were refused), he was sent back without achieving success to the Christian army at Damietta, on the eastern branch of the Nile.

The traditions of St Francis persisted, however, and in 1335 the Order opened a convent in Jerusalem, presided over by a friar with the title of the Guardian of Mount Sion. Owing to sporadic harsh treatment meted out to the monks by the authorities, life in the convent was often hard. Besides dispensing hospitality as far as they could, the duties of the Franciscans included assisting the pilgrims visiting the shrines in the Holy Land, and providing religious succour to the European merchants, from whom they obtained alms to supplement what money they had to eke out their existence. However, in the fifteenth century, by chance things took a turn for the better. During the Guardianship of Friar Francis Rosso of Piacenza (1467–72) there were in exile in Jerusalem two amirs, al-Ashraf Qaitbay and Yashbak al-Faqih. Qaitbay had been purchased for thirty drachmas by a former sultan, al-Zahir Jaqmaq (ruled 1438–53) and was his Mamluk. During the period the two amirs were in exile, they were forbidden to ride, or take servants, or leave the city. They were even unable to visit the houses of other Muslims, who dared not show themselves as friends. In contrast, the friars treated them with great sympathy and plied them with good food. Qaitbay was pleased to frequent the convent for recreation and the Friars 'received him not as a prisoner but as a lord, and they gave him to eat most solemnly, providing spoons, sweets and other fine victuals: but above all, liking the vegetables and omelettes made by the Friars, he came with great eagerness to the place.' The Guardian, a shrewd man, knew well that the fortunes of this unhappy world, lucky or unlucky as they may be, are not stable but turn as the wheel, and conjectured that these men could easily return to the sultan's favour. Therefore he lavished food and drink on them and offered them money.

When finally their innocence was proved and the amirs returned to Cairo, Qaitbay was installed as the new sultan in 1468. He reigned for 28 years and Yashbak was made his vizier. As day follows night, on the Guardian's arrival at Cairo, he was received with much joy. Henceforward during the reign of Qaitbay the friars in Jerusalem were given precedence at court and enjoyed the royal protection because of the great and cordial kindness offered during a period of anguish and tribulation. Without fail, the sultan meted out punishment to any who molested them. When Friar Jacomo Magnavaccba (Father Guardian 1475–77) had been unjustly imprisoned by the governor of Jerusalem, he went in person to court to complain of this oppression. Yashbak had the offender brought forthwith to Cairo in chains, and on arrival the governor was cruelly beaten in front of the Guardian, deposed from office and sent to prison for five years. It was related that all the country was in such terror and fear on hearing of the above, that the chief enemies of the friars humbled themselves before them. The omelettes and vegetables had paid handsome dividends.

Al-Malik al-Ashraf Qaitbay, considered a wise and respected ruler even by the amirs surrounding the throne, was renowned for his courage and erudition. He was a man of discrimination who caused many fine buildings to be erected in Cairo and Jerusalem, where he built a *madrasa*, eventually completed to his liking in 1482. He over-hauled the administration and encouraged trading relations with Europeans. In 1486 he received a delegation from Lorenzo de' Medici and the following year, on 11 November 1487, the arrival of a very beautiful graceful giraffe caused great excitement in Florence. It was brought as a gift, together with a lion and other animals, to the Signoria by the envoys of Qaitbay, the 'Sultan of Babylonia'. The animals arrived at the Medici Palace with a green Moorish straw mattress and with oriental perfumes from the land of the Nile. The giraffe lived for a long time in Florence and was kept in a stable, petted by nuns. Luca Landucci, who kept a Florentine diary at the time, said that it was the

subject for many artists whose paintings could be seen all over the
city. Exotic African animals were prized by Renaissance rulers; Anne
of France wrote to Lorenzo that she desired a giraffe above anything
else.

Qaitbay died in August 1498 after a reign of just over 29 years. His
portrait was included in a famous collection of portrayals of illustrious
men in a museum owned by Paolo Giovio (1483–1552), which he built
between 1536 and 1543 in a villa in the Borgo Vico at Como. Paolo
was a prolific writer. Among an outpouring of literary works, he
published many volumes about the museum and its contents, in which
he included short biographies he had composed of the famous men
shown in his collection. Woodcuts of the portraits, including one of
Qaitbay and another of the penultimate Mamluk sultan, al-Ashraf

1.11 The sultan Qaitbay

Qansuh II al-Ghawri (ruled 1501–17), were made after Paolo's death by Theobald Mueller for *Musaei Iovani Imagines*, published in Basle in 1557. Directly after Paolo died his friend Duke Cosimo de' Medici sent his painter Cristofano (di Papi) dell' Altissimo to the museum to copy the portraits, which were later placed in the Uffizi in Florence, where today many of them, including that of Qaitbay, hang in the corridor.

Paolo extolled the giraffe Qaitbay sent to Lorenzo de' Medici: 'For a long time it was a wonderful sight, not only in Tuscany but throughout Italy.' He observed that such an animal had not been seen there since Roman times and that its transportation from Ethiopia at the source of the Nile was very difficult. Qaitbay also sent an elephant and a tiger ('terribile per il natural fierezza') to Duke Galeazzo Sforza. Paolo related that the beasts could be seen, well painted, in the castle at Milan.

It is not known where Paolo obtained the original likenesses of the sultans, but possibly they were included in an ivory and ebony box containing miniatures or coin representations of eleven sultans, lent to him by the nobleman Virginio Orsini. Virginio acquired the box as part of an exchange of gifts by the corsair Barbarossa during a sojourn in Marseilles. In any case Paolo had many contacts. He was created Bishop of Nocera in 1538, in addition to being a renowned humanist, linguist and historian whose museum attracted many from far and wide. He moved constantly in Italian court and papal circles and was acquainted with many princes, ambassadors and military leaders besides having access to diplomatic letters and correspondence. On 29 January 1533, he attended the Bologna consistory during which the Portuguese explorer, the Franciscan Francesco Alvarez, who had just returned from Ethiopia, presented Pope Clement VII (in office 1523–34) with four letters (two were addressed to the king of Portugal) from the king of Ethiopia, Negus Lebna-Dengal, who reigned under the name of David from 1508 to 1540. Paolo, who translated these letters from Portuguese into Latin for the pope, acquired a portrait of the Ethiopian king for his collection which Alvarez had brought to Italy. Paolo died in Florence on 10 December 1552 while a guest of Duke Cosimo.

With all the displays of pomp and grandeur, the Mamluk state was expensive to maintain, and the lavish lifestyle and position of the ruler depended on large payments made to his adherents. The taxes raised from towns and the countryside were not sufficient to keep the army happy, nor the large opulent court, with its myriad retainers ever on the lookout for favours. Turkish-speaking themselves, for obvious reasons the Mamluks chose Arabic speakers to run the bureaucracy; a wide gulf separated the rulers and the native population, who could never aspire to military positions, great riches or political power. The livelihood of all was attuned to the needs of the Mamluks, who were paid part of their salaries in kind. Tradesmen in the Cairo markets supplied saddles, arms and armour for the Mamluk cavalry, and all kinds of food, especially grain. Massive grain stocks accumulated by the sultans and amirs enabled them to become dealers par excellence, sometimes causing dire shortages and disrupting the economy.

Christian renegades, Copts and Jews had vital roles as tax collectors, accountants, money-changers and masters of the mint, though in times of trouble, having no political power and few rights, they were the subjects of persecution and extortion. While the peasantry eked out their existence along the Nile valley, only the independent lawless Bedouin, who sometimes partook of this agricultural way of life, rebelled against the foreign yoke and made persistent armed attacks against the Mamluks. At times, however, when they found it expedient, the sultans allied themselves with certain Bedouin tribes, lived among them and wore their dress. For services rendered to the Mamluks and military service, they received lavish rewards.

Oppressive though the Mamluks may have seemed to the local population, providing visiting Europeans did not transgress the strict rules laid down concerning the Muslim faith, did not travel away from prescribed routes and paid the required taxes, they were fairly free. Even if individuals overstepped the mark, justice was not always unduly harsh. A fourteenth-century *fatwa* issued as a result of alleged misdemeanours by some Frankish merchants at the port of Acre showed that the case appeared to have received a fair judgment:

The town of 'Akka on the coast of the province of Safad [in Syria] has a harbour to which the Franks resort by sea to sell what they bring with them and buy other goods instead and return to their homeland. And it was not their custom to celebrate their festivities publicly in 'Akka nor did they practise the usages of their native countries. Then one day the Franks gathered together and engaged persons who cut down olive branches for them, and they laid these on the shoulders of Muslim carriers with beams of wood. Then the Franks mounted on

1.12 The penultimate Mamluk sultan, Qansuh al-Ghawri

the beams a number of their boys with drums and flutes, And the said boys, while in the harbour, prayed publicly for the Sultan al-Malik al-Salih. Then all went to the ruins of 'Akka and at the head of the procession were the 'Muqaddim' of the province and the harbour and a number of Muslims with drawn swords. When they reached the church, the boys riding [on the shoulders of Muslims] prayed to the Christ to succour the religion of the Cross; and one of them raised a lance with a banner attached to it.

The local governor, having apprehended the Franks and the other Muslims implicated in the affair, asked for a ruling from the nearest judicial officer. After much deliberation it was decided that 'we should detain those Franks here until they set free the Muslim captives in their countries, for they have the means of doing so by influence or money… For such measure at this time is preferable to execution, or to showing mercy to them or to enslaving them and God the Exalted knows best!'

At the end of the fifteenth century, the decline of traditional military training in the Mamluk sultanate coincided with the rise of firearms, so successfully used by the Ottoman Turks. Even as early as 1346, Edward III of England had employed guns as a secret weapon to defeat the French at the battle of Crécy. Unwilling to adapt to the new technology, ill prepared in the manufacture of new cannon, the Mamluks still clung to their old military skills based on cavalry and it was this tardy policy that lost them their sovereignty in battle against the Ottoman Turks in 1517. Too late did the elderly sultan al-Ashraf Qansuh al-Ghawri try to modernise his army. Ibn Iyas, the historian of Mamluk descent, described his visit in 1510 to inspect the new cannon that had been cast. He related that when they fired the powder in them they all exploded: 'Their bronze flew into the air and not one of them was sound… The sultan was exceedingly upset on that day and returned quickly to the Citadel. He intended to give a feast for his amirs, and spend the day rejoicing but it was not to be.'

Notes

General: Al-Maqrizi, *Histoires des sultans mamlouks de l'Egypte*; Wilson (trans.), *Behâ Ed-Din*, *Life of Saladin*, vol. XIII, p. 1; Garcin, 'The Regime of the Circassian Mamluks' (sultanate of Qaitbay, pp. 295–97); Giovio, *Gli elogi e vite brevemente* (his portrait gallery, pp. 97–199); Rovelli, *Paolo Giovio nella storia e nell'arte*, pp. 25–28; Cragg, *An Italian Portrait Gallery*; Müntz, *Le Musée de portraits de Paul Jove* (possible origin of portraits, p. 260); Glubb, *Soldiers of Fortune*; Hildebrand, *The Crusades: Islamic Perspectives*; Holt, *The Age of the Crusades* (see especially 'Institutions of the Mamluk Sultanate', pp. 138–54, and 'Diplomatic and Commercial Relations', pp. 155–66); Lewis, *The Arabs in History*; Maalouf, *The Crusades Through Arab Eyes*; Mayer, *Mamluk Costume*; Weit (trans.), *Ibn Iyas, Histoire des Mamlouks circassien*; Leclerc, *Histoire de la Médicine Arabe*, I, pp. 568–70; Popper, *Egypt and Syria under the Circassian Sultans*; Lapidus, *Muslim Cities in the Late Middle Ages*, pp. 44–58 (trade and the *Karimi* merchants, pp. 124–27). **The army:** works listed by Ayalon, especially *L'Esclavage du Mamelouk*; 'The Plague and its Effects upon the Mamluk Army', pp. 67–73, 'Furusyya Exercises and Games in the Mamluk Sultanate', pp. 46–51; Lapidus, *Muslim Cities in the Late Middle Ages*, pp. 44–56; Petry, 'Late Mamluk Military Institution and Innovation', pp. 464–95; Smith (ed.), *Medieval Muslim Horsemanship*; Dopp (ed.), *Le traité d'Emmanuel Piloti* (education of young slaves, pp. 14–18); Esposito (ed.), *Itinerarium Symon Semeonis* (polo, p. 77); Popper, *Egypt and Syria under the Circassian Sultans* (sultan's emblems, of sovereignty, bands, music and tents, classes of amirs, Mamluk army and bureaucracy, pp. 84–100). **Sultan Al-Malik al-Nasir:** Popper, *Egypt and Syria under the Circassian Sultans*, pp. 184–95. **Relations with the Franks:** Holt, 'The Treaties of the Early Mamluk Sultans', pp. 67–76; Dopp (ed.), *Le traité d'Emmanuel Piloti* (favoured by Faraj, p. 20); Bellorini and Hoade (ed. and trans.), *Francesco Suriano* (Qaitbay in Jerusalem, pp. 126–30); Fischel (ed. and trans.), 'Ascensus Barcoch', pp. 57–74, 152–72; Wansburgh, 'Venice and Florence in the Mamluk Commercial Privileges', pp. 483–95; 'A Mamluk Ambassador to Venice in 913/1507', pp. 503–30. **Qaitbay and Lorenzo de' Medici:** Babinger, 'Lorenzo de' Medici e la corte ottomana' (Anne of France's desire for giraffe, p. 351); del Badia (ed.), *Luca Landucci* (giraffe in Florence, p. 44). **Justice to Franks:** Atiya, 'An Unpublished XIVth Century *Fatwa*', pp. 55–63.

CHAPTER 2

Egypt Imagined and the Realities
of the Voyage

Even if Europeans felt some hostility towards the Muslims, this did not deter them from risking their lives on dangerous sea voyages, intent as they were on making pilgrimage to the Christian holy places and increasing the lucrative trade with the infidels. This mercantile outlook was typified by men such as Francesco di Marco Datini of Prato, a wealthy Florentine merchant who headed his account books 'In the name of God and of profit'. Foreign travel too had a certain cachet: the traveller became a focus of attention, a person of importance on his return. It was considered that a Florentine who was not a merchant, and had not travelled through the world seeing foreign nations and peoples and afterwards returning to Florence with some wealth, was a man who enjoyed no esteem whatsoever. Boasting of achievements, however, did not win friends and displays of wealth could well attract unwelcome taxes; Cosimo de' Medici (the Elder) (1389–1464), a cautious and somewhat secretive man, ever watchful of potential enemies, warned against winning too much attention, advising that envy is a weed that should not be watered.

Little was known about pharaonic Egypt in fourteenth-century Europe; it was considered as being shrouded in the mists of antiquity, full of mystery and wonders. But with the revival of classical learning a rather incomplete picture of that ancient country, composed of both fact and fantasy, gradually unfolded. In his preface to the *Lives of the Artists*, Giorgio Vasari was 'fully aware that all who have written on the subject firmly and unanimously assert that the arts of sculpture and painting were first derived from nature by the people of Egypt'.

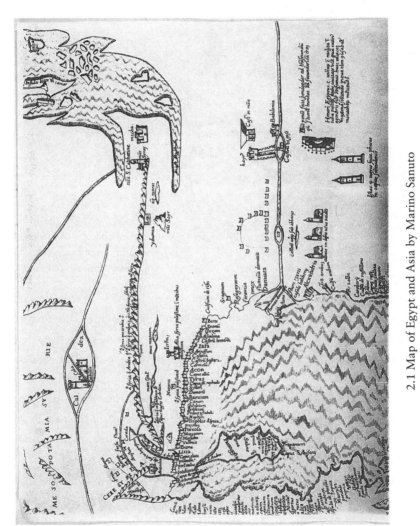

2.1 Map of Egypt and Asia by Marino Sanuto

2.2 Joseph parading in his carnival chariot, with vases containing the seven full and seven thin ears of corn

Biblical stories of Egypt told of Joseph the vizier of Pharaoh, and of Moses discovered in the bulrushes by Pharaoh's daughter. Egypt was the country that gave shelter to Mary, Joseph and Jesus when they fled from the persecutions of Herod; these narratives were familiar even to the illiterate who saw them as subjects of paintings, frescoes and mosaics in their churches. The artists who had never been to Egypt used local models, perhaps with a few idealised camels thrown in to give an Eastern flavour, painted against a background of their own familiar countryside.

In medieval Italy, Old Testament tales of Joseph in Egypt almost had a life of their own. They were popular subjects for the decoration of *cassoni* or household coffers. Sometimes Joseph could be seen arrayed in fanciful clothes, adorned with regalia and seated on an elaborate cart, decorated with the emblems of the seven full and seven rank ears of corn, playing his part in one of the festive street processions which wound their way through the narrow streets of the principal Italian towns. *Trionfi*, as these processions came to be called, usually took place at the times of ducal weddings and grand entrances into the city. Classical figures were portrayed in the form of Greek gods and goddesses who played prominent roles in the decorated vehicles. In sixteenth-century Florence such cavalcades became very sophisticated, so much so that some stage managers and their costume designers became bored with the Greek pantheon and looked elsewhere for novelty. In *Le dieci mascherate delle bufole*, performed in 1565, produced by Giorgio Vasari for the Spanish merchants in Florence, the god Osiris appeared seated on a black calf. He wore a garland of ivy leaves made of green silk on his head, together with a red velvet cap decorated with little masks of lion, wolf and god. His face mask portrayed him as a good-humoured old man with a beard, and was completely gilded. Over his coat of red satin he had a rich golden cloak which hung from his shoulders. It is doubtful if the crowds lining the route could recognise some of the more bizarre aspects of the Egyptian gods who were paraded before their unsuspecting gaze. Most would not have read the classical author, Apuleius, who described them with such assurance and from whom costume designers drew their information. Indeed so complicated did everything become that those responsible for the parade were forced to issue a handbook by way of explanation.

In the eleventh-century Byzantine basilica of St Mark in Venice, the Joseph cycle was depicted in mosaics in the ceiling of the north narthex. With meticulous detail the artist portrayed the principal scenes of his adventures in Egypt: the attempted seduction by Potiphar's wife, the hero's incarceration in prison, the golden-crowned pharaoh in classical garb dreaming in his bed, and Joseph as the vizier overseeing the husbanding of the grain. This was shown conveniently stored in the pyramids, depicted by the artist as sharply pointed structures, five in number and provided with windows. The notion that the pyramids were the granaries of the pharaohs (or Joseph's barns) had a long tradition that lasted well into the sixteenth century. It caused confusion to some of those later travellers to Egypt who had become acquainted with such classical writers as Herodotus of Halicarnassus who visited Egypt in c.450 BC. The latter described the pyramids of Giza and recorded the manner of their construction as related to him by the priests.

Familiar too were stories of the third- and fourth-century AD

Christian fathers and hermits, the ascetics who retreated to the bleak caves amid the privations of the arid Egyptian deserts. Their idealised portraits painted against the imaginary harsh mountainous terrain of the Thebaid, particularly by artists of the Sienese and Florentine schools of the fourteenth and fifteenth centuries, left the onlooker in no doubt as to the hermits' disciplined piety. Saints such as Marcarius and Onuphrius were shown as cadaverous figures, usually naked, covered only by their long thick beards. Other well-known characters were Paul the father of monasticism, the patrician Anthony of Egypt, who left his rich estates for a stark cell near the Red Sea, and Mary of Egypt, sometimes portrayed by painters peeping out from her cave dwelling. Shrouded by her long wavy locks, she was shown gazing at an angel hovering above, who coyly offered her an apple wrapped in

2.3 Hermes Trismegistus (mosaic said to be by Giovanni di Stefano)

a napkin. Stories of their lives made popular reading, some of which were included in *The Golden Legend*, a pious work by Jacob of Voraigne (1230–98), a Dominican friar who became Archbishop of Genoa when he was 62 years old. In the fifteenth century, soon after the invention of printing, more than 150 editions appeared, making it the most popular book after the Bible. Though these stories were despised by later Renaissance humanists, who thought they were historically worthless, they were revered by the unlearned for their spirit of devotion, particularly if the fame of a favourite patron saint was enhanced.

Ancient Egypt was further understood to be a place of magic and astrology. Exodus (7.11) spoke of the wise men, the sorcerers and magicians of Egypt. Prominently displayed in coloured marbles in the fifteenth-century floor of the *duomo* at Siena is Hermes Trismegistus, a legendary Egyptian philosopher priest, associated with the god Thoth and credited with having piety and wisdom. Both Christian and pagan ancient authors, impressed by his learning, had sung his praises. A number of treatises attributed to him, known as the *Corpus Hermeticum* and written in Greek, were translated into Latin in 1463 by Marsilio Ficino for Cosimo de' Medici (the Elder) of Florence. Marsilio, who was engaged by Cosimo at the time to translate an important manuscript of Plato, related that he was ordered to put it aside so that he could finish the *Corpus*. The artists in the *duomo* (probably Giovanni di Maestro Stefano and his assistants) portrayed Hermes the Egyptian as being grandly dressed, wearing a tall brimmed hat, proffering the tablet of laws to representatives of the native and Greek populations of Egypt. A caption stated that he was a contemporary of Moses. Elsewhere, this mysterious figure was portrayed dressed as a king with the title of 'Mercurius Re Degitto', holding a naked manikin in his hand in the manner of a magician. In his turn, Trismegistus, like Joseph, took part as a character in street carnivals, and in the triumphal entries of illustrious sixteenth-century Renaissance princes, together with unlikely fellow travellers such as Isis and Osiris, who had crept into the usual procession of the pantheon of classical gods, whose presence was considered necessary to enhance the dignity of the local ruling house.

Apart from their knowledge of countries relatively close to them, most medieval Europeans had scant knowledge of geography in the modern sense. There were few explorers in the thirteenth century, and apart from the account by Marco Polo, the East remained a place of speculation. Contemporary travel books were a mixture of fact and fantasy, cobbled together from compilations of earlier works, only serving to perpetuate some of their inaccuracies. One such work was purported to have been written by an enigmatic author commonly known as Sir John Mandeville (d. c.1372). Mandeville's notes of his travels and social descriptions were woven into earlier accounts, taking over all their errors. His tales of wonders, wound about with myths and rumours, beguiled his readers to such an extent that demand for them led to manuscript translations into a wide variety of languages from the mid-fourteenth century, before the appearance of the printing press. About two thirds of the work, based on fairly reliable sources, was concerned with three regions, one of them being the Christian pilgrim circuit of Egypt and the Holy Land. Despite his intrusive fantasies, travellers following him to Egypt could see for themselves that Mandeville had described correctly some of the customs, flora and fauna in the Nile valley, and many believed too in his conclusions as to the origins of the pyramids: Mandeville said that some people maintained that they were the 'sepulchres of great lords', but firmly dismissed this notion, insisting that everyone believed they were the granaries of Joseph, since it was corroborated in the scriptures and chronicles: 'besides if they were the sepulchres of great lords, they would not have been empty or so large and high, and have porches before them and gates. For this reason they should not be looked on as tombs.'

Mandeville's fables included one of the Egyptian phoenix, a mythical bird taken to be a symbol of resurrection and rebirth. In the time of the Renaissance, the phoenix was the subject of learned discussions by humanists who quoted references to it from classical and early Christian authors. The phoenix motif also crept into religious art. In 1570, the artist Antonio Corberelli incorporated a phoenix into the front of the inlaid marble altar in the church of the Holy Crown at Vicenza. It was shown with outstretched wings perching on a bundle of sticks used as kindling for the flames. The head was coloured red and blue with a blue crest and looked towards the sun, the three rays of which shone down upon it. It was rumoured that real phoenix feathers were in circulation and that Pope Clement VIII sent a phoenix feather to Hugh O'Neil, who had defeated the troops of Elizabeth I at Blackwater in 1598. According to Mandeville, the priests of Heliopolis showed him a book describing the bird's death and resurrection after five hundred years. At the end of this time, it came to the altar of the temple where it was consumed in the ashes. From the ashes emerged a worm which became a new bird, taking the place of the old. Its neck was yellow and the back indigo, its tail striped with red, green and yellow, and the head crested like that of a peacock. Mandeville gave a graphic description of the aged bird burning in the embers and of the resurrection of the reborn chick flying away. 'Vidi duabus vicibus' ('I have seen it twice'), he declared. And why should his readers doubt him? After all, he had correctly described the rearing of poultry in the Nile valley, something mentioned by the classical authors. There remained, however, some sceptics. An amusing note in an eighteenth-century hand, written on a fragment of a 1503 edition of the *Travels*, summarily dismissed Mandeville's marvels: 'No occasion to Travel to write such stuff. A Fool with a whimsical head-furniture may do it at home.'

In the fourteenth century, map-making was relatively undeveloped. Navigation at sea was aided by mariners' charts (*portolani*) indicating coastlines, islands, ports and distances. Most ships hugged the coast whenever possible, which prolonged the journey, since both landsmen and the average sailor were scared of the open sea. The Nile delta had become familiar through the establishment of trading posts and crusading attacks against the Saracens. Cardinal Pelagius and John of Brienne attacked Damietta in 1219 and St Louis IX of France landed there in 1249 before being captured at al-Mansura in 1250. Gradually there followed attempts at drawing world maps, many of which were based on those of Claudius Ptolemy, the second-century astrologer and geographer, who was probably a native of Alexandria. His works, such as a richly decorated copy of a Greek original (in the Marciana library in Venice) commissioned for the library of Cardinal Bessarion of

Trebizond, were prized possessions. The frontispiece shows an idealised portrait of Ptolemy in royal regalia. Such a depiction by the artist showed him to have a dual role, as a Ptolemaic king of Egypt as well as a geographer surrounded by scientific instruments and codices. This particular confusion was by no means uncommon.

Simple *portolani* blossomed into pictorial imaginations of the known world. A beautiful nautical chart drawn in 1375 by two Majorcans, Abraham and Jafuda Creques, depicted the Red Sea as truly red, camels and turbaned figures abounded, and India was shown to be south of Egypt, emphasising a common notion of the time. Other pictorial maps to delight the eye followed, such as the Laurentian portalan world map of c.1351, and the Borgian world map, ante 1450. The Borgian world map may have been drawn by travelled and observant contemporary authors, describing what they saw and heard. It did not rely on scholars of older authorities, although some legends were included as well as stories of the Magi and the Gospels. Probably commissioned by the Venetian Senate, a notable pictorial round world map in colour was drawn in 1459 by one Fra Mauro, a monk of the order of the Camaldules at S. Michele di Murano near Venice. Little is known of Mauro except that he had obtained distinctions in mathematics and physics and was an incomparable cosmographer. While Mauro relied on Ptolemy, he also embodied geographical descriptions by Marco Polo and used Portuguese charts of the west African coast, of which he had many in his possession. In addition, he included information from the travels of intrepid missionaries, seeking converts to the Roman faith, who had penetrated the little known land of Ethiopia. While Ptolemy was generally recognised as a knowledgeable man, Mauro was not convinced by his notion that the Nile's rise emanated from the mythical regions of the 'Mountains of the Moon' in Ethiopia, and cautiously incorporated first-hand information about the area side by side with Ptolemy's beliefs. He also included the oft repeated biblical story of the source of the Nile (called Gihon) as one of the four rivers emanating from the Garden of Eden or the romantic 'Terrestrial Paradise' (Genesis 2.10-13).

Together with the development of map-making, travellers wrote down their personal experiences for those at home and, particularly during the fourteenth century, Italian writers were predominant. Individual details of the dangers and discomforts of voyages at sea were graphically told, and practical advice was given about supplies to take on board ship, as well as warnings about contracts to be made with the captain before embarkation.

In April 1346, a Franciscan friar, Niccolò of Poggibonsi (a town between Siena and Florence), made preparations for a pilgrimage to the Holy Land and an extended tour of the holy places in Egypt. He was a singular character of great curiosity, not of the missionary type like many of his brethren, and had in mind 'to visit everything and not to return to my country without doing so'. His narrative, one of the first to be written in Italian, reveals that he refrained from passing judgment on native customs. He noted that the lands ruled over by the sultan of Cairo enjoyed a good economic situation, their cities having great attraction, being rich and populous and the highways free from danger. Niccolò took care to carry his gypsum writing tablets with him so that his descriptions of holy sites and Christian churches were immediate while fresh in his mind. He delighted in the unusual flora and fauna which he found in the deserts and cultivated land. Niccolò's spring sea voyage to Egypt was unenviable even by the standards of fourteenth-century travel:

> Few were the days of March in the year of our Lord Jesus Christ 1346 when I departed from Poggibonsi, and passed by Florence and Bologna; and then by water canal unto Ferrara, and then I kept by the Po river as far as the city of Chioggia; and then I entered a boat and by sea proceeded to the noble city of Venice.

Having spent some days in Venice, on 6 April Niccolò made the sign of the Holy Cross and embarked on a ship with two masts and with two crow's nests. After the second day of the voyage, there was such a tempest that night that nine ships were lost in the Adriatic, known to seafarers as the 'Gulf of the Venetian Sea':

> And no person on board could stand upright, not even could he lie prone without being tossed to the other side of the ship; wherefore

everyone was below deck, and only the sailors above striving to escape perdition. But amid the murmur of asking for mercy, and amid screams and wailing and beating of the breast could be heard: 'Whereto are we come to die!' and frequently the ship's clerk went below to see if the ship was damaged, and he used to say: 'You Friars and other good people pray God that we escape such a cruel death!'

But the storm continued, despite litanies being sung to the Virgin and exhortations made to their favourite saints, for they had no peace all that night and during the following day. At any moment they expected shipwreck, while the barrels rolled from one side of the ship to the other and objects of all sizes tumbled down without pity on their heads and shoulders:

> And all the pottery was broken, so that after the storm we had none for stools; and we all confessed ourselves guilty, pardoning one the other, and confessing, none could speak for the many tears, and again, from the great screaming we were all hoarse. As it pleased the Lord who did not wish that his people should die in this manner, the next day we had a calm, and in the morning one looked at the other as if we had forgotten one another, for all of us appeared as if we had emerged from a tomb, so pale and yellow were we, and this all from fear.

In 1597, John Donne wrote a verse letter to his friend Christopher Brooke describing his boat in the grip of a violent storm during the reckless expedition under the Earl of Essex to Cadiz and the West Indies. His experience was strikingly similar:

> Some coffined in their cabins lie,
> Grieved they are not dead but yet must die;
> And as sin burdened souls from graves will creep
> At the last day, some forth their cabins peep
> And tremblingly ask what news...

It was a pity that Niccolò had not waited to set out until June, when the trade winds habitually blew from west and north without raising the sea. These predictable summer winds enabled a mariner to calculate the length of a voyage and estimate the time of arrival. The friar was a bold as well as a brave traveller. On this same perilous journey, the ship was later attacked near Cyprus by a *panfano*, a long armed boat manned by Barbary pirates, and he readily joined the crew, who were divided into eight parties to repel the intruders:

> And it came full on our lee side and therewith we set to don arms and pull up the crow's nests on the masts with many things for those who were above to enable them to fight and also stones beyond number, and so we emptied the armoury. I did not believe that in any castle there were so many arms as of a sudden I saw in that ship. And to make haste, one handed [out] cuirasses, one helmets, one crossbows and lances in great number; for these wicked people were bearing swiftly upon us. When we were close, the Captain said to the man who held the rudder: 'Hold forward all square and hit them sure and strong, because our ship is new and stronger than theirs, so that perchance you will shatter the panfano.' And as we rammed them down firing our crossbows, for they did not wait blows, of a sudden these ruffians of the panfano avoiding the crash, began to signal and say they were friends. The Captain said: 'Wicked men, you make yourselves as friends, because you see us; but otherwise you would not be friends'; and so we passed them by. All our men were ready to kill all of them, or all of us to die, for this they would have done to us, to take everything we had, and thus we would be saved; but they would have carried us into a strange land and sold us all; for this reason every man would rather die than become a bought slave.

Capture by the Moors was a dreaded fate. If there was no money for hefty ransoms, those unlucky passengers sold into the underworld of the North African slave markets could vanish without trace. Even two centuries later, pirates continued to menace shipping. Khayr al-Din, known as 'Barbarossa' (c.1482–1546), an Algerian corsair, ally of the Turkish sultan Sulayman I, terrorised the coasts of Italy. In one raid he captured 7,000 inhabitants whom he carried off as slaves to

Constantinople. Christian pirates did not hesitate to follow Muslim example. In 1574 Teodorino Roditto, sailing with his barque a hundred miles from Alexandria, was assaulted and robbed of his merchandise by the galley of Marchese Vico, a Neapolitan corsair. Labour shortages after the ravages of the Black Death of 1348 caused the widespread importation of slaves into Italy. In 1336 a decree in Florence issued a proviso that the slaves must be infidels and not Christian. By the end of the fourteenth century there was hardly a wealthy household in the Italian city states without at least one slave, many of whom were Tartars, Circassians, Russians and Moors, including children of nine or ten. Sick, wounded or pregnant captives in chains were merely goods whose value might appreciate or depreciate; doctors accepted them in lieu of fees, brides listed them in their dowries. Contrary to received wisdom, slavery did not start with the

2.4 Venetian merchant

exportation of Africans to work the sugar and cotton plantations of the New World. The West African slave trade was not an early modern invention as is now commonly supposed. Western European traders took over, adapted and profited from a system already nurtured by the Africans themselves. Fourteenth-century captives of all kinds were not imported to Europe in special slave ships, but were transported in mixed cargoes by merchantmen and attracted duty like any other commodity. They could also be insured along with other merchandise in the hold. Both Genoa and Venice had lucrative trading posts on the Black Sea where they bought silks, furs, caviar and above all slaves. From Tana, Venetian traders travelled as far as Astrakhan and Tashkent to inspect prospective merchandise, while back in Venice the Signoria prepared the documents stating the maximum allowable costs for transporting and feeding slaves on the three-month journey between the Sea of Azov and disembarkation. From Caffa (Feodosia in the Crimea) in the fourteenth century the Genoese exported about 1,500 slaves a year, nearly all destined to bolster the regime of the Mamluk sultans of Egypt.

A frightening sea voyage to Alexandria in a trading vessel was the fate of the pilgrim Nicolas de Martoni, a notary who departed from the small town of Carinola near Naples in June 1384. Small of stature, full of fear, Nicolas admitted that he could not even swim and, thinking he might die in the raging storms which hit them near Crete, he took refuge in a corner of the boat crying hot tears. He owned that all his anguish made his hair and beard grow white, but took comfort in the pious thoughts of the merit of undertaking such a journey. Nicolas professed particular devotion to St Catherine and was patron of a chapel founded in her honour by his family in his home town.

In the fourteenth century, smaller groups of travellers took their passages overseas in cogs, one- or two-masted broad-based sailing ships, principally merchantmen carrying an increasing amount of goods to ports throughout the Middle East and North Africa. Such vessels were slow, often resulting in frustrating delays, so it was impossible to predict the time of the journey. But by the following century, besides operating the merchant fleets that traded between their Greek colonies, the Venetians had developed a most efficient travel service, hedged about with strict statutes to protect pilgrims going to the Holy Land and the more intrepid who wished to extend their journey to Egypt and Sinai. In the busy Venetian dockyards, together with the great war galleys that were manufactured to fight their numerous battles and protect territorial conquests, pilgrim ships were constructed large enough to carry 100–170 passengers with a large crew. In exceptional years, the dockyards employed up to 4000 men. The contract for the round trip from Venice to Jaffa was a package that theoretically included food and wine, tolls, taxes and the necessary papal permission for the pilgrimage. Special guides licensed by the Venetian magistrates were on hand at the Rialto and St Mark's to accompany travellers to their lodgings, advise on appropriate shops where provisions could be bought and conduct them to their ships. Guides were told to accept free-will payments only for services to pilgrims. Gratuities from money-changers and shops were forbidden and there were rules laid down for a just division of gains.

Before departure, travellers were advised to purchase such necessaries as a frying pan, a stewpot and twig basket for shopping on shore. Some added a hencoop to house chickens to be replenished at ports of call. Three ducats purchased a feather mattress, a pair of sheets and a quilt, all refunded at half price if brought back on return. Besides these comforts, there were aperients for constipation, plague pills and a basin in which to be sick. Few could fail to be beguiled by this care and attention. While they idled in Venice waiting for their ships to make ready, this astonishing city provided countless attractions. In contrast to many other cities, the streets were cleaned of rubbish, by a guild of refuse men. Rainwater was supplemented from the Brenta river and channelled into elaborate cisterns purified through sand filters. The water could be drunk from the carved well heads in the squares coming from great underground storage tanks that sometimes filled the area of the *campo*. Besides going the round of the many monasteries and churches, pilgrims passed their time playing *pallone*, a game that took place every Sunday in the Piazza Santo Stefano, and visiting the glassworks at Murano, where they saw costly vases of crystal and other glass vessels of various shapes manufactured and wrought with the most exquisite art.

2.5 Venetian woman bleaching her hair

At the sumptuous procession of Corpus Christi at St Mark's cathedral on 29 May 1480, Brother Felix Fabri, a Dominican monk from Ulm who was waiting for his ship to go on pilgrimage to the Holy Land and the holy places in Egypt, was severely critical of the extravagant dress of the women, the dissolute behaviour of laymen and the disorderly conduct of the clergy in the crowd. Rich Venetian women were decked out in low-cut dresses of silk and damask, adorned with jewels; their locks, artificially bleached in the sun, were padded out with strands of false hair, which could be seen for sale waving in the breeze on poles in St Mark's Square. Venetian brides were celebrated throughout Europe for their sumptuous attire. They wore their hair long to the altar, cascading down their backs intertwined with golden threads, crowned with jewelled coronets. In contrast, widows were clad in black and veiled, and if they remarried, had to do so on the stroke of midnight. In spite of their costly clothes and painted faces, Venetian women were generally pitied, as fashion dictated that they walked on great high soles covered with cloth three fists high, requiring them to be supported on either side.

On display at the crowded markets of the Rialto, apart from the vast range of food, were quantities of white wax, exotic precious stones and pearls. More important still were the tons of eastern spices, particularly the valuable pepper on sale (almost used as currency), waiting to fill the apothecaries' jars of Europe. Each year on Ascension Day pilgrims could witness the splendid festivities when the Doge, amid the clanging of all the city bells, was rowed by 300 oarsmen into the lagoon for the ceremony of blessing the sea and the casting of his ring on to the waters. His ornate ship the *Bucentaur* (named after the horse of Alexander the Great) was propelled by privileged oarsmen. Gilded and decked out, it was fashioned like a tabernacle and shrouded with silken hangings; a gold brocade awning embroidered with stars sheltered the Doge, who was seated on a golden throne. As many as 5000 craft could be in attendance.

In 1481, the Cavalier Santo Brasca, twice Quaestor of Milan and Ducal Chancellor of Ludovico Sforza, published a description of his travels to the Holy Land and Egypt, a voyage he undertook in the pilgrim galley owned and commanded by the Venetian patrician Augustino Contarini. In case he might die on the way, he was careful to nominate his brother Erasmo as his heir, and he warned all pilgrims to follow his example and be sure to put their affairs in order for the sake of their descendants. To others contemplating this arduous voyage, he advised them 'to go to Venice', because from there they could take a passage more conveniently than from any other city in the world. Every year, one galley was deputed solely for this service. 80 men were on hand to defend the passengers and the galley was ordered not to stop in ports for more than two or three days except for tempests. A contract was made that regulated the financial arrangements between the captain and pilgrims wishing to make the further journey on to St Catherine's monastery in Sinai.

Santo Brasca urged the would-be pilgrim to carry with him two bags: one 'right full of patience, the other holding 200 Venetian ducats

2.6 Voluntary soldier on board a galley

freshly minted as the Moors would only take such coins'. He added that 150 would just suffice: 100 was the absolute necessity for any man who valued his life and was used to living delicately at home, with 50 kept by for sickness or other emergencies. As well as cash,

> he should cause to be made an overcoat reaching to the ground when sleeping in the open air and buy a long chest, two barrels one for wine and one for water and a night stool or covered pail. He should not forget a warm long upper garment to wear when cold on the return journey and a good many shirts so as to avoid lice and other unclean things.

Santo Brasca was an advocate of syrup of ginger to settle the blood after vomiting, but not too much as it heated the blood. Fruit syrup was desirable, as it kept a man alive in the great heat.

Once on board the pilgrim ship, however, it was a different story.

For ordinary passengers an early arrival was necessary to secure a place in the open air, and not to be herded below under the main deck, where it was hot and stinking and where the pilgrims' beds were crammed in with no space between them. Sleep became a luxury owing to the noise, the lice and the fleas. This was compounded by the ceaseless trampling hooves of the animals tethered next to the kitchen on the deck above. By day, passengers passed the time in drinking, playing, sleeping, each one as he pleased. Although the captain was bound to provide two hot meals, bread, good wine, eggs and fresh meat daily, travellers soon learnt not to rely on optimistic promises. In reality meat often slaughtered from sick animals was hung in hot sun, served with warm wine and foul water. Fresh bread, supplied to the ships from the bakery close to the vast Venetian arsenal, and then replenished in foreign

2.7 Galley slave

ports, did not last long. As a replacement the customary biscuit was hard as stone. Meals were generally hurried affairs. When the four trumpets sounded, passengers had to run hastily to the poop if they wished to eat at table, the laggards being forced to eat on the benches with the rowers in the blazing sun and wind. Contrary to popular opinion the oarsmen were not all slaves in the fifteenth century; it was only later that they conformed to the image of manacled wretches. Though some were the riff-raff of the population, others were poor men seeking to scratch out a living by buying and selling in the ports, mending shoes and doing rough sewing.

At night huge rats scampered over the passengers' faces and heedless sailors indulging in disgusting practices walked over the sleepers crying 'Pando', shifting position for a change of sail. It was no wonder that many became ill or died. Wealthy pilgrims such as the noble Santo Brasca could afford more luxurious accommodation and were bidden to have their food and drink served in the silver and gold dishes and goblets at the captain's table, to which they were summoned to a second sitting by the ship's trumpets. Indeed Santo Brasco said that Augustino Contarini treated him *come figlio*. The pitching and rolling of the ship prevented the full celebration of Mass. 'Dry Mass' only (the Host was not consumed in case of sickness) was observed. A barber was sometimes found among the ship's complement, his work being confined to bleeding and the care of wounds with the aid of herbs.

When credible first-hand accounts of Egypt were circulated back home, Europeans soon came to realise that the prevailing conditions, as propounded by the strict views of the church, were not all of wickedness and vice even though they were alien and unpredictable. From the confrontations during the Crusades there emerged aspects of positive gain, namely the increased peaceful communications through commerce between the Christian and Islamic people. There followed an increasing number of European merchants venturing to the ports of Alexandria and Damietta. Amalfi and Pisa had established trading posts in the tenth century, and in 1238 the Venetians negotiated a treaty with the sultan whereby a general guarantee of security was given to persons, ships and chattels, enabling them to trade freely within agreed terms, and to adjudicate in disputes with Venetians and other Christians. They were allowed to maintain a chapel and a bath-house and import wine for their own use. Soon a great deal of rivalry arose among nations and city states, and the dominant influences in the area became subject to the profit and loss of the merchant's ledger according to which group was predominant.

Even if communication with the Muslims was through interpreters, travellers to Egypt gradually saw for themselves the extent of Saracen culture and hospitality, the efficient administration, the sumptuous buildings and opulent wealth. Coupled with all this, they were at times witnesses of unpredictable barbaric cruelty and flamboyant displays of oriental splendour.

Notes

Venice, general: Norwich, *A History of Venice*; Morris, *Venice*; *The Venetian Empire*. Portrayal of biblical and legendary figures: Letts (ed.), *Mandeville's Travels* (phoenix, p. 34 and n. 2); Demus, *The Mosaics of San Marco Venice* (mosaics in the vault of the Capella Zen, pp. 179–87). Representations of Hermes Trismegistus: Cust, *The Pavement Masters of Siena*, pp. 84–86; Colvin, *A Florentine Picture Chronicle*, p. 5, plate 51. Egyptian gods paraded in Florence: Anon, *Le dieci mascherate delle bufole 1566*, pp. 21, 22. Venetian fleets to the Near East, general: Hyde, 'Navigation in the Eastern Mediterranean According to Pilgrims' Books', pp. 521–40; F.C. Lane, *Venetian Ships and Ship Builders*; *The Merchant Marine of the Venetian Republic*; *Fleets and Fairs*, I, pp. 651–65. Geography: Claudius Ptolomaeus, *Cosmographia*; Ball, *Egypt in the Classical Geographers*, pp. 85–91; Kimble, *Geography in the Middle Ages*, p. 117 n. 2, pp. 182–83; Almagia, *Il Mappamondo di Fra Mauro* (see especially maps 16, 17, 22 for Egypt, the Nile and Abyssinia). Venice and the sea voyage: Lepschy (ed.), *Viaggio in Terrasanta di Santo Brasca* (treatment of Brasca by captain, p. 52; instructions for pilgrims and requirements for journey, pp. 128–30; expenses of journey, p. 144); Newett, *Canon Casola*, pp. 4–13; Mitchell, *Spring Voyage*, pp. 16–61; Stewart (ed. and trans.), *The Wanderings of Brother Felix Fabri* (description of pilgrim galleys, conditions laid down for pilgrims, pp. 85–92; life on board ship, pp. 125–63); Bellorini and Hoade (ed. and trans.), *Fra Niccolò of Poggibonsi*, pp. 3–6; Legrand, 'Pélérinage de Nicolas de Martoni', pp. 556–67; Bellorini and Hoade (ed. and trans.), *Frescobaldi, Gucci and Sigoli*, pp. 34–35; Bull (ed. and trans.), *Travels of Pietro della Valle*, p. xxi. Slavery: Spufford, *Power and Profit*, pp. 338–41.

CHAPTER 3

The Maritime Port of Alexandria

At first sight, to those approaching the coast of northern Egypt, the low-lying country with its peculiar light suddenly seemed to rise out of the sea. In the greenish-yellow currents of the debouching Nile hippopotami could be seen swimming out to sea from the delta swamps. When passengers crowded the decks on arrival at Alexandria, the city appeared to be a shining noble place, surrounded by stout double walls protected by 'towers, moats, warlike machines and having fair palaces within'. On closer inspection, however, the streets were narrow, ugly, tortuous and dark, full of dust and dirt.

Founded in 331 BC by the charismatic Macedonian, Alexander the Great, on the site of the ancient Egyptian town of Rhakotis, Alexandria was advantageously positioned between a natural deep harbour at the north and Lake Mareotis at the south. It had easy access to fresh water and the limestone materials used for its illustrious buildings. This sophisticated Hellenistic city, capital of Egypt for over 900 years, became renowned throughout the civilised world. Emulating that of Athens, the renowned library, initiated by the insatiable Ptolemies, housed the accumulated knowledge of scholars who bickered at will among its columns and porticos. After the rediscovery and translation of Latin and Greek classical literature by Italian humanists, and its subsequent dissemination through printing, a trawl through even the most incomplete Renaissance library lists indicates the numbers of books they contained by ancient authors who wrote about Egypt. The works of Herodotus, Diodorus Siculus, Strabo, Theophrastus and Pliny were prominent. These accounts were woven about with tales of the fabulous Queen Cleopatra, 'Egyptia femina, totius orbis fabula' and the widely read disparate Alexander

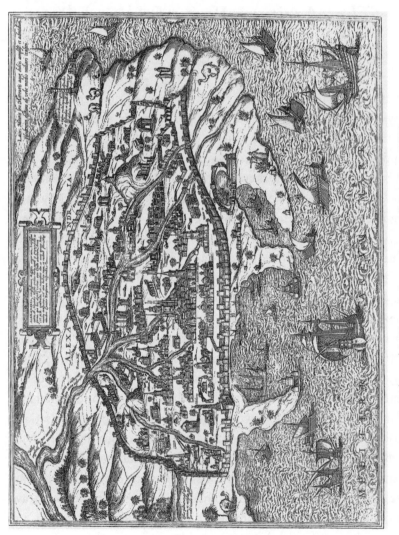

3.1 Alexandria Vetustissimum Aegypti Emporium, 1619

Romances, which resounded down the centuries that followed.

Alexandria became one of the earliest centres of Christian teaching and the seat of the senior bishop. Side by side with the classics on the shelves of Renaissance libraries were the works of the early Church Fathers, such as Clement of Alexandria (AD c.150–c.215) and his pupil Origen. In the mid-second century AD, the neo-Platonic Alexandrian school of philosophy nurtured such pupils as Longinus, Plotinus, and Theon, whose ideas influenced Renaissance philosophers such as the Florentine Marsilio Ficino. Marsilio subsequently translated the works of Plato, printed in 1484, and of Plotinus, printed in 1492.

But while the unfolding classical source material absorbed the erudite European scholars, it is doubtful whether the bulk of pilgrim and merchant travellers to Egypt were as knowledgeable; though now and then, increasingly so in the sixteenth century, a smattering of quotations from Latin and Greek authors would erupt into their accounts as and when they struck a personal chord.

In AD 642, when the Arabs arrived as easy conquerors with a small force under the general 'Abu 'Abdallah 'Amr Ibn al-'As, Alexandria's magnificent buildings still gleamed with limestone and white marble. Topped by the statue of mighty Zeus, the majestic Ptolemaic pharos, probably about 400–500 feet high, one of the seven wonders of the ancient world, towered over the double harbour of east and west and projected its fiery light far out to sea. Arab legends told of other statues, one whose finger followed the daily course of the sun, another which announced the hours of the day in a melodious voice, while a third sounded an alarm when a hostile fleet set sail. Although Saladin effected restoration works in 1272, the lighthouse had suffered badly from about 22 earthquakes between 320 and 1303, the last being one of great severity. With heedless neglect the decline of the once proud pharos increased, as witnessed by the widely travelled Moroccan explorer Ibn Battuta (b. Tangier 1304) on 5 April 1326:

> I went to see the lighthouse on this occasion and found one of its faces in ruins. It is a very high square building and its door is above the level of the earth. Opposite the door and at the same height, is a building from which there is a plank bridge to the door; if this is removed there

is no means of entrance. Inside the door is a place for the lighthouse keeper and within the lighthouse there are many chambers. The breadth of the passage inside is nine spans and that of the wall ten spans, each of the four sides of the lighthouse is 140 spans in breadth. It is situated on a high mound and lies three miles from the city on a long tongue of land which juts out from the sea from close by the city wall, so that the lighthouse cannot be reached by land except from the city. On my return from the west in the year 750 [1349] I visited the lighthouse, again, and found that it had fallen into so ruinous condition that it was not possible to enter it or climb up to the door.

One of the first genuine antiquarian travellers, Cyriaco de' Pizzicoli (1392–1452), a native of Ancona, visited Egypt in 1412, 1418 and later in 1436. Cyriaco was a merchant and a political agent operating in the Middle East who took a great interest in unusual animals, antiquities and inscriptions, which he sketched and transcribed for like-minded friends in Italy. Though many of his letters and sketchbooks are lost, the material was copied and circulated within educated Italian circles. His correspondents included such famous fifteenth-century humanists as Niccolò Niccoli in Florence, known for his knowledge of antiques and ancient history, and Filippo Maria Visconti of Milan, to whom Cyriaco sent a letter for the New Year in 1443. To his friend Pope Eugenius IV, in 1441, Cyriaco related that he had arrived at length at Alexandria, the most noble city of Egypt, in a ship under the command of its captain Benvenuto Scotigolo of Ancona, and that he saw the remains of the ancient high and mighty lighthouse, and the walls of the excellent city and massive gates. Later, in 1447, Cyriaco acquired a copy of Strabo's *Geography* (folios 18, 19 are autographed by him) with its topographical description of the Ptolemaic city in chapter XVII. Eventually all traces of the lighthouse disappeared when the sultan al-Ashraf Qaitbay built a fort with a mosque on the site as a defence against the Turks in June and July 1477. The conquering Turks further fortified the building after 1517 with artillery to repel piratical attacks. After his Egyptian visits, Cyriaco went to the hauntingly beautiful city of Mystras, with its harmonious

3.2 Interior of part of the double walls of the city

frescoed buildings, in the hills of the Greek Peloponnese to visit the school of classical learning founded by the inspired philosopher George Plethon Gemistus.

Although the Arabs subsequently fortified Alexandria with great walls, they enclosed only about half the area of the original Greek city, and in time many of its shining buildings fell into neglect. Due to the accommodating harbours, however, its importance as the major port of Egypt continued, and by the fourteenth century the disparate Frankish trading communities had become well established. From Ptolemaic times there had been a respected and flourishing Jewish colony which had remained there, some of the Jews serving as officials at the port under the Muslim rulers.

At the beginning of the fifteenth century, Emanuel Piloti, the long-standing Venetian merchant from Crete, was well aware of the amount of merchandise that passed through the great Alexandrian customs house by the shore. In his account of Egypt, which he began in 1420, he could speak with authority when he asserted that 'without the town of Alexandria, Cairo with the whole of Egypt could not survive'.

Pepper and spices were of such importance that of the four major city gates of Alexandria, the southern gate (opposite the Marine Gate by the sea to the north) was called 'Pepper Gate' or 'Gate of the Spices', through which the merchandise was funnelled into the city on camel back from the Nile via the artificial canal to Alexandria. Of the other two, the Rosetta Gate faced east and the smaller gate near the old castle lay towards the west. Pepper was considered so valuable that it was sometimes used as currency by merchants, who paid in this commodity for the transit of their goods and entry fees.

After Vasco da Gama sailed from the Tagus river in 1497 with four prime ships under the auspices of King Manoel 'the fortunate', he rounded the Cape of Good Hope and landed on a beach near Calicut on the coast of western India on 17 May 1498. The Sanudri (the Sea King), the Hindu ruler of the Calicut state, maintained that Calicut was always open to any who wished to trade there and the Portuguese could buy as much pepper as they liked, providing they paid the due price. In spite of this encouragement, the first Portuguese traders suffered fatal attacks by the nearby villagers, though these did not deter further expeditions, making acquisitions of hundreds of tons of spices to enrich Lisbon. Thus the established monopoly of the overland spice trade via the Red Sea and Cairo, hitherto enjoyed by the Mamluks, became suddenly and severely interrupted and the consequences were viewed with alarm. To the merchants of Venice and the Egyptian sultans, the loss of revenue was likened to depriving a newborn babe of its milk. Few spices were to be found in Alexandria at the beginning of the sixteenth century and prices fluctuated wildly. However, towards the middle of that century, partly due to the presence of Turkish ships (built at Suez) in the Red Sea and Indian Ocean, sent to harry Portuguese shipping, as well as the increasing difficulties experienced by the Portuguese in maintaining regular services on the long route from Portugal, the old spice route via Egypt somewhat revived.

Although prohibitions were issued periodically by the Vatican, forbidding the supply of wood and iron to the infidels, these splenetic utterances were mostly ignored by the prosperous merchants, far from the confines of Rome, who traded via the Venetian Rialto. Occasionally the shifting Muslim relations with European states took a plunge, particularly after the brutal onslaught on the unsuspecting citizens of Alexandria under the pretext of one more crusade in 1365. After about two years combing through the courts of Europe to whip up support for his venture, Peter Lusignan, King of Cyprus, who had cobbled together a polyglot fleet, eventually set out from Rhodes for his destination, undisclosed to the participants until they had reached the open sea.

On the evening of 9 October, the Alexandrian citizens first mistook the sails of the armada of 165 ships for the larger than usual Venetian fleet that converged on the port for the autumn fair, with many other vessels from around the Mediterranean. Unsuspecting traders and youths strolled out for amusement, unprepared for an enemy. Consternation set in, however, when Peter's forces entered the western harbour, known as the 'Basin of the Fortress' or the 'Sea of the Chain', reserved for Saracen vessels and usually secured at night by a chain against pirates. In describing the attack by the invaders, the Arab historian al-Maqrizi did not hesitate to speak of the great numbers of martyred Muslims who fell in vain while defending their city. In their lust for rich pickings the Franks spared no one: native Christians, Jews and even the European merchants were pillaged indiscriminately. Five thousand inhabitants were sold into slavery. A mournful procession of pack animals loaded with spoils was driven to the shore only to be slaughtered at the journey's end, while throughout the city there arose the stench of killing. But so rapacious were Peter's forces that many precious objects had to be jettisoned from the overloaded ships as they set sail for home, For months afterwards divers came from the stricken city to salvage what they could from Aboukir Bay. The Venetians, who had been inclined to encourage the expedition and naturally interested in success, were extremely displeased with Peter, who had not only broken his promise over the date of the attack, but had caused substantial losses to their trading business, and had even caused their consul Andrea Venier to suffer in the looting. Although the Genoese, whose ships lay in the harbour, did not at first participate in the onslaught, when they saw that the Muslims were defeated they could not resist joining in the general pillage. In Europe, propaganda showed a different slant. In the *Monk's Tale*, Chaucer described Peter, King of Cyprus, as 'fine and true, that conquerest Alexandria by right of arms and did woe on heathens too'. As always truth was the first casualty of war, and it all depended on which side you happened to favour.

As a result of the attack, the Muslims took revenge. Many of the local Christians were arrested and imprisoned, and for some time no Frankish merchant dared to risk his ventures in Alexandria. The prices of Eastern spices rose astronomically and the event, which festered for some time in the minds of the Mamluk sultans, caused their behaviour to be choleric and suspicious. Commerce, however, was far too important to ignore indefinitely; both the Franks and the sultans had need of each other.

Accurate news as opposed to rumour was scarce and communications slow. But practical information was available to merchants in handbooks, such as *La Practica della Mercatura* by one Francesco Balducci Pegolotti, who wrote specifically about 'things needful to be known to merchants of divers parts of the world'. As one of the most trusted agents for the powerful Bardi company of Florence, with widespread business interests throughout the Levant, Francesco was an ideal man to advise traders as to the state of Middle Eastern currency, weights and measures of particular goods and the types of merchandise traded in Alexandrian and Levantine ports. Many companies employed resident agents stationed in Alexandria and elsewhere to buy and sell merchandise, see to the loading of their goods, keep them in touch with fluctuating tariffs and protect their pecuniary interests. It was important that a bond of trust was established between all parties. As might be expected, if the trading company back home was rich and influential, an agent tended to give priority to the wealthier merchants. Poorer traders of small consequence might find their goods badly placed in the ships' holds, unprotected from the elements, or hidden in inaccessible places, so they could not be displayed to purchasers at ports of call. Andrea Barbarigo, a Venetian merchant of medium standing, exhorted his agent Andrea Capello to load his cloth well in position and not where it could be damaged by sun and salt water. Large sums, however, could be made by the able and fortunate, even though trade was always at the mercy of such hazards as shipwreck and piracy, and subject to the heavy taxes extorted by the Mamluk and Turkish rulers. The ledger of 1470–81 of another Venetian merchant, Alvise Michiel, shows that when the book was opened there were over 10,440 ducats in the capital account and 7,700 ducats of profit in the profit and loss account. The main business recorded is the purchase of oil in Apulia and its shipment to Alexandria whence some pepper was imported back home, the size of his shipments often being worth about 3,000 ducats. Even quite small merchant ships were required to carry two scribes mainly to keep a record of goods carried.

In the train of sixteenth-century merchants came a few curious scholars who were interested in the strange fauna, flora and antiquities of Egypt. Prospero Alpini (b. Marostica 1553), who sailed to Alexandria in 1582, was a doctor and naturalist who had graduated at the renowned Padua University, a mecca for students from all over Europe. Padua was famous for its forward-looking medical school, where cadavers were dissected in an oval theatre, in which a channel of running water coursed under the operating table, watched by medical students from the steeply tiered rows of benches.

Prospero, who accompanied Giorgio Emo, the incoming Venetian consul, as his medical adviser, was convinced that his study of medicine was incomplete without the examination of rare plants and animals in their natural habitat, for which Egypt was renowned, as already described by many Greek and Latin authors. Because an outbreak of plague in Cairo delayed his onward journey he spent some time studying the natural life of the delta. He was a systematic botanist and his writings were finely illustrated with somewhat fierce likenesses of crocodiles and hippopotami, then common in northern Egypt. Besides recording rare plants and animals, Prospero made sketches of some *ushabti* figures (which he called *idola*) made of glass, stone and bronze. In 1588, Aloysius Donato, the current Venetian vice-consul of

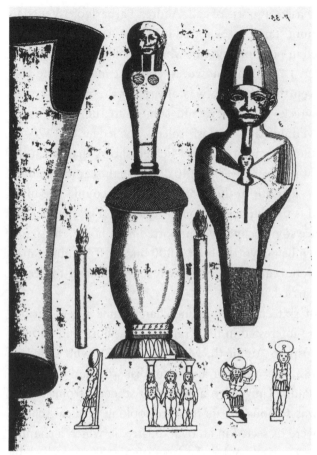

3.3 *Idola*, said by
Prospero Alpini
to be of glass,
stone, or bronze

Alexandria, even procured some mummies, but he soon realised that
unless they were well hidden in the merchandise out of sight of the
sailors on board ship, they would be thrown overboard. It was believed
that such macabre corpses attracted bad luck.

According to the merchant Emanuel Piloti, urban Alexandria was
badly administered by the Mamluks, who cared little for its upkeep.
After the sack of 1365 by King Peter, the decay accelerated further and
Emanuel saw that in his time the price of a certain house, which
formerly cost three or four thousand ducats, had an asking price later
of four hundred only for the use of its building materials. Over the
years the mosaics, cut from multi-coloured stones in squares and
circles arranged in beautiful patterns, had been extracted from the

floors of dwellings and reassembled, often by Jewish craftsmen, to adorn the buildings of Cairo.

As well as the disparate Frankish merchants who landed at the port, numbers of Christian pilgrims arrived, seeking papal indulgences granted at the legendary holy places of Egypt. Their customary itinerary, usually an extension of a visit to the Holy Land, followed a much trodden tourist circuit that touched on Alexandria, Cairo, the balm gardens at Matariyya, and St Catherine's monastery in Sinai. Even though the pilgrimage was regarded as an adventure and a means of seeing a foreign country, the way was long and hard and many died in the attempt.

Such fourteenth-century pilgrims to the Holy Land and Egypt were the Irish Franciscan monks Symon Semeonis and his beloved friend Hugo Illuminator or 'Le Lumineur'. In 1323 they sailed from Dublin to Holyhead, beginning their six-month journey through Europe. Their road took them through such cities as Chester, Lichfield, London, Canterbury and Dover, where they embarked for France and proceeded overland to Nice via Paris. Symon's enthusiasm for London was only surpassed by his admiration for Paris, which he described as 'the mirror and lamp of all moral and theological virtues'. From Nice, they took ship for Genoa and finally reached Venice on 28 June 1324. Waxing lyrical, Symon considered that the city deserved to be placed between the stars of Arcturus and the shining Pleiades. Probably of Anglo-Irish origin, Symon was an intelligent and imaginative observer; he described with great accuracy many details of the distances and prices charged, as well as the customs of the people of the countries through which they passed. In keeping with contemporary monastic life in Ireland, he was educated in some of the Latin authors, as well as (unusually) having some knowledge of the Qur'an, although his reading of it only exacerbated his abomination of the Muslim faith, an attitude entirely compatible with the times. After a short sojourn in Cairo, he was forced to proceed on his journey alone, as his beloved companion Hugo 'of happy memory', 'who having been afflicted without pause for five weeks, with quartan fever and dysentry, died in the city of Cairo on 26 November in the house of a Saracen'. The loss was severe, and amid great tears and lamentations Simon buried his friend's body, leaving it to lie for ever in a foreign land. Eventually, when the first shock diminished, 'I began to cease from my laments and manfully to control my tears, commending the soul of my brother and dearest companion to God Almighty, who summons those whom He loves and makes those whom He has killed live again'.

Relations between the Franks and Muslims in Egypt were fairly stable in 1324 during the third reign (1310–41) of the Barhi Mamluk sultan al-Malik al-Nasir Muhammad. Even so, all those arriving at Alexandria were subjected to rigorous inspection by the authoritarian customs officials at the Dogana del Gabbano ('customs house of the scales') near the Marine Gate. Ships' captains found the entrance to the port narrow and difficult and had to be careful not to founder on the jagged rocks submerged below the surface of the water. The sea, which almost reached the city gate, was unsavoury, since it was often polluted with algae and detritus. When a vessel had reached the port, the officials on watch in the guard tower on a small hill in the town, alerted by the raising of a flag, ordered the steering gear and sails to be removed until all dues were paid. Only then could the jaded passengers leave the ship, and the camels and donkeys on the quayside carry away the merchandise and luggage for assessment at the customs house. Though dues varied, a tax of 10 per cent plus brokerage of 2 per cent was usual on all goods as well as an additional fee of 0.25 per cent. Money was also declarable, on which a further 2 per cent was demanded. Immediately on disembarkation, the new arrivals were assaulted by the sights and sounds of the clamouring populace shouting in different tongues, the calls to prayer, the braying of donkeys and the pungent smells of dung and dirt.

As they waited for permits to enter the city, Symon and Hugo the Irish friars were detained inside the double walls of the customs gate and reviled as Christians by the inquisitive Muslims. While officials were examining their luggage they found some images of Jesus Christ, the Virgin Mary and St John the Baptist, reverently brought from Ireland. Breaking into loud abuse, the Saracens proceeded to spit on such blasphemous objects. Fearing the Muslims and wanting to please them, some Christian renegades (Europeans who had renounced their religion) cried out that they were surely spies and their arrival there would bring no good. They should be expelled from the city and made to return to the countries of the Christians or Idolaters from whence they came. Stung into a reply, Symon said:

> If Mahammed be the true prophet, then remain in peace with those with him and praise him; but to us there is no other Lord but Jesus Christ whose adopted sons we are and not spies, wishing to visit His glorious tomb, kiss it with our lips, and moisten it with our tears.

Impoverished clerics were not particularly welcomed by bureaucratic officials in Egypt. Little money could be made from them, since they were excused from the customary dues levied on the merchants.

Up to the Arab conquest the majority of native Egyptians were Christian, belonging to the Coptic church in Cairo. But some of the differing Christian sects in fourteenth-century Egypt caused confusion to Westerners who could not speak their language. The Copts, often called Jacobites (so called after Jacob Bardeus of Syria), were sometimes confused with 'Christians of the Girdle' (the Maronites). It was believed that their girdle was a replica of that worn by the Virgin Mary on ascending into heaven.

At the express command of the governor, Symon and his friend were taken to the hostelry, the *fondaco* of the consul of Marseilles, where they rested for five days in the chapel until they were granted further permits to continue their journey. On the way to their lodging they were reviled again by the bystanders, though this did not prevent Symon observing the kaleidoscope of colourful costumes in the crowded streets. Dark-skinned Ethiopians from the interior mingled with Saracens, Jews and Copts, who could be recognised by their differently coloured turbans. Symon saw the Saracen nobles and horsemen wearing their broad silk belts adorned with gold and silver 'like those of ladies'. The women were enveloped in linen and cotton mantles whiter than snow; only their eyes could be seen with difficulty through a narrow veil of black silk. All women, especially noble women, wore very fine silk trousers adorned with gold, reaching down to their ankles after the fashion of horsemen. Some of the women wore slippers, some red boots and others white. Symon likened their trousers, boots and ornaments to those of 'fictitious devils' seen in miracle plays:

Tartars, Turks and some Syrians were among the numerous men at arms guarding the town, they wore no armour on the back or head and except for certain corporals [leaders] seldom had a cuirass or breastplate. On their heads they wore a small hat bound about with a white mechelin [cloth made in Malines], twisted Saracen fashion with a linen cloth. Some carried a Scythian bow and a scimitar at the belt. Their horses, kicking up the dust in the streets were almost like those of Barbary and of one size. They were good runners, kept in a stall without bedding or a manger; the feed was put in a bag and tied to the head with two cords in such a way that the mouths could be put inside. The Saracens rarely or never wore belts but bound a towel round their waists which they laid before them when going to pray. They do not wear boots but simply red slippers which only cover the foot in front. Only camel drivers and poor people wear the same shoes as Irish boys. Only the horsemen who were high noble officials wore boots either of red or white leather reaching to their knees, their rich robes were encircled by broad silk belts adorned with silver of which they were very proud.

The *fondachi* or inns of varying sizes were available as welcome sanctuaries for visiting Europeans. Animals and merchandise could be guarded safely in the large cloistered courtyards, while on the floor above lay the offices, reception rooms and sleeping accommodation. A strict curfew was enforced by the Muslims, who ordered the large double entrance gates to be firmly shut at night and during Friday prayers. Sometimes these hostelries included cool gardens where exotic trees and plants afforded rest and shade and tamed wild animals roamed freely in the precincts. Infuriated by the pinpricks they received from the Saracens, the Venetians kept a pig in their *fondaco* out of bravado. Food was not free, though there was use of the bathhouse and bread ovens. Above all they were places where travellers could relax, attend the chapel and even consult a doctor in the larger establishments. Such establishments were leased by the sultans, but maintained by the foreign states, where individual state laws and administration prevailed.

All acceptable applicants were accommodated by the presiding consul who was usually one of the leading merchants. According to the knowledgeable Emanuel Piloti, each Christian state usually had its own consul who negotiated for his countrymen (and at times for men of other nationalities), saw to their well-being and had a care for their merchandise and shipping. They were remunerated by a certain percentage of the money that passed through their hands. In matters of dispute, when no satisfaction was obtained from the amir in Alexandria, consuls had the right to take their case to Cairo. A consul in chief from the most prominent trading nation of the time was elected by his fellows, a post that was not without its difficulties. If the whimsical ire of a particular sultan was roused and the dispute incurred his displeasure, the unfortunate representative, often through no fault of his own, could find himself chained up in prison and even suffer the *bastinado*. Many of the *fondachi* had private chapels and some of the major consulates owned churches. Travellers worshipped at St Mary of the Genoese, St Nicholas of the Pisans and St Michael of the Venetians. By courtesy of the Jacobites, burials took place in the graveyard of St Michael.

On 27 September 1384, Lorenzo Morosini, the noble Venetian captain of the *Pola*, a brand new merchant cog of 12 barrels, arrived from Venice and dropped anchor amid a heaving swell in the Alexandrian harbour. On board were a party of 14 Tuscans, including three notable citizens from Florence, Lionardo di Frescobaldi, Giorgio Gucci and Simone Sigoli, accompanied by their servants, all on pilgrimage to Egypt and the Holy Land. Lionardo's doctors in Venice had advised him against the journey and particularly the extended tour to Egypt, since he had fallen ill on the journey from Florence. But after Lionardo had persuaded his friends to allow him to proceed as planned, Lorenzo Morosini put his own cabin beside the helm at his disposal. So having taken Holy Communion, the party boarded a brigantine of 16 oars to ferry them to the *Pola* and having made the sign of the Holy Cross they embarked and finally departed on 4 September. As the captain had been anxious to set sail, the cockboat had not been completed in the shipyard either in the deck or in the capstan, so many of the workmen remained on board. In addition to the passengers who had paid 17 ducats per head, the boat carried 15 good bowmen, in all a goodly crew. The ship's cargo included Lombard cloth, silver bullion, copper, oil, and saffron. During their pilgrimage, Lionardo, Giorgio and Simone wrote independent, lively accounts of their journey for the domestics who served them, and for those at home who thought of venturing overseas.

In spite of the shabbiness of the city, all pilgrims found plenty to do. Native guides who acted as interpreters lost no time in conducting their charges to the legendary historical landmarks. In the Middle Ages a persistent Arab legend linked the tomb of Alexander to a site under the mosque of Nabi Danyal in the centre of the town – a story that has persisted to this day. Rumour had it that there existed a wondrous figure of a crowned king lying in a subterranean vault. The mosque was built around an open square, planted with rows of trees, and had a beautiful lofted interior supported by many columns. As the Nabi Danyal was the principal mosque of the city, all the others took their cue from it to start the calls to prayer.

But above all, the Christian sites took precedence on the city tour. According to tradition Mark the Evangelist had arrived in Alexandria bringing Christianity to Egypt in AD 41–42 or 42–43. Travellers were taken to the church, allegedly marking the place of his execution situated in an area known as *bucholi* (cattle yard) inside the walls at the east of the city. It was cared for by the Copts and was 'small and dark, poor and badly kept'. To curious Europeans who attended Coptic services, their rites seemed rather bizarre. Every time the priests celebrated mass they sang 'alleluia' many times, while striking a small board with sticks amid cries of rejoicing. The congregation were required to take off their shoes on entering the church and the youngest priest touched the hands of all present. They prayed for the Pope, and professed to be of the same faith as that of the king of Ethiopia, called Prester John. Near the church lay the long broad street where it was said that St Mark was dragged at the horse's tail, to the place where he was martyred by rocks and stones.

For many centuries Venice had enjoyed a proprietorial interest in

St Mark. Around AD 828 or 829, the saint's corpse was alleged to have
been transported to their city in a barrel of pickled pork by two
Venetian merchants, Buono di Malamocca and Rustico di Torcello,
with the aid of two Greek monks, Stauriacus and Theodore. Tradition
had it that the sacred body, wrapped in a shroud, was carried through
the main gates of the port to an awaiting Venetian ship in the harbour.
The odour emanating from the bundle was such that the suspicions of
the Muslim officials were aroused. 'If all the spices of the world had
been gathered in Alexandria they could not have so perfumed the city'
wrote a thirteenth-century chronicler, Martino da Canals. However,
the merchants, aware of the dangers, took the precaution of covering
their prize with carcasses of pork, at which sight the devout Muslims
fled away in horror. When the ship was safely out to sea, delighted
with their success the sailors hoisted up the corpse, wrapped in a sack,
to the yard arm, and proceeded on their voyage to Venice. The city
fathers, who regarded themselves as the first-born sons of St Mark
(believed to have been the apostolic missionary to the northern
Adriatic), lost no time in depositing the revered bones in the ducal
palace until such time as a worthy church could be built. When the
Basilica of St Mark was consecrated at the end of the eleventh century
and housed the sacred relics, it became the most important religious
centre of the Adriatic, a monument of Byzantine splendour to enhance
the increasing prestige of the Venetian republic. Such an audacious
capture of a coveted heavenly prize was graphically advertised in
twelfth-century mosaics in the Capella di San Clemente in the *duomo*.
Viewed by many of the departing pilgrims from all over Europe, it was
a statement proving to everyone the divine right of the Venetians to
be the rightful owners of the relics. Like a strip cartoon, the story
unfolds with the portrayal of classical arches with the caption
'Alexandria'. It continues with a scene showing the removal of St
Mark's corpse from the sarcophagus, the body held in the sturdy arms
of the two merchants assisted by Stauriacus and Theodore wearing
their tall hats. Next come the merchants with the remains crammed in
a basket slung over their shoulders on a pole, watched by a Saracen
customs officer. This was instantly recognisable by the words 'Khinzir,
Khinzir' ('Pig, pig'). There follows the examination by the guards of

3.4 St Mark's body in transit to Venice

the three-masted boat in the harbour and the vessel's departure. With some degree of satisfaction at the completed mission, when the boat was out to sea, the caption reads: 'Having retrieved the body they took it away and fled.' The final scene depicts the gathering of mitred clergy, in the richest of robes, anxious to take possession of their precious prize on the quayside.

As the power of Venice increased, so did her acquisition of saintly bones. At the church of St Giorgio Maggiore could be seen the head of St George and his left arm covered with flesh. Elsewhere were the heads of Ss Cosmas and Damien in a gilt bowl, the left arm of St Lucia the Virgin, and the head of St James the Less, though it was noted that this latter could also be seen at Compostella in Galicia, Spain. Overall the unsuspecting saints provided a lucrative focus for enhancing the medieval tourist industry.

But Mark was by no means the only saint for which Alexandria was famous. Catherine the virgin martyr was at least equal in importance to pilgrim visitors. According to popular legend, the saint was a beautiful high-born maiden who protested publicly to Maxentius against the worship of pagan idols. After she endured many tribulations, including attempts to break her on a spiked wheel to make her recant, the emperor angrily ordered her to be beheaded. From her severed veins, it was said that there poured forth not blood but milk, while the saint called down blessings on all who should remember her. There were many versions of this colourful tale. Afterwards it was believed that her body, 'radiant with light', was transported to the summit of Mt Catherine, the higher of the two peaks of Mt Sinai, where her body lay whole and entire for several hundreds of years. From there it was transported reverently by ascetic Christian monks, who had been alerted of its presence in a dream, to the basilica in the valley below. The emblem of Catherine and her wheel was seized upon by Renaissance artists who perpetuated her cult, depicting their subject in many guises according to the choice of their patrons. They took their source from the *Legenda Sanctorum* compiled by Jacob of Voraigne. The Monastery of St Catherine was the supreme point of the Christian pilgrims' circuit; the long trek through the Sinai desert was arduous and dangerous, and many papal indulgences were granted as a reward for climbing the twin peaks of the mountain and worshipping at the tomb of the saint. In the second half of the sixteenth century, the church marking her alleged death in Alexandria had been despoiled by the Moors and was in a sorry state. But the Turkish sultan Murad III (d. 1595) ordered it to be reconstructed anew, a pious act that the local population considered to be astonishing.

Before embarking on the *Pola* lying at anchor in Venice, in spite of his illness, Lionardo di Frescobaldi had carefully chosen a small chest to take on board to keep books of the Bible, 'the Morals of Gregory the Great, silver cups and other delicate things'. Lionardo was a resourceful man:

> from the chest we detached one of those bands which are set in the lower part of the cover and with a bodkin we emptied a part so that inside we hid 600 brand new ducats two hundred each for the three of us; and I carried two hundred ducats of silver Venetian grossi and a hundred gold ones, and the balance of up to seven hundred ducats per person we carried by letters for Guido [de Ricci].

Guido de Ricci was the Alexandrian agent for the powerful Portinari trading company in Florence. The Tuscans, who were aware of the preference of the Muslims for newly minted coins, were the first Italian travellers to give a list of their expenses disbursed in Egypt. Giorgio Gucci, who acted as treasurer for the party, stated that from Florence and back, the expenses for each of them, 'that is for one with one servant', were 300 gold florins. But the detailed expenses were only accounted for from the day they reached Alexandria, when they made a common purse, up to the day they reached Damascus. The party would have been warned in Venice before leaving that travellers should be careful to have with them plenty of money. In 1431, a priest, one Mariano da Siena, gave a warning to pilgrims travelling in the lands of the sultan that he should not go to Palestine, if he had not the means to do so, as it would be woe to his skin. He would be sawn in twain, or other pilgrims would have to pay for him, or he would have to renounce his faith. Sawing unfortunates in half at the waist was not uncommon, should a supposed miscreant happen to displease the whimsical authorities.

In 1384, Lionardo and most other travellers to Egypt would be apprised of the currency situation. It was known that the Muslims accepted both Venetian ducats and Florentine florins, because their weight and size were constant, in contrast to the local dinar, which could vary. In his handbook for merchants, Francesco Pegolotti stated that in Alexandria, gold besants or florins (the beautiful *fiorentino d'oro* stamped on the reverse with the Florentine lily) could buy all kinds of merchandise because the coins remained constant in weight. By 1398, there was a silver famine in Egypt (the *Pola* imported silver bullion) and the minting of silver dirhams became infrequent, mostly due to the fact that there were large demands for silverware, including the costly accoutrements for the Mamluk horses. With the accession of the sultan Faraj in 1399, copper coins became dominant in most of the population's business transactions and according to Lionardo di Frescobaldi, out of all the silver currencies, only the Venetian grossi were current. For a short time from 1422, the Florentine florin ran concurrently with the Venetian ducat, until an order in 1425 issued by the sultan Barsbay officially forbade the use of foreign currency, which was replaced with the *ashrafi* dinar. In spite of this edict, ducats and florins continued to circulate.

After the Venetian captain, Lorenzo Morosini had brought the *Pola* into the eastern harbour on 27 September, the boat lay at anchor tossing in a rough swell. At length the sails and rudder of the cog were removed by port officials, and the names were taken of Lionardo di Frescobaldi's party, together with those of all the other weary passengers on board. No doubt news of the cog's arrival had been sent off from the ship by a pigeon despatched to the amir of Alexandria, who in turn relayed the information to the sultan in Cairo. The royal pigeons, fed in the dovecotes of the citadel and taken in cages to the coast, had a distinguishing mark and no one but the sultan was allowed to detach the message concealed in their tails. Thus the ruler had first-hand news of the arrivals and departures of all shipping at the port, and was immediately aware of the costly merchandise on which heavy dues were exacted to fill his coffers. Even if he was dallying at his ease, playing polo, or on hunting trips with his prized falcons, he was accompanied by a basket of pigeons. Falcons were so important to Egyptian rulers that they were prepared to pay 150 écus for a live one and half that price for one that had died on the way.

Once inside the great customs house, Lionardo's party were registered by the tax officers, numbered like animals and 'searched even unto the flesh'. After all of their bundles and bags were untied and closely inspected, they were made to pay their 2 per cent on silver and gold money and on their things, as well as a ducat each as tribute. Though a religious man, Lionardo was hot tempered, but even if he disliked this treatment it was prudent to remain silent: 'truly I doubted that they would not find the six hundred ducats that I had placed in the lining of the chest for they would be lost and we would be treated worse'. But by God's grace his fears did not materialise. As opposed to pilgrims with personal luggage, traders of each major state with large amounts of merchandise had the right (by separate treaties) to use the vast locked and covered shops within the enclosure, where their transactions were conducted under the watchful eyes of the inspectors.

Like Symon and Hugo, the Irish friars, Lionardo's party was lodged in the *fondaco* of Marseilles, where they were allotted four rooms

3.5 Monkey on display
from the interior of Africa

above a courtyard in which each was assigned only a space, and a big
cage like a hen coop, on which they unrolled their mattresses. Below
their rooms there was an unroofed vault on pillars like a friary cloister.
Having agreed a price for their lodging, the consul introduced them to
his colleagues in the city, the consuls of the Venetians, the Catalans
and the Genoese and then to Guido de Ricci (the agent of the Portinari
company of Florence), to whom they delivered their letters of recom-
mendation. They were well received by everyone, invited to dine and
accompanied through the town as if they were ambassadors.

On the way to their lodgings, travellers passed through the narrow
street of the bazaar where the booths and shops were covered over
with matting against the heat. The bazaar sold a mixture of all kinds
of exotic merchandise: wide ranges of spices, sandalwood, cloves,
porcelain, balass rubies and pearls. Wild animals and birds were on
display from the interior of the continent: ostriches, gaudy parrots,

screeching macaws, monkeys, young lions and leopards ('an animal dreadful to look at with head and throat like a lion and reddish hair with black spots on its body').

Owing to Alexandria's further decline under Turkish rule, it seemed there were few inhabitants left. By 1577, the Venetian consul had moved to Cairo, leaving a vice-consul in his stead. The most important consul left in the city was the French representative. This remunerative office, which could be bought and sold, remained under the jurisdiction of Marseilles and endorsed by the king of France. A little time before, there had even been a mysterious unknown: 'a French lady, who through merit possessed that authority to be consul of Alexandria, gaining from it many benefits'. Under the Ottoman Turks, most consuls kept two janissaries to protect them and many dragomen clothed in violet, who acted as interpreters with the Turkish officials.

During the long time he traded in Egypt, Emanuel Piloti the Venetian merchant became highly favoured at the court of the sultan al-Malik al-Nasir Faraj. In spite of being cruel, Faraj was a somewhat tragic figure, who had tried to lead and defend Syria against the Mongols. He appeared to warm to Emanuel, who was a versatile, gregarious man, having the advantage of speaking Greek and Arabic, though he lacked Turkish, the language used by the Mamluk sultans.

But probably because he was favoured by Faraj, in 1402 Emanuel became the focus of unwelcome attention when trouble loomed for the Venetian community in Alexandria. An armed corsair, Peter Laranda, had captured an Egyptian galley with a rich booty of about 700 sacks of merchandise. On board were about 150 Muslim prisoners whom he subsequently sold to Jacopo Crispo, Duke of Naxos. The dukes of Naxos had been feudal chiefs and clients of Venice since the island's capture in 1207 by Marin Sanudo; they resolutely remained Venetian citizens and spoke in Venetian dialect. They were hated Catholic rulers of a Greek population with their headquarters in the *kastro*, the twelve-towered citadel, high on a hill and guarded by fortified walls, built by the Venetian Sanudo, Duke Marco I. They spread themselves around the countryside in farmhouses with crenellated walls and squat towers, rather resembling the pele towers decorating the houses of northern Cumbria on the borders of Scotland.

Their relations with Venice, however, remained turbulent. In 1397, Duke Niccolò Adoldo, Lord of Serifos, who usually resided in Venice, returned to his domain on Naxos with a band of Cretan brigands and threw a number of the island notables into prison, where they were subsequently tortured. It was alleged that the islanders had not paid him a sufficient amount of tax. Since the whereabouts of the money was not disclosed – if indeed it existed at all – the unfortunate islanders were summarily hurled over the ramparts of the city to their deaths. The chronicles of the Cyclades were often bloody and it was usual for the pirate princelings ruling the Aegean Islands, under the overlordship of Venice, to milk the revenues and overtax the people. On this occasion, however, the Republic, which often turned a blind eye to local upsets, was forced to intervene. Niccolò was condemned to be imprisoned for two years, deprived of his office and forbidden to visit the island again. Jacopo Crispo, the duke in 1402, seemed to follow the normal patterns of piracy practised by the former rulers of Naxos. And perhaps encouraged by the events of 1397, it was understandable that Faraj looked to Venice to redress any injuries he suffered in the area.

Accordingly, the young sultan in the Cairo citadel threatened to seize all Venetian ships in the harbour, together with goods ready for despatch, unless Venice agreed to act in the release of the prisoners. The consul and council of Venetian merchants in Alexandria, prudently wishing to avoid personal conflict and maintain relations with what was an unpredictable, sometimes hostile regime, decided to comply with the demand, and duly accepted the 2,000 ducats that the sultan had sent them towards the ransom. Because of his linguistic abilities and knowledge of the area, Emanuel was the obvious choice by the council to mediate between Faraj and the duke. Although he was reluctant, he eventually agreed to set off on the mission to Naxos. After two months of negotiations, which involved a total payment of 4,000 Venetian ducats, Emanuel succeeded in bringing back the released prisoners in triumph to Alexandria. Before departure from the island, the Muslims had caused to be made a golden banner with the emblem of St Mark, so that Emanuel could take it back on the boat he had hired for the homeward journey. It seems however that the flag was not a gift, as Emanuel related that he personally had to pay out 35 ducats.

On arrival at the port, amid the acclamation of the citizens he paraded the prisoners together with the flag, and was welcomed at the house of the amir in charge of Alexandria at the end of the town. But the Christian merchants, fearing that the wrath of the people might be aroused because of parading the Venetian flag, fled from the city after closing the doors of their *fondaco* and shutting the windows, only returning when they realised they were safe!

After three days, Emanuel departed with the prisoners and a large party for Cairo. Because of his successful endeavours, he was cordially received by Faraj, who publicly professed his favour to the Venetians above all other Christians. As a reward Emanuel was granted, at his own request, the import of five barrels of *malvoisie* (malmsey) wine a month into Alexandria free of tax. This would net him 50 ducats a time as profit, though he owned that the sultan's promise was not always kept. Faraj also implied that he would be recompensed for the 2,000 extra ducats he had disbursed, though it was not recorded if this was honoured.

With his attractive and friendly personality, Emanuel was popular with his fellow merchants of all creeds, who affectionately called him 'Mannoli'. And unusually he could even talk with the Saracens on the delicate matter of religion. One can only surmise that he took advantage of his favour in high places, as he made a hole in the customs house wall, adjacent to his own warehouse, through which he extricated his goods to evade tax. Emanuel described the imports of woollen cloth from Flanders, Barcelona and Venice. Coral in great quantity came from Barcelona. Brass, copper, silver plates, silk and velvet, *zambelloci* (camlets, material made from the long hair of goats or camels and much prized by the affluent), saffron, *armelins* (ermine) and *marters* (sable) exported from Russia were shipped on from Venice. Besides spices representing untold sums of gold money, great quantities of sugar, perfume, fine linen and silk cloth were exported, some of it woven in the famed though declining workshops of Alexandria in the west of the town. This was in addition to the local foodstuffs such as the raisins, sugar, lemons, dates and capers.

Into the port came the adolescent boys, the prized Christian slaves, kidnapped from in and around the Caucasian area to be indoctrinated as Muslims and taught the martial arts to perpetuate the Mamluk regime in Cairo. Other slaves in Alexandria were captured from the interior of Africa and exported in great quantity to Venice and throughout Italy. They were supplied as household servants (particularly the females), who were depleted in numbers after the Black Death in the fourteenth century. The Tartars kept a flourishing slave market in their Alexandrian *fondaco* where Christian men and women, boys and girls were sold daily for very little money according to their rating. Their limbs were first inspected to see whether they were healthy, strong, sick or lame. The Venetians and Genoese ventured to all parts of the known world to collect young people to sell in Egypt.

Every year during the September *muda* (the periods allotted for loading) the large flotillas arrived from all over the Mediterranan for the great annual exchange of goods. They took on the merchandise which had been brought over the desert to Cairo on camels from the Red Sea in April, May and June, thence up the Nile and along the Alexandrian canal during the inundation. Although winter trading did not cease altogether, most ships departed before the middle of November before the autumn winds gave place to sea tempests. Those pilgrims currently travelling around the country hastened to Alexandria to secure a berth on one of the crowded departing vessels. Under the Ottomans, who used Egypt as a granary, fleets of galleys, increasingly attacked by pirates, were sent to the delta ports twice a year to take up wheat, sugar and rice to feed the ever-increasing population of Constantinople.

Although earlier visitors of the medieval period were not generally interested in antiquities, most of them were attracted by a strikingly tall column over 80 feet high, topped by acanthus capitals, near the Pepper Gate outside the walls of the city. Dedicated to Diocletian by Publius, prefect of Egypt, in AD 300, it was popularly known to medieval Europeans as 'Pompey's Pillar'. Cyriaco of Ancona, who attempted to decipher the alleged dedicatory inscription, mistook some of the Greek letters he managed to read, declaring them to be part of the name of Alexander's architect Deinocarates, and declared

3.6 The so-called Pompey's Pillar

that the pillar was the 'Alexandrian column of the king'.

Others pondered over the two 'needles' covered with strange signs and other whimsicalities, said to be on the site of Cleopatra's palace by the harbour. One was still erect but the other lay broken on the ground. Some compared them to the obelisks exciting so much attention in Rome, which in the sixteenth century were being zealously resurrected and restored from the antique ruins to punctuate the squares in front of important churches. In 1588, Michele Mercati, a Roman antiquarian, wrote the first treatise (citing 79 ancient authors) on his city's obelisks. Moreover, he was one of those sixteenth-century writers who attempted to decipher the hieroglyphs on the obelisks he examined. Among contemporary travellers' accounts of Egypt quoted by Michele was that of al-Hasan ibn Muhammad al-Wazzani al-Fasi, known as Leo Africanus, who had been captured by pirates off Jerba in Tunisia in 1518. Later Leo was presented to Pope Leo X, son of Lorenzo de' Medici, who baptised him in Rome as Giovanni Leone. When he was taken prisoner, Leo Africanus had with him a rough draft in Arabic of his *History and Description of Africa and Notable Things Contained Therein*, which was translated and completed in Italy in 1526 and published by the erudite printer Ramusio in 1550. Leo had visited Alexandria probably between 1515 and 1517, and wrote of its ancient buildings, including the lighthouse and the ruined columns.

In 1547, Pierre Belon du Mans (1518–64), a French doctor and naturalist, travelled to Alexandria from Constantinople in the train of the French ambassador M. Fumet, who had been accredited to the court of the Turkish sultan by King Henry II of France. Pierre commenced his medical education as an apothecary's apprentice before travelling in Europe to study under such teachers as Valerius Cordibus at Wittenberg. Among his patrons were the cardinals of Tournon and Lorraine, and he counted Ronsard among his acquaintances. He was not quite thirty when he arrived in Egypt, where he spent the months of September and October. From the start of his visit it was evident that he had eyes only for the countryside which harboured the strange plants, animals and reptiles. He did not waste his words on recording events and the people he met on the journey. Like Prospero Alpini, besides the flora and fauna, he was filled with curiosity about all kinds of medicinal plants and their habitats. He used to question the merchants and examined the different spices in the Alexandrian bazaar, together with the ostrich skins and feathers

3.7 Ichneumon or 'pharaoh's rat' drawn by Pierre Belon

on sale, noting that the feathers adorning the turbans of the Turks were used in France to decorate the hats of the French cavalry and the caps of the infantry.

Two particular animals caught Pierre's attention, the ichneumon (or pharaoh's rat) and the civet (or hyaena). The ichneumon had a pointed black nose, short round greyish ears and a long tail; its fur, which resembled that of a wolf, was whitish or yellow interspersed with grey. It kept itself as clean as possible and caught the domestic rats and mice. Dextrous and agile, it lived off other prey such as serpents, lizards, frogs, snails and hens. Although it was small, it did not fear to fight with a large dog and equally, if it chanced on a cat, it strangled it with three bites of its teeth. M. Benoit Badiolus from Avignon, the French consul, who also acted for the Florentine community in Alexandria, owned a civet which Pierre said was so tame that when it played with humans it nibbled their noses, their ears and lips without doing any harm. The reason why such a wild animal, usually difficult to tame, was so docile was that from birth it had been suckled with human milk. It had a pointed nose like a cat, its eyes were glittering and red and its whitish coloured body had black spots. Its legs and feet were black and it had a long tail. M. Badiolus was a collector of Egyptian antiquities, and showed Pierre his statues, vases and money, as well as papyri found inside some mummies. After further travels in the Near East, Pierre returned to Paris where he was given the use of a residence in Saint Germaine as well as in the Chateau of Madrid to enable him to write up in peace his various works on the natural history of Egypt. One evening in 1564, however, his life was sadly cut short at the age of 46 when he was set on and cruelly murdered by robbers in the Bois de Boulogne. Even in a short space of time he had managed to accomplish the work that proved to be the foundation of zoological science. Pierre was a true humanist of the Rennaissace; he translated Theophrastus and Dioscorides, using their knowledge as a foundation from which he could build on for his own *Observations*.

Besides its winter rainfall, Alexandria depended on the Nile's annual flood, which was directed from the canal to flow under the southern foundations of the walls. In 1422, Gilbert de Lannoy gave a report to King Henry V of England on the state of the region of Alexandria. He spoke of an iron grating in the canal to the south-east, in a ditch where conduits were placed to divert water into the city. As the water from the inundation was full of silt, initially it was unfit for drinking and the people had to wait until November for it to clear. The waters ran through the ancient conduits and passages into the subterranean reservoirs and private cisterns underground before debouching into the harbour. Many of these antique cisterns were vaulted, built of inlaid marble, bricks and blocks of stone, and big enough for even soldiers with lances to ride through. Some were very large and deep, having two ranges of columns one above the other, connected together, divided into four or more compartments with round holes in the walls by which one could climb down easily. Others were isolated, filled by means of machines and water wheels with jars attached, mounted over large wells connected with the nearest branch of an underground canal. There were also a few fed by the winter rainfall. Samuel Kiechel (1563–1619), a keen young German traveller from Ulm who came to Alexandria from Jerusalem in 1588, was filled with curiosity about the wells, and accordingly spent some of his time in climbing down the notched sides into the old subterranean reservoirs. While he admired their construction, he saw that they had become haunts of thieves and beggars who could use them as hiding places before emerging to pillage the houses above.

After the annual inundation surged into the subterranean channels from the Alexandrian canal, Prospero Alpini from Padua warned those who used the fresh water that mingled with the old putrid residue in the subterranean places. He said that the mixture was so unsavoury that those who drank it suffered from many pestilences and fevers. At this time too there arose a most obnoxious smell from the unsavoury ordure flushed out by the flood, which was particularly noticeable by the harbour.

By the time that the erudite Filippo Pigafetta from Vicenza arrived in Alexandria in 1577, he was already a seasoned traveller. He came from a family of explorers, as his noble uncle Antonio had accompanied the Portuguese Magellan (whom he outlived) on his voyage round the world. The natural son of Matteo Pigafetta, whom he called 'uncle', Filippo was recognised by his contemporaries as being a philosopher, a mathematician and a student of classical authors, from whose works he studied military and naval affairs. He was a prodigious and detailed writer, had fought in many wars and was fortunate in having many influential friends.

Besides his description of Egypt, Filippo wrote extensively of his other travels. In a later account he produced a charming vignette of his visit to the English court of Queen Elizabeth I in 1582. He found the journey slow from Vicenza, with a speed of thirty miles a day if they were lucky, as at times they were forced to carry the coach. At Dover the customs searched their bags thoroughly for any subversive religious material, but on producing letters from Elizabeth's foreign minister, Francis Walsingham, they were allowed to proceed. The wooded roads to London were dangerous and beset by robbers, but on arrival they were pleased to find good lodgings with an attractive flower garden. Filippo noted that Walsingham spoke beautiful Italian 'like all English noblemen'. At court there were a number of Italian musicians and the richly apparelled courtiers, though small in number, were the most noble of the island. On entering the room where the Queen gave audience, Filippo doffed his cap and perceived her sitting on a gold chair covered with a baldachin of gold velvet. He described her as 'thin with a long face, not displeasing', and stated that she knew Greek, Latin, Italian, French and Spanish. Soon after, he watched her depart for prayers in a small church amid the sounds of an organ. Her ladies with flowers in their hair followed her in a long line.

Like the tale of his English visit, Filippo's narrative of Egypt was in the form of a tourist diary, though he often repeated himself in his zeal to include the smallest detail. Besides being a pious pilgrim, it is quite possible that he was sent to Egypt on a journey of espionage, as the long title of his work mentions the military forces of the Turks who occupied Egypt. The threat of the Turkish armies in Europe was grave and Filippo warned all Catholics to unite against the dangers. Though his Egyptian account remained unpublished in his lifetime, Filippo dedicated one of the manuscripts to Pope Sixtus V, for whom he had acted as legate to the king of Persia to make common cause against the Turks.

3.8 Fort of Qaitbay on the site of the ancient pharos

Although spying on the Turks was dangerous for a Christian visitor, Filippo meticulously described the old fort of Qaitbay with its crenellated retaining wall and the extent of the military guards. Though he did not see them, he ascertained that there was a quantity of artillery pieces in the castle, so he counted the number of portholes that could be used for guns and which way they faced. He described three other towers guarding the port, how the mole was situated, and noted that of the two harbours, the one allowed for Christian use was exposed to a strong wind from the east. Moreover he warned of the hazardous rocks hidden in the shallows of the harbour.

During the one and a half months Filippo spent in Alexandria, he noted that the remaining inhabited areas were roughly divided into three distinct parts. The bazaar flourished with the business quarter and the *fondachi*, except that of the French which lay beyond it in the same street. The area near the church of St Mark was inhabited by the Copts, the Greeks, some Cypriots and those Franks who did not wish to live in their own hostelries. The third and most beautiful part stretched from the Rosetta Gate almost up to the centre of the city, where there were some very good houses, mosques and other buildings. Here and there along the street were many large columns hewn of the same stone as those in St Mark's square, though smaller.

Elsewhere, except for the baths near the old castle and a few houses by the Pepper Gate, everything was in ruins, the friable stone reduced to powder by the hot desert winds. Filippo found it 'cosa degna di compassione' (something worthy of compassion.).

Outside the city he saw a group of new houses surrounded by gardens and orchards, stretching for about a quarter of a mile near the shore on the plain between the isthmus and the walls. Jews, foreigners with their merchandise and Turkish officials lived there, all preferring the fresh sea breezes to the stale air in the town; there were also some small shops, a food market and a large building constructed by one of the pashas for his profit. To the west of the isthmus there was an area of shipbuilding, while to the east of it there was nothing save some Bedouin tents with their openings away from the prevailing wind. Inside the walls there still remained the two main routes which crossed in the middle of the town linking the four gates, following the pattern of the old Greek city, whose columned streets had been laid out in a grid.

The crenellated city walls included much of the old stone taken from the ancient buildings; Filippo compared their architecture to those of Constantinople and Salonika. They were punctuated at regular intervals by towers with rooms reached by stairways to house the garrison. Some were abandoned and dangerous; Filippo noted that they were now stables and habitations for crows and other birds, and that wolves and foxes were seen there. During the Mamluk era, in times of suspected attack, the Christian community was enlisted to man the battlements, where at night they were obliged to display lanterns, similar to those to be seen in the Coptic churches. Between the double walls was a wide passageway where people could walk in safety.

The massive Marine, Rosetta and Pepper Gates (the western gate by the old castle was smaller) appeared both larger and different in form to those of European cities. Their bases, architraves and columns, each of one piece of stone, were of granite, which Filippo called *pietra tebaica*. The stone was similar to that of the Alexandrian obelisks, whose different grains of two or three colours Pierre Belon had likened to the spots on the breast of a starling. The Rosetta and Pepper Gates contained four doors in the walls leading out from an interior vaulted vestibule. One door gave access from outside and faced the door leading into the city. The two others opened into each side of the walkway. Exceptionally, the Marine Gate on the shore had no gate on its left-hand side, where the customs house was situated with its open and covered courtyards. The major gates were guarded not by armed men, but only by some Alexandrians who opened and closed them with large wooden keys. Jewish customs officers diligently searched both the incoming and outgoing travellers as well as their sacks and bags.

Filippo left for Cairo with Niccolò Giustiano, a Genoese merchant, on 7 February 1578. They joined a large flotilla of boats at Rosetta, its leader, which did not have to pay customs dues, displaying a pennant. Filippo had found the winter air in Alexandria 'torbida e malenconica' ('cloudy and dismal'). It was difficult to breathe and life was not tolerable because of the rain, the winds and the mud. At night it was necessary to have two blankets, and by day to put on warm clothes. Early in the morning there was fine mist, cold, unhealthy and born of the night, smelling of sulphur, afterwards dispersed by the rising sun.

Occasionally the citizens of Alexandria were enlivened by the arrival from Europe of important ambassadors who were travelling to the court of the ruler in Cairo. In 1512 Domenico Trevisan, the Venetian Ambassador Extraordinary, had been sent on a mission to the penultimate Mamluk sultan, Qansuh al-Ghawri (ruled 1501–17). In his eulogistic report to the Signoria, Zaccaria Pagani, the ambassador's secretary left no stone unturned in informing them of the rightful honours paid to their emissary. The Venetian merchants of Alexandria had dispatched to the ambassadors' galleys in the harbour two large decorated *palischermi* (pinnaces) decked out with crimson cloth to transport him to the quay. Awaiting the party were the amir of Alexandria and his attendants and a vizier (a master of the pen, one of the sultan's high officials). The amir had brought seven horses to the quayside for the ambassador and his family to ride. This underlined the envoy's status, as only Mamluk officials and ambassadors were allowed to ride horses in Egypt; all others were forced to travel on mules, asses and camels. When the procession arrived within a bowshot of the *fondaco* of the Venetians, they found that the road was decorated with red cloth. The door of the *fondaco* was decked out in crimson and red silk together with the ambassador's coat of arms.

On arrival at the amir's residence, formalities were exchanged in a large open courtyard where Domenico was invited to sit on a *mastaba* (a low platform). The amir who awaited his arrival was similarly seated nearby, his *mastaba* covered by a costly carpet. Ordinary travellers, such as Lionardo di Frescobaldi and his Tuscan friends in 1384, who had sought permits to travel in Egypt and favours such as the purchase of wine, were obliged to remove their shoes and stockings before going into the courtyard. When they entered, they had to kneel and kiss the ground three times. After mounting the staircase to the audience room they were not invited to sit, nor allowed to stand on the carpet which covered the *mastaba* on which the amir was seated cross-legged like a tailor.

Zaccaria Pagani was greatly impressed by the opulent guest house allotted to his party. The marble floors were of precious stones and the doors, of which there were more than sixty, were inlaid with ivory and ebony. He estimated that its cost must have been more than 70,000 ducats, a sum he found incredible. The amir sent the ambassador plentiful baskets of food which included ten *castroni* (castrated lambs), three *cesti di piselli freschi in erba* (baskets of fresh peas), two *cesti di ravi* (baskets of radishes), two *cesti di naranze* (baskets of oranges) and ten *Galline paja* (ten pairs of chickens). In return, the company of the Venetians provided opulent gifts of cloth including *Restagno d'oro per una vesta* (a particular gold brocade for a garment) and *Raso arzentin* (silver fabric from Brescia). These were popular presents, as Mamluk lords delighted to dress in Venetian cloth and their ladies rejoiced in gowns of *tele di Renso* (fabric from Rheims). The ambassador had brought six blocks of cheese from Venice as a personal gift to the amir. These rich presents were only small samples of those ferried by barges from Rosetta to Qansuh al-Ghawri, his chief wife and officials in Cairo. Zaccaria's subsequent account of their reception at the citadel at the beginning of May resembled a fabulous story taken from the *Thousand and One Nights*.

Notes

Alexandria, foundation and early history: Fraser, *Ptolemaic Alexandria*. Lighthouse: Breccia, *Alexandria ad Aegyptum*, pp. 107–10; Fraser, *Ptolemaic Alexandria*, I, p. 20; Forster, *Alexandria*, pp. 145–52; *Pharos and Pharillon*, pp. 15–24; Gibb (ed.), *Ibn Battuta, Travels*, p. 46; Lehmann, *Cyriacus of Ancona's Egyptian Visit*, p. 13; Van Essen, 'Cyriaque d'Ancone', p. 297. Traditions of Coptic church in Alexandria: Burmester, *Ancient Coptic Churches of Cairo*, pp. 7–9. Trade, general: valuable general reading in works listed by Ashtor; Braudel, *Wheels of Commerce*, II (difficulties of Portuguese in maintaining spice route, pp. 543–70); F.C. Lane, *Fleets and Fairs*, pp. 649–65; Day, *Medieval Market Economy*, p. 126; Heyd, *Histoire du Commerce du Levant*, II (ports, ships, pp. 427–37; spices, pp. 443–47; taxes and flotillas, pp. 449–53; slaves, pp. 556–53; cotton and sugar, pp. 611–14; pepper, pp. 658–61); F.C. Lane, *Fleets and Fairs*, pp. 649–65; Lapidus, *Muslim Cities in the Late Middle Ages*, pp. 6, 24; Van Gennep, 'Le Ducat Vénetien en Egypte', pp. 373–81, 494–508. *Fondachi*: Heyd, *Histoire du Commerce du Levant*, II, pp. 430–34. Italian traders: Evans (ed.), *Francesco Pegolotti, La Practica della Mercatura*, pp. 69–72; Dopp (ed.), *Le traité d'Emmanuel Piloti* (price of houses, products of Alexandria, pp. 36–38; commerce of Cairo and Alexandria with Europe and the Middle East, pp. 45–76); F.C. Lane, *Andrea Barbarigo, Merchant of Venice* (company's agents in Egypt and Syria, pp. 93–113). Attack by Peter Lusignan: Runciman, *History of the Crusades*, III, pp. 441–49; Holt, *Age of the Crusades*, pp. 125–27. Canal and cisterns: Breccia, *Alexandria ad Aegyptum*, pp. 78–83; Heyd, *Histoire du Commerce du Levant*, II, pp. 436–37; da Schio (introd.), *Viaggio di Filippo Pigafetta*, pp. 86–88; Sauneron (ed.), *Voyage en Egypte de Pierre Belon*, p. 94b; *Voyages en Egypte, S. Kiechel, H. Teufel*, pp. 34–36; Dopp (ed.), *Le traité d'Emmanuele Piloti*, pp. 23–24. Venetian attack on Naxos: Dopp (ed.), *Le traité d'Emmanuel Piloti*, pp. 95–103. Topography, importance of port: Dopp (ed.), *Le traité d'Emmanuel Piloti*, pp. 6–10; da Schio (introd.), *Viaggio di Filippo Pigafetta* (fortifications, gates, walls, Church of St Mark, pp. 65–86). Ruined state: Dopp (ed.), *Le traité d'Emmanuel Piloti*, p. 6; da Schio (ed.), *Viaggio di Filippo Pigafetta*, p. 92. Further observations by pilgrims: Esposito (ed.), *Itinerarium Symon Semeonis* (religion, manners and customs, pp. 45–65); Bellorini and Hoade (ed. and trans.), *Frescobaldi, Gucci and Sigoli*, pp. 149–150; Sauneron (ed.), *Voyage en Egypte de Pierre Belon* (fauna, pp. 93a–95b). Venetian embassy: Barozzi (ed.), *Zaccaria Pagani, Viaggio di Domenico Trevisan*, pp. 12–19.

CHAPTER 4

Sailing Upstream to Cairo

When I came to Alexandria, a city of Egypt, I, longing for novelty
(as a thirsty man longs for fresh water) departed from these places
as being well known to all and entering the Nile arrived at Cairo.
Ludovico di Varthema, *Travels in Egypt, Syria and Arabia*

Once travellers left the bustling decaying port of Alexandria they were
absorbed into the atmosphere of the countryside, where the fellahin
had followed the daily round according to the rhythm of the Nile since
the time of the pharaohs. No matter which conqueror had invaded the
land, later to recede as the tide, the life of the native Egyptians kept to
its inexorable pattern, varied by the levels of harsh taxation levied to
enrich the rulers.

On 5 October 1382, after a week of rest and sightseeing, Lionardo
Frescobaldi and his companions prepared to set off for Cairo. Presumably the wine granted to them as a favour during their audience at
the house of the chief amir had all been drunk, since the Tuscans asked
the Venetian consul to fill up their barrel of malmsey for the journey.

Having paid an exit toll from the city of four ducats each, they were
committed to their Muslim guide and interpreter, who with his son
would conduct them to the Grand Interpreter, a Venetian renegade
and high official at the court of the sultan Barquq. Sa'id was then an
old man of 70, and Simone Sigoli thought that he was, for a Saracen,
quite a good man. He told Simone that in his life he had accompanied
the pilgrims who went to St Catherine's and the Holy Sepulchre 67
times. One of the pilgrims he had so carefully looked after in 1347 was
Niccolò di Poggibonsi on his journey to St Catherine's monastery (see
Chapter 8 below).

The party rode away from Alexandria on asses with camels to transport their baggage. The road afforded a good view of the high walls, punctuated by towers and surrounded by moats. About a mile or more from the city, 'in very great and immeasurable heat', they reached Fuwa, the port on the canal that supplied the sweet water to Lake Mareotis and Alexandria. Though the beginning of October marked the end of the Nile's rise, the high water still flooded over the bordering plains, which resembled the sea, an astonishing sight to the Franks whose rivers at home had mostly dried up in the summer's heat. As soon as the flood subsided, the peasants turned the mud over with their implements or drove out the sheep to trample the grain into the wet earth, a practice that had remained unchanged since pharaonic times. The delta of Egypt, one of the most fertile lands in the world, yielded two crops each season.

In his third reign (1310–41), al-Nasir Muhammad started up many ambitious and expensive engineering projects intended to catch and

4.1 Camel drawn by Prospero Alpini

control the Nile waters, one of these being the dredging of the brick-lined Alexandrian canal. Due to his efforts the canal remained navigable throughout the year for the greater part of the fourteenth century. It was dug out twice in 1326, and though the sultan Barsbay effected further repairs they did not last long. Because of economic problems many of al-Nasir Muhammad's successors adopted a hand-to-mouth policy in the maintenance of water systems, which were only spasmodically renewed. In the sixteenth century, under Turkish rule, renewal and dredging work seemed to have lapsed, so instead of a leisurely trip on the water to Fuwa, travellers often had to ride to the port of Rosetta along a sandy road near the shore lined with high feathery tamarisks and groves of tall palms.

The Tuscans were either rowed or pulled along the canal in their flat-bottomed Nile boats (called giarmas by the Franks) by their Saracen boatmen. Lionardo di Frescobaldi estimated the depth of the water to be 14 braccia (one braccio equalled about two thirds of a metre). Thirty-five miles away from Alexandria they saw Damanhur receding towards the land of the Arabs on the right-hand side, surrounded by good hunting and camping country. On the way they caught great quantities of good and beautiful fish, though they found the oil for cooking them was distasteful. They passed by a 'great number of beautiful and fine gardens with great quantities of the most perfect fruits: oranges, cedars, lemons, Adam's apples, walnuts, dates, figs, pomegranates, water melons and cassia'. Besides the banana trees, Lionardo had never seen the fig trees of pharaoh, 'thick, high as oaks with small leaves producing white fruit of good taste about seven times a year'. When the winter winds brought rain and the thrushes grew fat feeding on the dates, the Frankish merchants came with crossbows and nets to catch the turtle doves and the migratory birds. Around Alexandria could be seen many suburbs and beautiful houses, 'after the Saracen fashion', which were used for holidays. The gardens were watered by wells and small canals with wooden sluice gates which were opened as necessary. By 1577, Filippo Pigafetta from Vicenza saw that many of the houses were empty, their owners had left and they had fallen into disrepair. Nevertheless, he enjoyed resting in the shade of the trees and fishing in the canal with some bread which he threw into the stagnant water. Bedouin girls working the land entertained the party by singing and dancing, adding to the merriment by lifting their skirts to show 'before and behind' without shame.

In the suite of the French ambassador to the Ottoman court, the Parisian doctor Pierre Belon was forced to ride along the shore road to Rosetta to reach the Nile's tributary, as the inundation almost covered the small nearby villages, which only showed their tips above the water. About half a league from the city, they reached sandy open country where Pierre found a spiny plant called kali by the Arabs, who dried it for burning, as firewood was scarce. The Arabs mixed the ashes with lime (Pierre called it soda), and they were carefully kept for sale to the Venetians. The ashes subsequently hardened into a stony mass which was loaded into trading ships for export to Venice as an ingredient for manufacturing the renowned crystal glass. The glassmakers of Murano mixed the imported material with pebbles from Pavia, making the paste for their wide range of fine crystal glasswares. These included such desirable delicate objects as goblets, bowls, tazzas, hanging lamps, beakers, jugs and reliquaries, so much in demand in Europe. Some, suitable for the Egyptian market, were exported to Alexandria and Cairo via such merchants as the Venetian Emanuel Piloti. At that time the two basic raw materials of vitreous paste were silica, obtained from quarried sand or quartz pebbles, and soda ash, derived from burnt vegetation of coastal origin, brought in from Syria and Alexandria. Stabilising agents such as lime, not available in Murano, were present in small quantities in the soda ash and were automatically absorbed into the mixture.

Dotted around the flat countryside of the Egyptian delta there were curious domed structures used for poultry rearing; the same methods had been employed since the time of the pharaohs. Pierre, versed in the classical authors, observed that only the Egyptians kept to their ancient ways and habits. Instead of eggs being incubated covered by the wings of the hen, they were placed in ovens and covered with manure from the stable; this manure, composed of cow and goat dung mixed with straw, was lit and replenished at intervals to regulate the temperature. As many as three or four thousand eggs brought by local villagers could be communally heated by this method. While living in

4.2 Fat-tailed sheep

Cairo, Emanuel Piloti, who frequented a hatchery between the city and Old Cairo, heard the farmers crying out loudly in the streets after the allotted days of incubation: 'A hatchment of chickens is ready and will be released tomorrow'. He watched the poultry-keeper drive the chickens along the busy streets where they scattered around among the pedestrians and the hooves of the animals, only to regroup miraculously once more in the middle of the road. Scooped up by the load and sold by weight rather than number, the chickens, with their legs protruding at all angles, were shovelled into containers and bought by the customers at the doors of their houses.

The sheep grazing in the countryside had surprisingly fat heavy tails. The sultan al-Nasir Muhammad had encouraged the Turkomans to bring their herds from Syria to Egypt to improve local breeds. He even kept a select flock of his own near Cairo, in addition to his studs of horses and fine camels. Flocks of goats with long ears trailing on the ground gleaned what they could from the scrub. Pierre Belon watched the goatherds whiling away the time as they sieved the sand in their search for fine antique coins and medals of gold and silver.

About three leagues (c.12 km) along the road to Rosetta from

Alexandria, Pierre's party found a vessel full of good Nile water, provided by the Turks 'for the love of God' from leather bottles brought by camels. To replenish the water along the major routes for travellers was considered to be alms of great merit. As they followed the shore of the Mediterranean, the darkness of the night overtook them, though they did not stop until they reached the sweet water gushing out of one of the tributaries of the Nile. After fording it where it ran into the sea, they chanced on a fisherman's house on the seashore. There was little there except salt, which was used to manufacture the relish made from mullet's eggs, a practice that had continued over the centuries.

When the Nile rose, hippopotami, taking advantage of the flood, waded ashore in good weather and ravaged the cultivation, devouring the tempting succulent plants within their reach. When the inhabitants saw them coming, they lit fires in their path to frighten them away, making them trundle off before doing further damage. Never having encountered at home these strange, brown, hairless animals, lacking horns on their enormous heads, with their tiny pointed ears, small pig-like feet and tails and enormous elephantine bulk, the Europeans called them 'river horses'. They feared their undulating cavortings in the

4.3 Hippopotamus drawn by Prospero Alpini

water, as they were liable to overturn the flat river craft swirling among the currents of the Nile.

Far worse than the hippopotami were the crocodiles, with wicked porcine eyes, short legs, long pointed feet, thrashing tail and snapping jaws devouring man and beast alike. They infested the shallows along the shores, sometimes even invading the villages in search of prey, the contents of their stomachs revealing pathetic corpses of children, dogs and other animals. A bird that some compared to a black and white partridge was seen perching on the reptiles' heads, occasionally diving into their mouths to peck out the regurgitated food (described by Herodotus, *Histories* 11.48 and Pliny, *Natural History* 37.90). The eggs laid by the females on the river bank were hatched in the sand by the heat of the sun; if it were not for the ichneumon, which found them irresistible, the country would have been completely overrun by crocodiles, some of which grew to a great length. When possible, they were hunted by the intrepid villagers, who trapped them with baits of meat placed in a pit over which a light covering of greenery laced with mud had been laid. When the crocodiles fell into the pits in seeking the lure, they were tightly secured with ropes and taken for sale in iron cages to Cairo. Their thick scaly hides were much in demand, not only as trophies but for lining the doors of strongholds; some even said that the meat was palatable and tasted sweet like chicken. Crocodile meat could be found for sale in the market stalls of Cairo where it was a popular commodity.

4.4 Crocodile drawn by Pierre Belon

Despite all these hazards, the Nile, the highway of Egypt, was revered by fourteenth- and fifteenth-century travellers as being the second of the four rivers (called Gihon) which issued from Eden and encompassed the whole land of Ethiopia (Genesis 2.10–13). A plenary indulgence was granted to those pilgrims who reached it. Father Francesco Suriano, a Franciscan friar born in Venice in 1450 of a wealthy mercantile marine family, knew Egypt well; as a child he had spent time in his uncle's merchant ship trading along the coasts of the Mediterranean. He spoke Greek and Arabic, and at the ports of call when visiting the fondachi he became familiar with the life in maritime cities. But at the age of 25 he gave up being a merchant and entered the Franciscan order, where his knowledge of languages and experience of the Middle East were immediately put to good use by his superiors. After an initial stay in Palestine, from 1493 to 1515 he held the office of Father Guardian of the Franciscan convent at Mount Sion in Jerusalem. At that time this post was a powerful one in the lands of the Mamluks, almost comparable with that of the Sovereign Pontiff himself. Francesco's duties included taking divine service in the shrines, looking after the pilgrims in the Holy Land and giving religious assistance to the European merchants in Egypt and the Middle East. In addition, he used to preach the Lent sermons to the trading community in Cairo and Alexandria (for which he was paid alms to supplement the intermittent, sometimes meagre funds from Europe). At these times Francesco frequently used the great Nile waterway: 'Its water has this property, as I experienced during my long sojourn in Cairo, that drinking it on an empty stomach, it satiates you as if you had eaten, and drinking it to your fill after meals it purges the body like medicine of rhubarb, gently without injury or haste.' Ancient authors extolled the properties of Nile water. Galen recognised three qualities: good taste, clarity of colour and a sweet smell. In order to clarify the water, having filled up some large vessels, the Egyptians used to take a handful of almonds which they rubbed against the sides, afterwards crushing them in the palms of their hands. Then, plunging their arms up to the shoulder in the container, they left the almonds to act as a filter at the bottom. After about three or four hours the water, clear as a glass, could be decanted into small jugs. When

Francesco Suriano embarked for the four-day journey in winter to preach in Alexandria, he often saw the sailors jump into the water to draw the boat off from a sandbank when it had grounded. Making the same journey after the inundation along the artificial canal in summer he thought it 'marvellous to see the feast and rejoicing of all the people of Alexandria when the said water arrives'. It was a time when many crocodiles were caught.

The port of Rosetta, which lay along the bank of the main western mouth of the Nile, was shaded by palm trees and described as a 'a fair town without walls'. Even large boats could moor right up to the houses built of dried mud bricks. Within the town there was a large fondaco belonging to the Venetians, who were well placed to observe the volumes of merchandise and shipping handled at the depot and the boats plying to and from Cairo. Both Rosetta and Damietta, on the eastern branch of the Nile, were guarded against piratical attack by strongly fortified castles at the entrances. Some of the larger river craft loaded with cargoes for Alexandria could venture out to sea, braving the sandbanks and the heaving waves whipped up by the north wind when they encountered the strong currents of the milky debouching Nile. It could be a dangerous shore, as experienced by a young traveller Hans Christoph Teufel, Baron of Gunderstaf in Austria. On 9 December 1588, he took ship from Damietta for Tripoli in Syria. Because it was winter, a time when sea communications were severely curtailed, the passengers had to pay double fare to the master of the decked boat on which they were booked to sail. Three days earlier, the vessel had been moored in the open sea after unloading its cargo; therefore, in order to reach it, the party was ferried for about eight miles in a giarma, which ran aground on a sandbank at the mouth of the river. The turbulence of the sea kept heaving them out of the channel, with one wave following another, so that their shallow boat became dangerously full of water. Invoking the aid of Almighty God, the passengers, by dint of pushing with all their strength with oars and rods, managed to extricate the boat and reach the caramusale which unfurled its sails before evening. All passengers gave thanks for their survival.

The story of Johann Wild (b. 1585?), a soldier and native of Nuremberg, is one of the most astonishing to be written by a European traveller to Egypt at the beginning of the seventeenth century. Johann was the son of Hans Wild and his wife Catherine and was baptised in Nuremberg on 26 or 27 December 1598. Otherwise nothing much is known of him except that he probably had a good education, since he cited the classics in his account of his experiences, and knew Latin. At the age of 19 he went to Hungary to fight against the Turks in the army of Rudolph II. Johann was born into the century during which

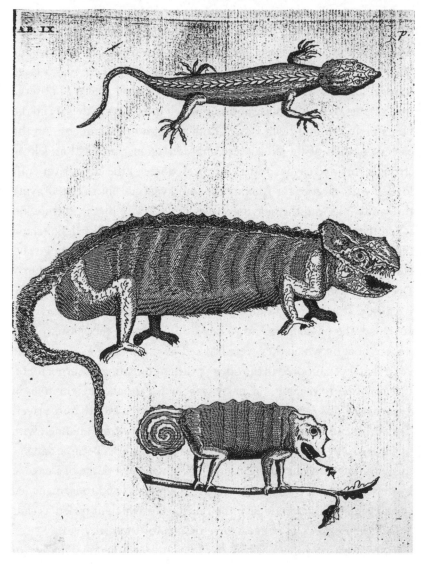

4.5 Lizards drawn by Prospero Alpini

the Turks were looked on as 'the present terror of the world', although in 1603 they found themselves fighting on two fronts: against the Persians, ruled by the powerful Shah 'Abbas (1557–1629), to the east, and the Habsburgs to the west

In spite of enduring great privations, Johann managed to write a gripping account of his adventures, as well as a graphic description of the manners and customs of the people of Egypt. He liked a soldier's life, was a brave man and happy when he had the whiff of powder in his nostrils and heard the cannon balls whistling around his ears. But his misfortunes arose while he was fighting in Hungary in the army of the emperor Rudolph II and was taken prisoner. Ten days later he was sold to a Turk who abruptly cut off his hair, which made him very sorrowful. After passing through the hands of further Turkish masters he was bought by a pasha, who meted out severe physical punishments to his unfortunate prisoner for alleged misdemeanours, eventually taking him to Constantinople. After the pasha's death, Johann was sold for 60 ducats to a slave merchant who travelled twice a year from Constantinople to sell his slaves, together with other merchandise, in Cairo. On the way, his habit was to stop at either Damietta or Rosetta to buy rice. Thus it happened that after Johann landed at Alexandria, with a fellow slave, they proceeded to Rosetta in readiness to transport the goods up the river to Cairo. After searching in vain for accommodation in the town, the merchant ordered Johann and his companions to carry all his goods into a mosque so they could shelter while looking for a boat to transport them. According to Johann:

> This church was never closed, neither by day nor night and many beggars and good for nothing villains lay down there for the night. My master could not find a lodging because all the rooms were full; this is why we had to be satisfied with a church. When it was night the sacristan came to light the lamps. But when he saw that we too lay down there, he warned my master that he must take great care of his belongings because there were many thieves there. When my master heard this he told the sacristan to fill up the oil right up in the lamps which were hanging above us, so that they would burn all night so we could see. And my master offered him a tip. As for us, we had to keep

watch that night one after another, we were three captive young men
as well as my master's valet. When we three young men had kept watch
the first half of the night, my master said that we must sleep which we
did; he and the valet wishing to take the rest of the watch up to the
day. But while there still remained one hour to the stirring of day, they
also slept. Then came a thief who wanted to extract the money from
my master's clothing. This woke him up and he started to cry out:
'Rogue, thief! Get up and catch the robber!' We were all frightened
and quickly sprang up with a jump, but the lamps had gone out and
it was dark as an oven, so much that we could not perceive the thief.
He had certainly not left the church but had lain down in a corner and
pretended to sleep. Besides there were a great many naked Moors and
beggars. Who would have been able to find the robber or the culprit
among more than two hundred who go barefoot? And in Egypt as well
as in Arabia it is the custom that a person cannot be arrested or accused
of something if he was not arrested in 'flagrant delit' and the object
has not been found on him; only then is it believed [that it is true] and
the thief condemned as he deserves.

When daylight came, they made a search to see if the thief had taken
anything away but found nothing lost except three or four ducats
which he had ripped from the coat of the merchant's valet, into which
they had been stitched. Their journey continued with further dangers:

On the third day, early in the morning, we carried our baggage once
more on to a boat and left for Cairo. But the boat which was well
loaded [carried] a few Turks. We travelled all that day (while it was
light and three hours more during the night) as we had a good wind.
Then the boatman stopped near a village, let down the sail and made
fast the boat to the shore; and [we] rested, ate and drank, each
according to what he had brought and what pleased him. After we had
eaten and drunk we lay down in the boat and slept. Each one took his
weapons with him, each loaded his gun and each made provision as
best as he could. But when midnight had passed and all were in a deep
sleep some loud cries rang out on our boat, so much that in our sleep
we were frightened, not knowing what was happening. Because on his

own one of the Arab servants on the boat shouted: 'Get up Sirs! Arm yourselves, the robbers are quite near.' The Turks seized their guns and their bows as well as their sabres, but they saw nothing. And to the man who had first cried out, they shouted 'Impudent dog! Where are the robbers?' But he replied 'Look now at the water. Do you not see the boat?'

They looked all around them, and at first could see nothing as it was very dark and they were frightened. But soon they saw the boat coming towards them in silence and a man sitting in it heading to the shore scarcely a stone's throw away. Then one of the Turks fired so accurately at the assailant that he fell backwards into the water. At this the man's companions jumped to their feet in the boat and shot their arrows, which fell thickly down on Johann's party as if it were snowing. The next day, the relieved travellers were able to dress their wounds with the aid of a bundle of barber's instruments, which the Turks habitually carried with them on their journeys. Being expert swimmers, the Nile raiders might surprise sleepers by swiftly climbing aboard, seizing as much as they could, even killing the passengers and making off with the loot. Some travellers placed lighted candles around the edge of their boats and fired their arquebusses at intervals to frighten off intruders.

Having satisfied his curiosity about the cisterns of Alexandria, Samuel Kiechel travelled to Cairo with the Venetian vice-consul of Alexandria. He was fortunate to go with someone experienced, as the consul had hired a vessel for the party of four which included two janissaries each armed with a large gun. Samuel was warned that only three weeks previously a Venetian merchant, accompanied by his two janissaries and the owner of the ship, had all been presumed killed as the boat, its cargo and all the inhabitants had completely vanished.

Samuel's party started the voyage in a favourable north wind. But the day after, a stifling sirocco blew up from the south-west, causing them to be stationary in the heat. It was enervating to proceed against both the high wind and the current, although at the dropping of the wind, crews often went ashore and resorted to dragging the boat along with ropes. When conditions were fair, the sails filled and the vessels,

4.6 Irrigating the fields

shaded from the sun by mats spread above the centre of the boat, glided upstream passing by a succession of villages. Along the banks of the river, there were endless scenes of cultivation, with the mesmeric sights of oxen at work turning the water wheels and the peasants working their shadufs. At the Nile's height, herdsmen forced their animals to cross the river by swimming a distance as much as two and a half miles. Having stripped off their clothes, they tied two long pumpkins under the arms down to the thighs, and drove the cattle to swim forward, goaded by a stick. Troops of boys and girls of about 14 years, all stark naked, customarily begged for lemons, which they picked up without any shame of nudity. Occasionally the girls sported leather belts from which dangled a small piece of skin about four fingers wide, cut into strips, which dangled in front of their private parts. The ribbons of skin twisted and twirled at the mercy of the wind when they ran, but some of them willingly displayed these intimacies for a piece of biscuit.

At length, when glimpses of the pyramids arose from the plain, an unforgettable sight in the pink light of dawn, even though Cairo was not yet in view, the boatmen prostrated themselves in prayer, knowing the journey was at an end.

Notes

River Nile, flora, fauna: Crawford, 'Some Medieval Theories About the Nile', pp. 6–29; Bellorini and Hoade (ed. and trans.), *Frescobaldi, Gucci and Sigoli* (sluice gates, height of canal 20 *braccia* on 5–6 October, pp. 42–43); *Francesco Suriano*, pp. 193–95; *Fra Niccolò of Poggibonsi*, p. 86; Leo Africanus, *La Descrittione dell'Africa* (danger from hippos, f. 98 v., r.); Alpinus, *Historiae Naturalis Aegypti*, pp. 218, 247; Belon, *Portraits d'Oyseax*, pp. 119, 105–106; Sauneron (ed.), *Voyage en Egypte de Pierre Belon*, pp. 97a–102a; Esposito (ed.), *Itinerarium Symon Semeonis*, pp. 65–71; Bellorini and Hoade (ed. and trans.), *Fra Niccolò of Poggibonsi*, p. 86.; da Schio (introd.), *Viaggio di Filippo Pigafetta*, pp. 94–99. **Rearing of chickens:** Jacquet, 'Des couveuses artificiels', pp. 165–74; Dopp (ed.), *Le traité d'Emmanuel Piloti*, pp. 38–40; da Schio (introd.), *Viaggio di Filippo Pigafetta*, pp. 156–57. **Glass and glassmaking:** Honey, *Glass*, pp. 50–53; Dorigato, *Murano Glass Museum*, p. 17; Sauneron (ed.), *Voyage en Egypte de Pierre Belon*, p. 97a, b. **Adventures on the journey:** Volkoff (ed.), *Le voyage de Johann Wild*, pp. 10–18; Sauneron (ed.), *Voyages en Egypt, S. Kiechel, H. Teufel*, pp. 43–47.

CHAPTER 5

Cairo: 'meeting place of comer and goer'

While Syria had suffered from the onslaughts of the Mongols and the wars of the Crusades, Cairo had escaped almost unmolested. Peace had enabled her to become the fabled cultural city of the Arab world. Foreign visitors were uniformly astonished by the opulence that unfolded before them. Ibn Battuta (b. Tangiers 1304) surpassed himself with his mellifluous prose when he dictated his memoirs on his return to Fez to Muhammad Ibn Juzayy, the current secretary of the sultan:

> I arrived at length at Cairo, mother of cities and seat of Pharaoh the tyrant, mistress of broad regions and fruitful lands, boundless in multitudes of buildings, peerless in beauty and splendour. The meeting place of comer and goer, the halting place of feeble and mighty, whose throngs surge as the waves of the sea, and can scarce be contained in her for all her size and capacity.

Mamluk Cairo was the backdrop against which were played out the fictional stories from the Arabian Nights, those romantic imaginings that took the listeners by the hand and led them round the markets and houses, the high and low life of the streets, and all that touched on the texture of life among the people. The infinitely varied skyline of minarets and domes on view in the capital was remarkable to all European visitors, who hastened to compare Cairo's size with Milan, Venice, Paris, or whichever city was theirs:

> Of the riches of Cairo it is unnecessary to write, for they cannot be enumerated on paper or described in speech. They consist of gold and

5.1 Plan of Cairo, probably drawn by Matteo Pagano in 1549

silver, of cloth of gold and silk, cotton and linen embroidered wares, of gems, pearls and other precious stones, vases of gold, silver and bronze uncomparably decorated in the Saracen style, glass objects most beautifully ornamented commonly made in Damascus, balsam oil, honey, pepper, sugar and various spices, and innumerable jewels of all kinds.

By the beginning of the fourteenth century, Cairo had a population approximating 250,000, though the number could be exaggerated by visitors among the jostling crowds in the streets. But due to the high mortality caused by the bubonic and the (even more lethal) pneumonic plague, which erupted with depressing frequency every few years, this figure fluctuated widely. Massacre and terror were not the only calamities brought by the Mongols in their ambition to conquer the world. The so-called Black Death, as unheralded as the horsemen of the steppes of Ghengis Khan, as devastating as wildfire, followed a relentless path from central Asia to the Black Sea area in 1346, before gathering its strength to lay waste the populations of Europe. Rumour had it that in 1347, when the plague-stricken Tartar army under the Khan Jani Beg was besieging the port of Kaffa, held by the Genoese, he ordered the heads of his soldiers to be catapulted into the fort to infect the defenders – a forerunner of germ warfare. The caravans of the silk route from China, via Baghdad, the Tigris and Armenia to the entrepôt stations of the Italian merchants in the Crimea, which had provided untold wealth to the traders, now transmitted the infection. Mortality took precedence over wealth. The plague permeated the ships, carrying their lethal cargo of rats, together with refugees from the area, some of whom fled to Alexandria to escape its horrors. From Alexandria and Syria in 1347–48, plague spread swiftly throughout Egypt, possibly laying waste about two thirds of the population. Not knowing who to blame, the people spread stories of how the pestilence had been carried by the furs imported for the autocratic Mamluks to trim their clothes.

While on business in Cairo, the Venetian merchant Emanuel Piloti watched the low Nile of 1403 and the consequent famine two years later in 1405, after which the debilitated people suffered a further major eruption of plague more disastrous than the scourge of six years before. The culling of the population in this fashion caused great economic problems for the sultanate, as it affected particularly the royal army of Mamluks and the impoverished peasants who tilled the land. As in other countries, the pestilence was responsible for a marked decline in building works and manufactures. At its height, the streets became littered with the dying, who remained grotesquely where they fell until their bodies were carted away for burial.

While he was a captive, Johann Wild lived in Cairo from 1606 for nearly four years. He was among those fortunate few who survived the bubonic plague. At its sudden onset, he discovered a small blister on his body about the size of a nut; in no time at all the blister grew as large as an egg, black as coal. The following day the tumour broke of its own accord and in suppurating left a hole large enough to contain a pigeon's egg, after which he lay stricken without moving, with a high fever for three days. When the barber was summoned to examine him, the man was reluctant to treat the hole, fearing that his patient would die 'under his hands' as it was near to the heart. For four weeks Johann lay amid great suffering, but after three months of illness he related that God came to his aid and delivered him. Few were the cases when the buboes had discharged and the patient recovered. Scenes of desolation were widespread. In Florence, Giovanni Boccaccio related that the plague 'first showed itself by the emergence of certain tumours in the groin or armpits, some of which grew as large as a common apple, others as an egg'. While it raged, both Christians and Muslims could only resort to prayers to the Almighty, most people regarding the visitation as the will of God to be endured fatalistically. Even the doctors in the *maristan* built by the sultan Qala'un, with their sophisticated medical and surgical instruments, bronze needles to suture wounds, ear tubes, tweezers, tongue depressors and carefully written prescriptions, could not staunch the onslaught of death in such numbers. The plague was the flail of God and the world of Saracen and Frank alike his threshing floor.

The Fatimids, who conquered Cairo in 969 and ruled until 1171, had fortified it with strong walls which enclosed an area of about half a square mile. To the west the city was bounded by the main canal, the Khalij al-Hakim, which traversed the plain issuing from the Nile opposite al-Rawda island, north of Fustat, and acted as a moat beneath the old brick fortifications. Later the canal formed a waterway through the centre of the enlarging urban development. At the north of the city where the fortifications were strongest, two stone gates were built by architects from Edessa, the Bab al-Futuh (Gate of Conquests), constructed in 1087, and the Bab al-Nasr (Gate of Victory), close to its eastern side. At the south lay the Bab Zuwayla, while other gates opened on to the east and west. The city contained a series of streets running north and south and a main street connected the Bab al-Futuh and the Bab Zuwayla, thus dividing it roughly into half. The two splendid palaces of the Fatimid caliphs, the large 'East' and the smaller 'West', lay in the centre of the city.

From its beginning, al-Qahira (later known as Cairo by Italian

5.2 Bab al-Nasr

merchants), built on the edge of the desert, as was the custom of early
Arab rulers, continued to expand and by the fourteenth century the
Bab Zuwayla, the gate in the southern part of the Fatimid walls, had
become integrated into the centre of the city. Cairo and its surroundings eventually became divided roughly into three parts: the main city
of al-Qahira, the outlying suburb which had grown up round the river
port of Bulaq about one kilometre to the north, and the rather decaying
area of Fustat (also known as Old Cairo or Babylon) about two or
three kilometres to the south-west. It was here that Abu 'Abdallah
'Amr ibn al-'As, the Arab conqueror, had first pitched his tent in AD
640 near the old Hadrianic Roman fort. Between the river and the
main city the land was green with trees and orchards, but was liable
to flooding from the Nile.

After describing the fortifications of Alexandria, Filippo Pigafetta

5.3 Bab al-Futuh

sailed upstream to Cairo in 1577. With his interest in topography, he
carefully paced out the urban area of the city and reckoned that its
length totalled about 6,510 steps 'de uomo ordinario', perhaps making
it about three miles and a quarter. He described Cairo as taking the
form of a half moon having wide corners instead of narrow horns, its
concave side following the bend in the river. By that time, many of the
old Fatimid city walls had crumbled and fallen into disuse. Filippo saw
the road leading from the port of Bulaq through orchards of orange
trees, acacias and groves of palms so thick that it was difficult to
discern the gate he called 'Bab al-Bahr' (this was possibly the 'Porto
del Mare' or 'Nile Gate') leading into Nile Gate Street which crossed
the Nasiri Canal. This smaller channel, emanating from the Nile, had
been constructed by the sultan al-Nasir Muhammad during his third
reign between 1310 and 1341 and joined up with the principal Cairo
canal.

To the north of Cairo caravan routes from Gaza and Syria led to
the Bab al-Futuh and Bab al-Nasr, which sucked in and spewed out
some of the richest merchandise in the world. Both gates had imposing
portals flanked by towers with curved fronts; arches spanned the
entrances and cool vaulted interiors contained stout iron bound
wooden doors. Filippo looked at two further gates to the south, the
massive Roman entrance with its round towers leading to Old Cairo
from the Nile, and a second, surrounded by caravans from the south
and Barbary which had brought prized collections of coloured parrots,
ostriches and baboons. By the sixteenth century, the striped ochre and
cream Bab Zuwayla at the southern boundary of the old Fatimid city
rose up as a marker from among the surrounding bazaars; close by
soared the two elegant minarets of the fifteenth-century mosque of the
sultan al-Mu'ayyad Shaykh (ruled 1412–21). Through the Zuwayla
gate ran a main thoroughfare known as 'Main Avenue', threading its
way northwards from the Bab al-Futuh to the citadel. Filippo described
all the gates as being very large, having architraves resting on square
granite bases each cut from a great long single piece. Renowned
throughout the Middle East, they were admired as being prime exam-
ples of military architecture. Off the main thoroughfares grew up an
intricate, confusing labyrinth of unpaved, narrow, dusty alleys, many

of which ended in culs-de-sac and were capable of being closed off at night against the criminal elements lurking in the suburbs.

By the end of the sixteenth century, hardly any of the old city walls remained except along the north side and by the citadel to the south-east. The Nile formed a natural boundary to the west. To the south of the citadel, Filippo mourned the dilapidated grandeur of the tombs of the Circassian Mamluk lords, among which were those of the renowned sultans Barquq and Qaitbay. A road ran through the middle of these proud memorial buildings, each with its domed mosque and minaret, courtyard and garden. Of the cemetery to the north he thought it was 'a thing worthy of marvel, to see so many buildings so large and built with care, which were well kept but now gone to ruin, their lords dead, no one overseeing their upkeep'.

Apart from the plague, ophthalmia had been endemic among the population in Egypt since pharaonic times. After only three months of enslavement in Cairo, Johann Wild had the misfortune to endure a painful eye disease lasting eight days, which made him fearful of going blind. By the grace of God, however, and with the application of egg white and rosewater he recovered. He attributed the illness to the great heat which affected the head and eyes, though others asserted that it was caused by the myriad flies amid the dust, whipped up at random in the sudden winds that swirled and twisted along the narrow streets and into the alleyways. Conscious attempts were made by the author-ities to organise gangs of lowly paid labourers to wash the roads and remove rubbish. As part of their civic duties, shopkeepers were ordered to whitewash their properties, sweep the areas in front of them, hang out nocturnal lanterns and keep fire buckets ready to quench the ever erupting fires.

Disparate nationalities who swelled the urban population – Syrians, Ethiopians, the north African Maghrebis, the Jews, Greeks and Copts – lived in their own quarters, while beggars roamed at will around the city, living off the patronage of the amirs while benefiting from alms and shelter from the mosques. They resorted to devious trickery to wheedle money from passers-by, faking pitiful illnesses and mutilation with unsavoury disguises; alert and cunning, they would resort to cursing those who refused to give. During the rule of the Mamluks, even a 'sultan' of the beggars was tolerated, who could act as a foreman to negotiate with the authorities. The cemeteries provided shelter among the complex of graves for the poorest section of the population. Pickpockets lurked in the shadow of the sepulchres and lovers found them a ghostly refuge for their trysts. The street crowds made way for holy men or saints, 'nude as when they came from the bodies of their mothers'. Though Europeans thought they were mad, they pilfered their food at will from the shops, such behaviour being tolerated by the indulgent population who revered their so-called saintliness. Lining the Bayn al-Qasrayn, the city's major artery, the grand mosques and colleges were surrounded by thousands of shops and booths where goods of all kinds were peddled and takeaway food, such as the so-called honey cakes made of syrup, was on offer. Another side of life was that of Cairo's homosexual community. Dressed in exotic silks, the men lounged on divans in their elegant apartments, indulged in alcohol and told erotic jokes.

In spite of initial opposition by religious fundamentalists, coffee drinking became a pleasurable social pastime in early sixteenth-century Cairo. Coffee houses quickly erupted all over the city, where men lazed around pleasurably on divans and sipped the freshly boiled coffee, which acted as a stimulant for conversation, from delicate cups. These establishments soon became popular meeting places for all classes of society. Illuminated at night by hanging lamps, they made a cheerful scene where story-tellers wove their tales and musicians played on their lutes, two-stringed violins, flutes and mandolins. Interminable games of backgammon, chess and trictrac whiled away the time, and customers were further diverted by the performances of beautiful young men, attired in splendid clothes adorned with gold or silver belts a hand's breadth in width, who danced to the tunes of drums and flutes. On such an evening, Johann Wild saw a youth advance into the middle of the crowd and start to dance, spinning around. In each of his hands he had two pieces of wood which he clacked together very skilfully to the beat of the music. Sometimes he bent his knees and clapped his hands on his breast or on his thighs, rising again to continue his act. After his last whirl, the youth mingled with the audience to ask for tribute. Johann, however, was particu-

5.4 Whirling
darwheesh

larly disgusted by the lascivious behaviour of the intemperate watchful
Turks in the crowd who revelled in such entertainments: 'Because these
ungodly and detestable rascals are the true defilers who taint these
boys. These [entertainments] are contrived only for lewdness and
wantonness. For often when they donate the money they devote themselves to knavery, they kiss them without fearing anyone.' Johann
estimated there were about a hundred coffee taverns in Cairo and if a
Turk, Moor or Arab had to forgo the drinking of coffee for an entire
day, they were unable to be happy or enjoy good health. They even
took coffee to sustain them when travelling round the country; they
boiled it up during the journey and drank it down very hot and strong.
European travellers soon latched on to the habit and brought coffee
back on their return home. In 1587, the Italian naturalist Prospero
Alpini was the first European to sketch a coffee plant as a novelty for
his collection of drawings of the flora of Egypt.

The general hubbub of the streets was heightened by dextrous
jugglers, daring snake charmers and groups of musicians whose
raucous, undulating tunes sounded so alien to European ears. The
evenings were animated by women, who with gay abandon sang songs
accompanied by their drums and mandolins. Johann described a
seductive performer dressed finely in taffeta and satin, with gold coins

adorning her head. She sang with her companions and then danced with her arms outstretched. Known as *ghawazi*, these artistes were in demand to entertain the harems for marriage feasts, circumcision festivities, birthdays and at the time of Ramadan. They frequently resorted to prostitution and were therefore not respected. Comedies enacting stories of knavery and social farce, illuminated by lanterns and torches, took place in the thoroughfares, in which women took parts as well as jesters or fools. The women were beaten harshly and told coarse jokes. If a fool was questioned and did not reply immediately he too was given a blow on the back. Pickpockets and robbers lurked among the audience; Johann's turban was lifted from his head by a thief who ran off with it, while others suffered the loss of their coats, roughly torn off their backs.

Threading their way through the crowds were the indefatigable, docile Egyptian donkeys. Numbers of these biddable animals were gathered for hire on street corners. With uncomplaining patience they carried every kind of passenger: veiled ladies elegant and proud, seated on embroidered cushions with attendants at their sides on their visit to the baths; merchants going about their business; newly arrived foreigners to Cairo – in fact everyone, except the privileged few who rode around on mules or horseback. In addition there were strings of camels plodding their way to and from the Nile, carrying water in goatskin bottles to replenish the jars placed in the courtyards of private houses. The city and its surrounds had a well-regulated system of fixed stops and prices on taking animals for hire. After the Ottoman conquest, the incoming Turks were shocked at the seeming immorality and unbecoming behaviour of the Egyptian women riding donkeys, exposing themselves to the public. They considered it a serious defect, because in their own land prostitutes were paraded on donkeys as punishment. Through the crowds dawdled itinerant water-sellers, who sold Nile water to passers-by from their evil-smelling bottles for a minimal sum. When the Nile was low, this water was drawn from the shores of the river which had been fouled by dirt and the urine of camels.

In 1382, the amir Jarkas al-Khalili, Sultan Barquq's Master of Horse, constructed the great *khan* with three floors off the Bayn al-

Qasrayn. It was a tall solid building which became the hostelry for rich merchants, particularly from Persia, who sold high-quality goods such as brocades, carpets, precious stones and pearls. In 1511 the sultan al-Ghawri rebuilt the Khan al-Khalili and expanded it into a fine trading palace with a fountain in the centre. It remained the major commercial centre, retaining its reputation for opulence and luxury. Large markets attracting jostling crowds were held on Monday and Thursday, selling almost anything money could buy. Europeans looked enviously at beautifully patterned swords inlaid with silver and gold from Damascus, daggers and guns, rich harnesses and exquisitely worked saddlecloths which the Turks treasured for their horses, as well as silks and delicate linen cloth to wind into turbans. There was a large building in the complex with a cool courtyard in the middle surrounded by rooms. Filippo Pigafetta noticed a large plant for sale, grown in the province of Sa'id, which produced a red dye popular for tinting women's nails and hair and the tails and manes of prized horses. He learnt that the trade in this plant earned 300,000 ducats a year.

5.5 How miscreants were punished

Behind the grander shops of the Khan al-Khalili were smaller stalls displaying amber, myrrh, and a bewildering choice of perfumes. In other quarters there sprawled the vendors of meat, fish, grain, vegetables and bread. Regardless of nationality or the status of the merchant, the transactions were spot-checked by overseers, who examined the weighing scales of the shopkeepers. If malpractice was found, the culprit was usually severely punished, which sometimes led to loss of life. Itinerant salesmen who sold food from door to door and thought they could escape the overseer were mistaken. If found to be cheating, they were paraded through the streets with a long rope tied through the nostril. Around the neck was hung a large bell which was clanged with a rod by a janissary advertising the salesman's alleged misdeeds. At the end of this humiliating spectacle an appropriate fine was levied.

Many of the individual shops took the form of a small recess or cell furnished with wooden shutters, securely locked at night. The floor was raised level with a *mastaba*, a stone seat about two or three feet high on which the owner or his customers could sit. Such shops provided the setting for some of the scenes from the *Arabian Nights*, which cast their spells on countless audiences. 'The Christian Broker's Tale' tells of a shopkeeper who has an intriguing encounter with a mysterious female customer; she raises her veil revealing a pair of large seductive black eyes, before asking about a piece of silk fabric. Such a beguiling prelude, heralding the onset of a hard commercial bargain, was certain to whet listeners' appetites, especially if they could identify the locations of the stories. The shop of Ma'ruf the cobbler was said to lie in Red Street, just outside the Bab Zuwayla, the venue for public executions, when the gateway was gruesomely decorated by bloody severed heads left to rot in the heat, impaled on spikes. Since pharaonic times there had been a long tradition of story-telling in Egypt. Audiences relaxing in the coffee houses could have identified with the tale of the Shipwrecked Sailor, written by a scribe, one Ameny's son, Amen-aa, originating in a papyrus of the early Middle Kingdom. The sailor's troubles began thus:

A stormwind broke out while we were at sea, before we had touched land The wind was lifted up, but it repeated with a wave of eight cubits... then the boat died. And of those who were in it not a single one survived.

Having spent three days alone on an island by the surf of the sea, he slept in a wood cabin and embraced the shade before stretching his legs to find something to eat. He found fruits and vegetables in abundance, cut a fire drill and made offerings to the gods. Suddenly there arrived a gigantic serpent, his body plated with gold, who took up the sailor in his mouth and carried him to his rest house. So frightened was the sailor that he feared he would be swallowed up. After this terrifying episode, however, the serpent showed himself to be a benevolent if somewhat sad character and proclaimed himself as the Prince of Punt, to whom all the myrrh on the island belonged. 'Do not fear little one, do not turn white' he said, and foretold that his captive would be rescued by people he knew, and return home to die in his village: 'How happy is the one who relates what he has tasted after painful affairs have passed.'

Christopher Harant (1564–1621), the Lord of Polzic and Bezdruzic, a nobleman of fine appearance from Prague, who had served as councillor at the brilliant court of the Habsburg King Rudolph II, arrived in Egypt in the summer of 1598. He was accompanied by his brother-in-law M. de Cernin and other friends who had travelled together from Jerusalem on pilgrimage. Lately a widower, Christopher was a humourous learned man of light heart, educated in the traditions of the time, and could speak Greek, Latin, Spanish, Italian and German. He was also an accomplished musician and an agreeable singer. He punctuated his tale liberally with quotations from the Bible, the classics, the *Golden Legend*, apposite mottos from different countries, as well as references from available travellers' guide books current at the time. King Rudolph of Bohemia, a Holy Roman Emperor of Germany, was a Habsburg by blood but a Czech by inclination, who delighted in the company of artists, scientists and above all astronomers, for whose company no price was too high to pay. Among these were Tycho Brahe from Denmark, the German Johann Kepler, and Copernicus. Rudolph even dabbled in the occult with the eccentric English alchemist, John Dee, who had often been consulted by Queen Elizabeth I of England. When the Turkish army invaded Hungary in 1591, Christopher served six years in the artillery of the defending imperial army. After this victorious but long campaign, he returned home, but at the premature death of his wife, he consigned his two children to the care of his parents and set off on a pilgrimage to the lands ruled over by the Turks. Having survived his perilous overseas pilgrimage, Christopher once more attained his homeland, but after a peaceful period writing his memoirs surrounded by his books, he took up arms once more, only to be caught up in the defeat of the Protestant armies who fought in the battle of the White Mountain near Prague against the emperor Ferdinand II. As chief of the 25 Czech aristocrats and the last representative of the nobles of the Kingdom of Bohemia, Christopher was among the first to mount the scaffold to be executed as a retribution for their defiance against the victorious emperor. With typical bravery his last words were to thank God who had spared him from all dangers far from home, so that he could 'die at the hand of the executioner'.

On their arrival in Cairo, Christopher and his party were received hospitably by the consul of the king of France, an erudite man who could speak several languages. At the end of the sixteenth century, the French enjoyed privileges in the city since they had negotiated advantageous trade agreements with the Ottoman Turks with whom they had an alliance against the Habsburgs. After leaving Damietta, Christopher's river journey had ended badly as the friends had been tricked by the boatmen, who instead of landing them at Bulaq had dumped them unceremoniously on the bank at a village outside. They were forced to hire donkeys to ride through the village to an inlet of the Nile, where a group of Turkish and Jewish customs officials were sitting in the shade of some large fig trees. The travellers were questioned closely about their movements, and when the officials heard they had come from Jerusalem and were on their way to Sinai, in spite of all Christopher's protestations that they carried little but some utensils of earthenware, wood and stone, they were ordered to open out everything for inspection and each pay one large piastre. Christopher noted that the Turks had been disposed to be more lenient, but the Jews were tenaciously resolute.

The Nile was so high that they were faced with fording two deep floods before reaching the city. Not wishing to swim in the nude like the natives, they hired some horses, ready saddled, costing four *medines* each. At times the horses were forced to swim, but by dint of perching on their backs like monkeys, with their legs drawn up, the riders kept dry. No horses were available to cross the second lake, so there was nothing for it but to pay the donkey men two or three *medines* each to carry them on their backs. On the other side they were attacked by some arrogant Turks who tried rudely to push their porters into the water. Although there had been attempts to control the Nile's flood bordering Cairo by expensive earthworks, they had been largely abortive, and their maintenance had been eventually thrust on the local population whose efforts were unenthusiastic.

By the time they reached the city it was nearly midday. Following the clear directions given by the consul at Damascus, they made their way to the French consul's house almost unaided. They found the consul to be a courteous man, living in style with many servants and dressed in silk like a Turkish lord. He conversed in Italian with his guests whom he immediately asked to dinner. After the meal, when the consul had learnt of his guests' native land, he was amazed that they had dared to visit a country with which they were at war. He therefore advised them to keep a low profile and to let no one know who they were, in case they were seized and cast into perpetual imprisonment. Above all, he exhorted them not to talk to the Jews, who would be the most capable of understanding their way of speaking and knowing their country of origin.

Christopher and his friends were lodged in a large house built of stone overlooking the canal, adjacent to that of the consul, which he let to all merchants and pilgrims of the nations under his jurisdiction. It consisted of two or three stories without a roof, similar to many others in Cairo. During Turkish rule, a great deal of secular building took place along the banks of the Khalij al-Hakim canal; amirs invested fortunes in palaces and buildings to rent. Spacious tall mansions with courtyards, central reception areas and north-facing balconies were occupied by the city's elite; private rooms were provided for women, who looked down on the public areas with their wall paintings and marble floors. Often there were multiple kitchens and two bathrooms. Some houses were surrounded by gardens, others encompassed small estates with mills and farms, and stables to house their prized horses. Later these large houses were frequently carved up because of multiple heirs and the complications of ownership. To settle disputes, the *qadi*'s court would send a builder to divide them vertically. Everywhere in the city, it seemed that Cairo houses were either half built or half falling down.

The French consul's house contained a little door opening on to the canal, where a boat could be summoned by passengers who pointed a finger towards the direction in which they wanted to go. On returning to their quarters after visiting their host, Christopher and M. de Cernin spent some time looking out of the window at the numbers of craft gliding past on the flooded waterway. After sunset, Christopher saw a party of well-dressed Turks in a boat, seated cross-legged in a circle surrounded by a quantity of flowers which perfumed the air. They were looking at the windows around them and enjoying the music from an orchestra that accompanied them. The Turks were enraptured by the music but the onlookers stifled their laughter. To them it was as if a sow was squealing and an ass was beating the drum.

Their house contained only about four or five rooms but they were large and high. The straw was replaced on the floors each day and fresh water replenished the cisterns in one of the rooms which cooled the air. There were no benches on which to sit so each had to manage with his 'own natural seat'. A few windows of dark-coloured glass could be seen, small and high up, which could not be opened. Lower down, there were other openings, closed by a kind of shutter like a lid which could be raised, similar to those securing street booths. A servant was supplied who cooked and did the marketing; he purchased limes and dates, newly caught fish and white bread for a modest sum, though Christopher would have exchanged the limes and pomegranates for a simple apple. Such importations from Constantinople were, however, expensive. Only Nile water was available to drink, as wine was strictly forbidden except at the consul's table. Instead of other human guests, the consul kept all kinds of strange animals in the house: monkeys, ichneumons and lizards under the care of a keeper. At first the party thought these diversions would be welcome, especially during the siesta in the heat of the day, but soon they found the animals an irritant, especially during their nocturnal rites when the house resounded with their thumps, gnawings and cries.

Christopher and his brother-in-law were frustrated in their attempts to make the customary visit to the pyramids and sphinx, as the route was flooded by the high inundation. Instead they toured the city, which provided them with a shifting kaleidoscope of scenes. Not far from the Khan al-Khalili, at the Wikalat al-Jallaba, lay the slave market in a small narrow street, where they saw a great many men and women of all ages and nationalities on sale, the Moors being in the majority:

> Most of them were naked except for a small piece of material hanging down in front... We saw the buyers coming to buy them, to examine this one or that, handling them, stretching and pulling them like beasts... we saw others who compelled the slaves to run, to jump, in order to judge their agility. These slaves were chained or joined together in groups.

M. de Cernin was keen to buy a little Moorish boy at any price and it was only with great difficulty that he was dissuaded from it. Christopher emphasised the dangers they would encounter, that they did not have the right, and that in any case they would be unable to take him on the boat at Alexandria.

Their walk led them to the horse market near the citadel where Arab and Egyptian horses, camels, donkeys and other animals were for sale. The Czechs were enraptured by the graceful horses, which were large, strong and lithe, with such shining manes that no description could do them justice. They were naturally fast, well groomed and in short their equal could not be found in all the world. The rulers of Egypt had always cherished their Arabian horses: the sultan al-Nasir Muhammad had a passion for collecting them and could recall the names of all the horses and their offspring he had ever purchased, which he kept recorded in a special office. In 1315, he acquired a beautiful mare at the enormous sum of 600,000 dirhams, consisting of

290,000 dirhams in cash, plus a village near Aleppo.

The friends regretted their lack of money and the difficulties of getting permission to buy horses and of transporting the animals by sea. Christopher saw the Cairo lords proudly ride their horses, richly decorated with embroidered saddlecloths and embossed harnesses inlaid with gold and silver. Everyone who was entitled to ride a horse had one at least, if not two, and they climbed into the saddle even to cross the road to visit their neighbours. The arrogance of the Turkish horsemen was unbounded, especially if they encountered Christian foreigners whom they imagined were obstructing them in the street. One such troop, intending to make sport, deliberately tilted their lances at Christopher's party while they were with the French consul. When they asked the janissary why such behaviour was permitted, they were told that among the horsemen was the current young favourite of the ruling pasha and no one dared correct him. On riding past a field where some Turkish soldiers were practising their feats of arms, the Turks put their horses to the gallop, pointing their arrows and javelins directly towards them. But for the presence of their janissary, detailed to protect them, they might have been killed.

While he was a slave, Johann Wild endured many privations in Egypt, all of which he regarded philosophically as the will of God. After he was taken to Cairo by his Turkish master he was sold once more, this time to a harsh unrelenting Persian merchant who treated him with the greatest severity. Johann did not suffer the indignities of the slave market, although he was paraded around the streets while his sale was negotiated by advertisement through a third party. For the Persian, Johann had to shop, cook and act as general servant to satisfy the needs of a tyrant who often rewarded him with blows. Through astute business dealings his master became rich; he sold his high-quality goods in the Khan al-Khalili and afterwards took Johann with him on trading journeys to Palestine and Syria, even once to the holy city of Mecca. It is not clear if Johann was forced to become a Muslim, but it is hard to believe that a Christian would have been allowed to enter some of the most holy places of Islam, even though he spoke some Arabic, having been ordered to learn it by the domineering Persian.

5.6 Turkish ladies on their way to the baths

When he was temporarily released from his tasks, Johann took the chance of bathing in the *hammams*, open to all comers, of which it was estimated there were about 100 around the city. Men and women were allotted different days to bathe and Johann was told of the cavortings of the women during their ablutions, their elaborate hair dressing and use of paste depilatories. Thoughts of these forbidden females must have proved a stimulus to male fantasies. Leading cloistered idle lives at home, rich ladies had slaves to anticipate their every whim; their long clothes were costly and graceful, their eyes accentuated with kohl and their hair, covered with the finest of veils, was tinted with henna. They were lavishly adorned with jewels: from their pierced ears hung ornate earrings, necklaces and rows of bracelets decorated their arms and ankles. They painted their fingernails and toenails and the two first fingers of their hands red and white. They wore straight narrow shirts with very wide sleeves of coloured wool or taffeta; their belted silk trousers, reaching to the ground, were wide and long in the manner of sailors, their legs were covered in light stockings and they wore soft slippers on their feet. The harem quarters were situated among the twisting corridors of the upper stories of the houses, hidden by lattice-work screens. Here the ladies, seated on a dais, entertained their female friends in high cool rooms, decorated with richly painted and carved ceilings. They wore tall hats intricately embroidered with pearls and other precious stones with long feathers sticking up at one side. Johann was told that on the days the wives went to the baths, the husbands were obliged to oversee the preparation of the food while they were away otherwise it would be a great disgrace. The mistresses of the household made sure that their female servants accompanied them, as they had no confidence in their husbands' behaviour in their absence. It was also apparent that the women delighted in giving their husbands the slip, sometimes leaving the house by a side door, thus outwitting the gatekeeper sitting on his *mastaba* by the main entrance, which led into the central courtyard hidden from the street. Their voluminous outer garments, which covered them from head to foot when

5.7 Interior of a Cairo public bath

outside the house, afforded them complete anonymity. Ruffian ass drivers took them wherever they wanted to go, the chains around the donkeys' necks tinkling along the alleyways.

Stories of women delighting in deception were included in Arab folk tales. The story of three merchants' wives at the baths described how they competed for a coveted robe of cloth woven with gold thread, hanging in the *hammam*; each tried to outdo the other with an account of how she had outwitted her spouse in order to pass the time with a lover. The prize of the robe was to be awarded to the woman judged by the bathhouse keeper to be the weaver of the most ingenious plot. In this story, however, the bathhouse keeper kept the robe for herself, as she deemed all three to be equally sinful. In the more affluent houses, bathrooms with running water were incorporated into the top storey. Although small in size, they had domed roofs lit by small pieces of coloured glass let into the ceiling. In these cases the unfortunate ladies, so confined, might have no excuse to idle in the *hammams* plotting and intriguing with their friends.

As for the men, after discarding their garments in the rooms off the first courtyard, they were wrapped in a blue loincloth and gave themselves up to hedonistic luxury. Sweat oozing from every pore, they were stretched out on marble trestles where their limbs were massaged and their joints were cracked. After their bodies were finally washed and dried with enveloping towels, their locks were cut and pubic hair removed. In the *hammams* they could idle the time away sitting up to their necks in the large round bath under the dome, where the fountain played and hot and cold water coursed through separate runnels. Steps provided convenient seats at varying depths around the edge. The baths were places where every pleasurable relaxation and secret need was catered for, amid the hot steamy vapours swirling through the cubicles of the marble rooms.

Cairo's principal canal, together with the Nasiri canal and small side canals, held the Nile's flood water, which stagnated with increasing deterioration in quality for about nine months. Gradually, the drying channels became filled with rubbish jettisoned from the windows of the houses along the bank. Because the stench was insupportable, it became impossible to stay in the rooms overlooking them.

But with the arrival of May, gangs of prisoners and beggars were provided by the government to work at a grand spring clean; they carted away the debris to mounds outside the city and scoured the waterways in preparation for the surging fresh water. As an experienced engineer, Filippo Pigafetta estimated that the main canal could be extended to return again to the Nile with little expenditure by the government. It would be a great convenience for the people, who would not have to suffer such stagnant water and its drying up, with the accompanying stench.

In August, when the inundation reached its height, it had been the custom since pharaonic times to take measurements of the flood, enabling the scribes to foretell the fertility of the land and estimate the level of taxation for the ensuing year. The Nilometer, a ninth-century column marked in gradations of one cubit, lay in a kiosk decorated with classical columns and accessed by descending steps, at the south of al-Rawda island. It was one of the 'must see' sites of Cairo. Emanuel Piloti, the Venetian merchant, described it as 'high and thick, of marble, blood red or violet in colour'. A great part of the island was taken up by the river fortress, built in 1241, containing palaces, mosques and stables to house part of the increasingly vast army of Royal Mamluks. Once the flood water reached the critical measurement of sixteen cubits on the column, all anxieties for the well-being of Egypt for the next twelve months could be allayed. It was the custom each day for the Nilometer to be inspected by men on horseback who carried banners on their shoulders, after which they rode through the city to reassure the populace with cries of 'The river has risen'. Poor floods brought religious communities into the desert around a plainly dressed sultan to implore God's clemency. Though he was in poor health, the sultan al-Mu'ayyad Shaykh bravely swam the Nile in 1419. His desperate act did not go unrewarded as the river afterwards recommenced its rise.

When the waters reached their peak, the event was celebrated between 6 and 16 August, during which time few thought of sleeping. The high point of the rejoicing came when the sultan arrived on horseback, amid acclamations from the crowds, and knocked three times with his golden hoe on the broad-based high dam which had been

5.8 Celebrations at the cutting of the canal at the Nile's annual rise

constructed to seal off the canal from the river on the east bank. After this, Emanuel Piloti saw that 'the business was finished by a great number of men with hoes who hurried to breach the opening'. As the water flowed into the canal, the people sang and danced with joy. Amid the flood, the gracious houses with their balconies and private boathouses on the canals were in great demand by the crowds to witness the celebrations. The windows were crowded, as craft decorated with flowers and branches glided past on the incoming tide, accompanied by the crackling of fireworks.

After the Turks came to power, the celebrations continued. Roughly 250 years later, Johann Wild watched the pasha process down from the citadel for the festival which lasted three days and three nights. There were about sixty decorated vessels covered with carpets, gaily decked out on top with flags and painted in different colours. Stands and bridges had been erected on the boats which were covered over with fine coloured linen material and closed around with curtains. These had been prepared by the amirs and distinguished lords in honour of the ruler. When the pasha embarked, cannon from the surrounding boats were fired to greet him: the pasha, who had four large cannon on his own vessel, had them fired in return to salute the lords. With the pasha leading the way, the flotilla assembled in the evening close to Old Cairo, by which time the number of the fleet had increased to about 100. Fireworks were let off to entertain the watching crowds, and the boats were dressed overall with lighted lamps. It was a magnificent spectacle. On the fourth day, just as the dam was cut, there was suddenly a terrific explosion when a burst of fireworks erupted, throwing up tableaux of two large castles on either side of the bank which took the spectators by surprise. The tableaux marked the culmination of the display, and it was only left for the pasha to cast money and baskets of food upon the waters for the poor, who swam out to retrieve them. The pasha's boat was a large oared vessel, gilded and painted all over and usually kept moored on the bank at Bulaq. Though it was smaller, Filippo Pigafetta compared it to the *Bucintoro* of the Doge in Venice. The poop and prow were *al antica*, mirroring those he had seen sculpted on the columns in Rome and Constantinople, and he imagined the vessel to be similar to the sumptuous, luxurious barge that transported Cleopatra and her courtiers along the Nile.

These annual events pleased rich and poor alike; the crowds passed the time gawping at the street entertainers with their performing animals by the water along the road to Bulaq. Their acts included monkeys and bears who jumped and danced. Vignettes were enacted, with the animals playing parts as humans to show how lazy servants and wives behaved when their masters and husbands were away from home. Johann Wild saw the owner of a performing donkey tie a bandage over its eyes and turn the animal round three times. Then he drew a ring from his finger, plunged into the crowd and hid it under the clothes of one of the spectators. With confident anticipation he ordered the donkey to walk towards the onlooker who had secreted the ring. As soon as the animal reached the man it halted in front of him. Triumphantly the conjurer announced that the donkey had found the ring and it was returned to him in front of everyone. Woe betide the donkey if it did not indicate the right person; it was subjected to blows. Donkeys often took part in street charades. Christopher Harant laughed at a knowing animal when it heard its master declare in a loud voice that people throughout the town were looking for donkeys to

5.9 Ezbekyya Pond, south side, during the Nile's inundation

transport limestone and other materials for a large building yard. He saw it fall down, seemingly stone dead and remain like a corpse with its eyes closed, and its legs in the air as if struck down by the plague. Its master, lamenting with all his heart the loss of his donkey, tried in vain to move its legs, and though he grew cross and beat the animal with a gourd, it lay still without moving. The owner resumed his story:

Know you dear spectators, that tomorrow, there will be an escort for the sultan's reception and that the most beautiful women will ride the most beautiful donkeys and that for the occasion they [the animals] will be given fresh water to drink and choice barley.

Hardly had he uttered these words when the donkey leapt to its feet and started to dance with joy.

In addition to the cool flood waters of the canals, to the west of the city lay refreshing pleasure ponds, their banks lined with the principal houses and palaces of rich lords and officials. Secreted behind large double doors lay hidden courtyards, separate apartments for men and women with mosaic floors inlaid with gold and precious stones. There were fountains that played in secluded gardens and long rows of stables for the horses. The surface of the Elephant Pond, south of the citadel, was covered with pleasure craft and yellow water lilies; a horse-racing track lay beside it. To the south of Old Cairo lay the Qarun and Ethiopian Ponds, the delights of the latter being lauded by the father in 'The Jewish Physician's Tale', one of the stories told in the *Arabian Nights*. To the north-west, the Ezbekiyya Pond provided a place to relax on Friday after prayers in the mosque. There was a raised promenade and gardens in which to stroll. The water in these small reservoirs lasted a few months only, after which it became unsavoury and a source of infection until it was replenished via the canals by the fresh flow of summer. When full, the ponds harboured many different kinds of birds, which gave pleasure to those who liked to stand at the windows to shoot at them with their bows and arque-busses. Surprisingly the birds continued to flock to the waters in great numbers.

Even as late as the sixteenth century, Cairo was called 'Babylon' or 'Babylon of Egypt' by Europeans. The site of 'Babylon', initially on the old Hadrianic fortress, was mentioned by Ptolemy (*Geography* 4.5), and later there grew up a Christian quarter in the district, which became the seat of an early bishopric. According to Coptic tradition, it was in this place that the Holy Family took shelter when escaping from the Herodian persecutions. Subsequently it was said that they left in a sailing boat for Upper Egypt, eventually coming to rest in a cave near Asyut where the al-Mubarraq monastery was constructed in the fourth century.

From time to time, during eruptions of religious persecution, the Christians and their churches in Old Cairo were attacked by Muslim mobs. During his pilgrimage in 1324, Symon Semeonis, the friar from Dublin, learnt that from 1320 to 1323 a number of Christians of the Girdle had been put to death, and the churches were closed. For this reason the buildings were fairly humble affairs, huddled among the surrounding houses so as not to attract attention. Unlike churches in

5.10 Crypt of St Sergius, Babylon (Old Cairo), said to be the resting place of the Holy Family

Europe they had no spires or steeples, their windows were high up and their doors small and narrow. In contrast, the dark interiors, basilican in plan, were richly decorated and lit by hanging lamps, sometimes of enamelled glass in jewelled colours with intricate designs and Arabic writing, or plain white with handles on the shoulders. The sanctuary screens (*haykals*) were of solid opaque woodwork enriched with ebony and sheets of ivory, decorated with arabesques and geometrical patterns and inlaid with superbly carved crosses and stars of ivory. The doors in the screen were covered by a magnificent silk or brocade curtain, while ostrich eggs were suspended in front as a decoration. Behind the screen, the main altar was topped by a canopy resting on columns; the paintings on the walls were of patron saints and biblical scenes. In the floor of the porch lay the Mandatum Tank, a square basin covered over with wood, used for the washing of feet on Maundy Thursday. Services were conducted with the congregation standing, the monotonous singing of the priests accompanied by (to European ears) strident atonal music with the clashing of cymbals and triangles.

For Christian pilgrims, the church of Abu Sarga (St Sergius) was an especially holy place. Its crypt was said to be the cave that had sheltered Mary and Jesus. With due reverence, on 2 February 1324, Symon the Irish friar went to pray at

> Sancta Maria de la Cave in which under the high altar is that most sacred place where, it is said the glorious Virgin remained concealed with her most sweet son Jesus... Here also is a stone well in which she used to bathe the infant; and opposite to it on the left, is an altar in honour of the Virgin, at which I, brother Symon celebrated Mass on the feast of the purification of the Virgin.

Symon would have worshipped in the crypt (perhaps dating from the second or third century, possibly from the sixth), which lies under the centre of the choir and part of the *haykal* of the main church; it is reached by two flights of steps, one from the north transept, the other from the south aisle. It is still a silent place, consisting of a nave with a wagon-vaulted ceiling and north and south sides divided by nine columns. The altar at the east end is about twenty inches high, lying in a semi-circular recess under a domed roof. Nile water that used to seep into the crypt was revered because of its association with such a holy place. In 1384, the Tuscan Giorgio Gucci heard Mass there several times with many of his companions, and 'confessed and communicated from two Friars Minor (the Guardian of Mount Sion, Fra Niccolò of Candia and his companion) whom we found there, come from Jerusalem on business in order to see the Sultan and obtain from him certain permissions to adorn some of their churches'.

Symon the monk described 'another glorious church in that same city, known as Sancta Maria della Scala, and properly so named because it is approached by way of steps'. The ascent to the 'Hanging Church' (so called because it was suspended between two Roman bastions) is by a staircase built close by the central bastion of the south side of the red brick Roman fortress with its two enormous towers. Symon would have admired the singularly beautiful interior, with aisles divided by white marble columns (one of basalt) topped with Corinthian capitals, and the original ancient pulpit upheld by fifteen slender Saracenic columns faced with vertical strips of coloured marble arranged in seven pairs with a leader, no two pairs being alike.

Close to Abu Sarga lay a large and lofty building dedicated to St Barbara. Yet another martyred virgin saint in the medieval pantheon, Barbara's fame as being a maiden of great beauty was proclaimed in the widely read *Golden Legend*. The story told of a brave, stubborn lady who was converted to Christianity by Origen, but subsequently put to death at the hands of her pagan father Dioscuros when Maxentius ruled Egypt. Retribution came swiftly, as a further legend relates that the cruel parent was immediately struck down by lightning and reduced to ashes. (There is no evidence of Barbara's existence but her cult became strong in the ninth century when she was invoked against danger from lightning.) When Symon tried to visit the church it was still closed after the Muslim persecutions and to his disappointment he was unable to see 'her most precious body'. Six years later, however, in 1330, a pilgrim named Antonio Rebaldi found the church open and was able to touch and kiss the corpse.

Nicolas de Martoni, the notary from Carinola, having miraculously survived his terrifying sea voyage to Alexandria in July 1398, eventually arrived in Cairo on 19 August. A devout pilgrim, Nicolas made sure to visit Babylon where he was granted a long audience with the Patriarch of the Coptic Church. For two hours they discussed the nature of Christ and his holiness and talked of Nicolas's arrival and journey. The Patriarch entertained his Italian visitors to a meal that included 'bread, honey, large plates of eggs, figs, peaches and cheese'. Nicolas said that with the repast they drank the best water, as wine was not drunk there. On leaving, the Patriarch blessed them and extended the cross (always in his hand) for them to kiss. Few Christians took time to describe the ancient Ben Ezra Synagogue with its arabesque ceiling, close by the Coptic churches. Perhaps their guides did not tell them of its strong associations with the life of the prophet Moses.

While vessels from the south, sailing downstream from the reaches of Upper Egypt, landed at the old Roman port of Babylon (Old Cairo) at the south of the city, the large sprawling port of Bulaq to the north harboured fleets of boats plying upstream from the Mediterranean. The suburb of Bulaq had become fashionably prosperous: Filippo Pigafetta described some 'beautiful houses and gardens along the shore formerly built by the Mamluk lords who used to go there for pleasure', and said that 'even today, people from Cairo still came on Saturdays to amuse themselves with their loved ones, to eat in the fresh air in the gardens and under the loggias with their pleasant views'. In 1571, the Ottoman Turks built an important mosque near the river, with the largest stone dome in Cairo. Passengers disembarking from Lower Egypt were faced with the inevitable customs, taking further wearisome tolls on their goods and money.

Filippo had landed by the Dogana del Rey, a large building on the bank of the river, manned by the Jewish officials wearing yellow turbans, employed by the administration. He claimed that they appeared to be more vigilant in overseeing the tolls exacted from the Franks than from other nationalities. It irritated him that despite arriving during the Jewish Sabbath, the Jews were still at work and he was forced to pay up. Many complained of the harsh treatment from the predatory Jewish custom officials, who sat comfortably installed on benches by the warehouses in the shade of the fig trees while waiting for passengers to disembark on the quayside. Although Filippo protested strongly that they had nothing with them of value, and it would be laborious to unpack their bags, after a long argument with the officials they were forced to comply and show everything down to the last object, with the result that each person had to pay a large piastre.

Even 200 years earlier Bulaq was already a busy port. On his arrival on 11 October 1364, the Florentine Lionardo di Frescobaldi was astonished to see many Saracen boats laden with goods and that despite the fact that it was a Muslim country 'in every one of them there was a great number of low-class women, very great merchant-esses, who were going to Alexandria and through the island of Roseto, to do their business'. After Lionardo's party had disembarked, they caught sight of the sultan Barquq himself, returning with his immense retinue from the chase. They estimated him to be 'a man of about forty-five years, having a very fine appearance'. The spectacle was impressive, as about 100,000 men on horses accompanied the sultan, as well as a very large number of gerfalcons, peregrine falcons, his pointers and his greyhounds. Most impressive was

a very great pavilion, among the richest thing in the world; and it is so big that there are one hundred camels to carry it, because it is divided into very many pieces and has many wooden poles used for pitching it. And it is true that when the above pavilion is pitched, it is said that it contains very many rooms and saloons, so that in the evening nobody knows in which room the sultan sleeps at night, except perhaps his greatest confidant.

When all the great tents for the sultan's court were in place, the enor-mous camp resembled a city, with orderly streets containing many craftsmen 'one selling this and the other that'. Vast herds of camels were necessary to carry food and fodder to meet the needs of this itin-erant population who had been camping about fifteen miles from Cairo at Siryacos in the desert, near the Coptic convent of Abu Hur. Such monasteries were often goals for pleasure trips, where wine could be drunk in the gardens in which the guests could relax from the desert heat, and indulge in their love of story-telling and poetry. The Tuscans learnt that such was the magnificence of the sultan that he changed his clothes, which were of great value, three times a day; afterwards they were laid in a room to be given to his courtiers and close companions. Even if this tale was exaggerated, in the fourteenth century a robe worn by the ruler himself became a customary gift which officials could consider as much due to them as their emoluments.

After leaving Bulaq, Sa'id, the Tuscans' faithful guide led them along the road through the groves of tall palms, sycamores, oranges and lemons to Barquq's Grand Interpreter, the important court official in charge of foreigners visiting the city. They crossed a bridge over a side canal, which led from a larger cutting through the city. But in spite of Sa'id's care, on arrival at lodgings they received an mean reception: 'When we reached the house where all the pilgrims put up, he [the Interpreter] got from us four ducats each, without giving us a bed or anything else in the world, save lodging in the house.'

Lionardo di Frescobaldi was a man steeped in the strict Christian tenets of the fourteenth century. He was was primarily concerned for the soul of the Grand Interpreter, a renegade Venetian 'married to one of our Florentines', also a renegade. Her father, a Florentine who had turned Muslim, had occupied the post at court before his son-in-law. Lionardo had brought several letters to the Interpreter, sent by old friends in Venice and from the consul of the Venetians at Alexandria. Though the Interpreter appeared pleased to see them 'It is true he got a little sad because the letter from Venice brought the news of the death of his father, which he had not known.' Lionardo, anxious that the man was living in a state of damnation, endeavoured to make him see the error of his ways. So, together with the Father Guardian of the convent of Mount Sion in Jerusalem (a gentleman of Venice), they tried to persuade him to ask the friar to pray to God for his father's soul, and to say the Gregorian Masses:

After long dealings and with great art, by the grace of God, we induced him to accept. We wished to speak with the wife to talk over the matter, and to see if we could bear any fruit for the honour of God; and he did not wish, telling us 'though she is the daughter of a Florentine

Christian, she is not experienced in our faith, and she has by me several sons, who are Saracens. I doubt but if she revealed the matter, both you and I would die. But I promise you that if the Sultan sends me to Alexandria, and I can in an honest way return to the West I will.'

Having obtained this doubtful assurance, they reluctantly took their leave, though Lionardo conceded that it was a hard thing for the Interpreter to leave the two wives he had acquired as well as his children, his riches and his influential position. The post was a very lucrative one: Giorgio Gucci noted that besides a toll of four ducats, the payments to the Grand Interpreter of Cairo were 'XLVIII ducats and again for permission to leave the city and go through the desert, VI ducats'. Other compulsory disbursements included one and a half ducats to disembark with their belongings at Bulaq.

To the south-east of Cairo, overlooking the city and the pyramids, stood the citadel, on a high spur carved from the limestone of the Muqattam hills. From the beginning of the thirteenth century it was the seat of government and residence of the Mamluk sultans and after 1517, of the Ottoman Turks. It was a heavily defended fortress, much of it built by toiling Crusader prisoners who acted as overseers and masons, many of whom died in the process.

Under the powerful al-Nasir Muhammad, the square (Maydan al-

5.11 Entrance to the citadel and the parade ground, 1798

Rumayla) to the west of the citadel became a site of the major military markets and a training ground for the Mamluks. Perhaps this was where Lionardo di Frescobaldi saw a number of jewellers in a 'piazza near the citadel', vendors of precious stones, emeralds, rubies, balas rubies, turquoises and pearls. One of their party, Andrea, servant of Messer Francesco Rinucci, bought for his wife some big pearls which Lionardo took to her after Andrea's death in Damascus.

Near the *maydan*, al-Nasir Muhammad had constructed a wall around the lower enclosure at the west of the citadel to house the royal stables, where his 4,800 horses were cared for by over 800 vets and grooms, who exercised them each day in pastures by the Nile. In addition there was accommodation for 5,000 riding camels, innumerable dogs and hunting cheetahs. Access from the stables to the citadel was through the Chain Gate along a private road which led in to the royal enclosure of the palaces. Al-Nasir Muhammad, who had greatly increased his private army of Mamluk slaves, built 12 barracks for them with accommodation for servants, schools and baths in the northern enclosure near the main entrance.

In addition, he took down many of the buildings existing in the royal enclosure where he built his graceful mosque, the Hall of Justice and the black and white striped palace with its lofty arcades and rooms used for official ceremonies and councils of state. To the south of these lay the sultan's private residence, surrounded by a wall, where there eventually grew up a complicated entanglement of palaces, audience chambers, numerous pavilions, walkways and gardens. The harem quarters were cramped, having separate dormitories for over 1,000 concubines and residence halls for the sultan's children, though each of the four wives had her own palace and staff within the compound. The crowded harem even accommodated the descendants of the Mamluk sultan Qala'un (ruled 1280–90) and female relations of former sultans. The royal enclosure was enlarged towards the south in 1335 to house the treasury and the buildings that stored the carpets, tents and sheets used by the sultans. As may be imagined, the thousands of inhabitants required large kitchens, with many cooks to prepare the five meals eaten daily by the court and its guests, as well as the 10,000 kilograms of food consumed each day by everyone else. The citadel kitchens were situated close to the harem and underneath them were kept hundreds of head of cattle brought in from the citadel stockade.

Due to the large increase of the citadel's population, al-Nasir Muhammad constructed the aqueduct (started in the eighth century) in Roman style, leading from the Nile at the old city of Babylon, and in 1312 caused four waterwheels to facilitate the flow of water as there was insufficient water from the deep well (known as Joseph's well) built by Saladin in the original fortress. The aqueduct, which had been further enlarged by the sultan al-Ghawri in 1509, contained more than 300 arches constructed of good worked stone, and the Nile water opposite al-Rawda island was elevated by machines whose wheels were turned by oxen. At the summit there was a large deep cistern, with about 500 steps (cut into the side of the wall) which descended to water level. From the cistern, water was dispersed by further wheels (turned by oxen) into stone and lead conduits which led to all parts of the castle.

While they were guests of the French consul in 1598, Christopher Harant and his brother-in-law from Prague asked their guide to take them to this fabled fortress. They rose early so as not to keep him waiting and to start while the air was cool. Having chosen three good well-saddled asses, they made their way through the streets, preceded by the attendants crying 'Dahry, dahry' ('Make way'). Once up the sloping ramp leading to the Gate of the Steps, the main entrance for all visitors to the citadel, they dismounted and told the donkey men to wait for their return. Ascending through two fortified gates separated by a steep stairway, curving round a ninety-degree bend, they perceived a large court surrounded by buildings apparently used for the guards. This was probably in the northern enclosure, which housed the headquarters of the janissaries, the elite troops of the Turkish army. They saw the great number of beautiful Arab horses with rich harnesses and saddles, their stirrups and bits decorated with carved gold and silver, their cloths and plumes cared for by some grooms who were awaiting the return of their master in audience with the pasha. Having crossed the court without hindrance, the friends were about to enter a very small low door which led into a further courtyard. Immediately they were confronted by a Jewish custodian who regarded

them disagreeably. Although the Jew also acted as an interpreter for
the French consul and knew that the two Czechs were under his protection, he attacked them angrily, asking where they wanted to go.
Having heard that they wished to see the residence of the pasha, he
severely reproached their guide, saying that he had exposed them to
danger and had not informed his master the consul or taken his advice.
The Jew told them to leave, to have a care of their liberty since they
should be far away from there before the Turks knew of their visit,
otherwise they would not escape prison. A story was circulating about
some German spies, recognised in Cairo, who had fought in the
Hungarian campaign. With heads down and in great haste, the friends
returned to their lodgings, mortified by anguish and overcome by heat

5.12 Giraffe drawn by Cyriaco of Ancona

and fatigue. They followed the Jew's advice without stopping to thank him for his warning, and never even gave a backward glance at their waiting donkeys whose keeper followed them back to the house for his payment. As for the consul, he disapproved of their lack of prudence. He told them that usually he could have arranged permission for such a visit, but now it was out of the question owing to the prevailing rumours circulating round the town.

In their haste Christopher and M. de Cernin could not have had time to visit the citadel menagerie, where the Mamluk sultans had collected a variety of exotic wild animals. To Europeans, the elephants with their enormous tusks were not such a novelty as the endearing, graceful giraffe in the citadel zoo, which had been sketched by the antiquarian Cyriaco of Ancona. In rather inexact Latin he described an elephant, a crocodile and a giraffe in a letter to Filippo Maria Visconti for the New Year in 1443: 'Among other animals of the same region I saw a giraffe, for this the natives call the beast. A foreign animal indeed, wonderful to behold with a neck of immense length spotted like a deer...' Opinions differed: to the Tuscan traveller Simone Sigoli, the giraffe resembled an ostrich except it had no feathers on its body but the whitest wool. It had the legs of a bird, but the feet of a horse. A foreign animal indeed.

Christopher and his brother-in-law remained at the consul's house while hastening to make their preparations for the high point of their pilgrimage, the arduous desert journey to the monastery of St Catherine in southern Sinai. The consul, solicitous of their welfare, accorded them every assistance within his power.

Notes

Cairo, general: E.W. Lane, *The Modern Egyptians*; Haag, *Discovery Guide to Cairo*; Lapidus, *Muslim Cities in the Late Middle Ages*, pp. 225–46; Lyster, *The Citadel of Cairo*; Garcin, 'The Regime of the Circassian Mamluks' (citadel residences of female dependants, p. 304); Hattox, *Coffee and Coffee Houses*; Raymond and Weit (ed. and trans.), *Les Marchés du Caire* (Cairo streets and alleyways, pp. 42–72; Khan al-Khalili, pp. 143–45; Cairo slave markets, pp. 223–29; horse market east of the citadel, p. 249); Levanoni, *A Turning Point in Mamluk History* (attempts to control Nile waters, pp. 164–68); Irwin, *The Arabian Nights: A Companion* (tales of Cairo street life, pp. 120–58); Bushnaq (ed. and trans.),

Arab Folk Tales, 'The Gown in the Bathhouse', pp. 334–38. **Old Cairo (Babylon), general:** Butler, *The Ancient Coptic Churches of Egypt*; Burmester, *Ancient Coptic Churches of Cairo*, pp. 14–35; Meinhardus, *The Holy Family in Egypt*, pp. 54–62. **Europeans in Cairo:** da Schio (introd.), *Viaggio di Filippo Pigafetta* (Bulaq, pp. 118–20; description of Cairo: tombs of Mamluk rulers, streets, bazaar, citadel, aqueduct, Nile and canals, festival of the inundation, pp. 128–39; officials, houses, costumes, climate, illness, pp. 144–57); Brejnik and Brejnik (ed. and trans.), *Voyage de Christophe Harant*, pp. 163–75; Esposito (ed.), *Itinerarium Symon Semeonis* (the city, pp. 73–81; Old Cairo, or Babylon, pp. 85–97); Volkoff (ed.), *Le voyage de Johann Wild* (experiences as a slave, pp. 18–22; descriptions of Cairo, manners and customs, pp. 124–72, 175–83); Letts (ed. and trans.), *The Pilgrimage of Arnold von Harff*, pp. 101–26; Bellorini and Hoade (ed. and trans.), *Frescobaldi, Gucci and Sigoli* (renegade officials, p. 53); Legrand, 'Pélérinage de Nicolas de Martoni' (patriarch at Babylon, Old Cairo, pp. 597–99). **Giraffe at citadel zoo:** Van Essen, 'Cyriaque d'Ancone en Egypte', p. 299; Cyriacus of Ancona, Ms. Ashburnam, 1174 Florence, Biblioteca Med. Laurenziana, f. 143 v. (drawing of a giraffe depicted in Egypt), and Ms. Can. Lat. Misc. 2801 Oxford, Bodleian, f. 69; Bellorini and Hoade (ed. and trans.), *Frescobaldi, Gucci and Sigoli*, p. 169.

CHAPTER 6

Venetian Diplomacy and the Arrival of the Ottomans

After a 250-year rule over Egypt and Syria, the Mamluk sultanate was on the wane. By the time the elderly sultan al-Ghawri reluctantly agreed to ascend the throne in 1501 at sixty years of age, the taxes that had customarily flowed into Mamluk coffers, culled from the lucrative spice trade, were seriously depleted, leaving a gaping hole in the treasury. To the north the power of the Ottoman Empire was steadily rising. These and other factors were the cause of friction, apprehension and increasing paranoia.

Because of threats to the frontiers of Egypt, the disparate Europeans in Cairo found themselves the objects of the sultan's displeasure. In 1511, Pietro Zen, the Venetian consul in Damascus, with Signore Contarini, the Alexandrian consul, four merchants from Tripoli, and three from Aleppo were imprisoned in Cairo on 6 January where they were interrogated and ignominiously subjected to the *bastinado*. They were charged with having favoured the Persian ambassador, who had been arrested near Aleppo and found to be carrying proposed plans for an alliance with Venice from the Safavid ruler Isma'il Shah, who had united Persia in 1501. Qansuh al-Ghawri, who tended to favour the French above the Venetians at this time, feared that Mamluk Syrian territories might be compromised, so proceeded to take immediate action. Among several other Cairo merchants incarcerated in the Cairo dungeons were the Franciscan friars Francesco Suriano and his superior the Father Guardian, Bernadino del Vecchio of Siena. They no longer enjoyed the grateful protection of the old sultan Qaitbay, who had died aged 80 in 1496. Qansuh al-Ghawri coerced Francesco into

6.1 Fifteenth-century Venice

writing to Albuqerqes, Master of the Knights of Rhodes, warning him to desist from impeding Egyptian trade, and threatening him with reprisals against the Europeans living in his territories and the destruction of the Holy Sepulchre. The friars remained in their prison for two long years before they were released in 1512 through the good offices of Domenico Trevisan, the special envoy from Venice who had disembarked at Alexandria in April of that year.

Leaving Alexandria for Cairo, Domenico, his son Marcantonio, and his 'famiglia di persone venti' had camped for the night on the road that bordered the sea shore, before they embarked on the Nile at Rosetta. They arrived at Bulaq late on the night of 6 May 1512. Three hours before dawn, the party extracted their coffers from the boats and loaded them onto forty waiting camels and mules, resplendent in scarlet cloth embroidered with the arms of St Mark and those of the ambassador. Among the dignitaries on the quayside was the sultan's dragoman, a renegade Veronese, one Yunus, formerly employed in the sultan's armoury.

Domenico might have met Taghribirdi, the sultan's previous dragoman, in Venice. He had been sent there by Qansuh al-Ghawri in 1506 to negotiate commercial treaties with the Signoria. Taghribirdi was a Mamluk born in Spain, possibly of Jewish lineage, who spoke seven languages and had been highly favoured in Cairo. He had served under seven sultans including Qaitbay and, because of his capabilities, had been previously entrusted on another mission by Qansuh al-Ghawri, to act as his representative in Florence.

The Mamluk embassy had left Alexandria in April 1506 in a Venetian boat commanded by Francesco Pasqaligo. Of the party was Alviso da Piero, a former secretary to Alviso Sagundino, a Venetian envoy who had been sent to Cairo to improve on the unsatisfactory terms regarding the pepper trade laid down by the sultan. The envoy, however, had died earlier in the year. The 20-strong embassy from the sultan, which included four pages and two mace bearers, was greeted at the Lido by a deputation of scarlet-robed merchants having business interests in Alexandria and Damascus. Al-Ghawri must have felt the need for allies – Mamluks were a rare sight in Venice and Italian crowds found their colourful costumes a great novelty. Taghribirdi's visit lasted ten months, during which time he stayed in lodgings on the Giudecca at the expense of the Republic, an expense that was calculated to yield a profit.

After protracted negotiations with the Doge and the Grand Council, a list of demands was sent to Qansuh al-Ghawri by one Francesco da Monte in early 1507, since any firm agreement had foundered due to Taghribirdi's lack of authority to grant Venetian demands. Both sides were eager to snatch what was left of the lucrative revenues that they had enjoyed for over two hundred years. When Francesco returned after five months in Egypt bringing clarification of the deal, the terms were much to the advantage of the Venetians, with whom Taghribirdi naturally enough gained high favour. On their departure on 26 July 1507, the Mamluks were given robes of honour and escorted through the piazza to the music of a band, before sailing off with the consul elect of Alexandria on a ship commanded by a Venetian captain, the notable Luca Loredan. A Carthusian prior, one George of Chemnitz, was one of the passengers and noted that the Mamluk ambassador received honour and proper ceremony at Alexandria. Taghribirdi proceeded to sail up the Nile to Cairo in style, with two of his wives, accompanied by a boat filled with his luggage and another that ferried his Mamluks. The prior and his party followed them in a vessel with a mixed crew of Jews and Egyptians. Each night all the boats were dressed with lamps rigged out pyramid-wise and by day little bells were attached to the sails to tinkle in the breeze. At Bulaq, Taghribirdi disembarked, wearing his golden robe of honour, and was met by the sultan amid a ceremonious reception, all of which was watched by Taghribirdi's harem of 35 ladies. Later, however, the Mamluk fell from favour, and was imprisoned after both the sultan and the Venetians discovered that the negotiations had not been to their liking. Because of his downfall, therefore, he was not to be seen among the party to welcome Domenico Trevisan. As a dragoman, Taghribirdi was notorious among European visitors to Egypt as being a tricky character. He had formerly led parties of pilgrims to Jerusalem and Mt Sinai and included an obligatory stay in his house in Cairo. His charges for forced hospitality appeared extortionate and were sometimes accompanied by menaces should the unhappy traveller wish to escape.

Domenico Trevisan rode into Cairo wearing cloth of gold and surrounded by four young men, his immediate companions; an escort of Mamluks followed and about 20 resident Venetian merchants rode behind. The palace at their disposal was of great splendour, judged by Zaccharia Pagani, Domenico's secretary, to have cost more than 100,000 ducats. The lofty rooms contained gilded inlaid ceilings, intricate mosaic floors of precious stones and impressive wooden doors inlaid with ebony and ivory. Residences such as this were furnished with utensils in a hierachy of materials in silver and gold, imported Chinese celadon bowls, delicate inscribed glasswares and inlaid brass trays. The rooms were illuminated by candles in sturdy squat brass candlesticks inlaid with gold and silver, and enamelled glass lamps in blue, gold and red that hung from the ceilings. The following morning, customary presents of food were received from the sultan: 44 baskets of sugar, five pots of Indian honey, two jars of fine oil, 40 lambs, 50 pairs of hens, 20 geese and two sacks of rice.

On Monday 10 May, Domenico was escorted to the citadel by the sultan's officials. He wore ceremonial dress including a brocade garment with tight sleeves, over which was a gold embroidered cloak lined with ermine. Though the heat in May would have been intense and no doubt wearing fur was uncomfortable, ermine was a prized status symbol so had to be endured no matter what the temperature. The party rode through a grand square where horses were galloping around in all directions and ascended a ramp road before dismounting at the entrance. After climbing about forty shallow stone steps (curving sharply round for the purpose of defence) leading from the main portal, they reached the first gate of the interior and passed through three courtyards full of slaves. The chief amir of the castle welcomed them while sitting on a low stool, surrounded by his slaves, who made a tremendous noise by clashing cymbals, playing flutes, rattling tambourines and banging iron shields. The embassy progressed through three more gates to the armoury where about fifty men were working, all of whom stood up at their arrival. At length they found themselves in a vast and impressive open-air enclosure (possibly the *hawsh*, a large space used for ceremonials in the sultan's complex in the southern quarter of the citadel).

At one end, the sultan was seen to be seated cross-legged like a tailor, on a *mastaba* of green velvet raised up over a foot from the ground. His large turban used for formal occasions was adorned with two long horns, and he was clad in a dark green camel's wool *cambelotto* (camlet) under which was a long red undergarment like a cassock. At his right side al-Ghawri wore a scimitar and shield, which, it was said, never left him. A little way off to the right stood about 20 men, amirs of a thousand lances all dressed in their summer white. The ambassador removed his velvet cap and, bowing low, put his hand on the ground, then placed it on his mouth and afterwards on his head, according to the customs of respect to such a powerful monarch. These exercises were repeated after fifteen paces. Finally he reached an area (which he was not invited to cross) covered with carpet, about twenty paces from the sultan, and having repeated his respects a third time he drew from his breast a ducal letter tinted in violet with the papal bull of gold hanging from it, tied with gold ribbons and written with gold letters. Before handing it to a vizier, Domenico kissed the letter and held it above his head. The vizier, acting as interpreter, read out the document while walking to and fro between them. The sultan asked after the health of the Doge and bade the ambassador very welcome. On taking his leave, Domenico took four steps backwards, with his four attendants holding up his cloak so he would not trip and fall. As a warning, Zaccaria wrote that before the Lord Sultan one must not 'spit or blow one's nose as it would be a great insult'. Eight scarlet-clad trumpeters, who had accompanied the embassy to Egypt, bringing their instruments decorated with new golden banners, played at the door of the residence on the ambassador's return.

The costly presents brought by Domenico Trevisan for the sultan had been sent in advance before the audience took place. Outstripping in value by far those dispensed to the Alexandrian amir, they included eight robes of cloth of gold, either embroidered or worked in fields of crimson or purple (costing 30 ducats for one *braccio*), 14 velvet garments of various hues, 26 of satin and two of damask. Zaccaria totalled 100 garments in all. There were also 120 sable skins in bundles of three and 400 pairs of ermine to trim the robes had been added to the pile of gifts. Italian cheese must have been popular at court, as Zaccaria's list of presents recorded 50 pieces.

Although these gifts were opulent, no doubt their worth would have been carefully calculated. The Mamluk sultans were accustomed to such offerings and rewarded their amirs and members of their harems who pleased them in like manner, as well as giving them real estate. Some of the chosen harem women amassed great wealth. When Ittifaq, originally a slave girl with a beautiful voice who married three sultans in succession, was eventually ousted from the citadel in 1345, she took with her 40 dresses inlaid with jewels, 16 dresses with silk hems embroidered with silver or gold and 80 veils each worth between 5,000 and 20,000 dirhams. When she bore a son the cost of her confinement apart from the bedclothes reached 95,000 dinars. Her tiara, which all of her husband sultans had competed in adorning with precious stones, was rumoured to be worth 100,000 dinars.

When they returned to their lodgings, Zaccaria and Yunus, the Veronese dragoman, were sent back to the citadel to hand over the presents personally to the sultan as was the custom. They were ushered up a staircase to a superb room in a different part of the complex, which Zaccaria found more beautiful than the council room of the Venetian Senate. The throne, on which was laid a carpet, was made of porphyry, marble and precious stones. The ceiling was inlaid and gilded and the windows were of bronze instead of iron. Qansuh al-Ghawri was seated on a cushion close to the window overlooking the garden full of orange trees, his feet bare. On being introduced by the dragoman, Zaccaria drew near the sultan until he was only two steps away and, gazing at him, he saw that 'he was a lord of a most grave and proud appearance about sixty years of age, although some said he was seventy. His black beard was interspersed with a few white hairs, his brown face, not close shaved was fat and corpulent.' When the gifts were brought to him, the sultan inspected them separately and through the interpreter he conveyed his thanks as the handsome presents greatly pleased him. Even more, however, was he gratified by the appearance of his excellency the ambassador, who struck him as a serious man of middle age and not young, as he had an air of wisdom.

The objects of Domenico Trevisan's visit were to give assurances of good faith, to smooth over the depredations of Taghribirdi the disgraced Mamluk ambassador, to renegotiate terms for the pepper trade, to pacify the sultan about the lack of Venetian ships (there were usually seven galleys at Alexandria and five at Beirut), and in particular to urge the release of the unfortunate Italian nationals. How much was known abroad about the finances of the impoverished Mamluk state is difficult to say, but the old sultan Qaitbay had already left the coffers bare and that, coupled with the loss of the spice trade, enabled the shrewd Venetians to guess the true situation. There was certainly much dissatisfaction in Cairo about al-Ghawri's actions of plundering the charitable endowments of religious establishments, which formerly the Mamluk rulers had sworn to protect, as well as milking any other bodies thought to have amassed property and capital.

6.2 Old costume of Venetian ambassadors sent to Syria and elsewhere

During his stay of nearly three months, Domenico Trevisan had seven audiences at the citadel. Each meeting was conducted in a different place. The sultan al-Ghawri delighted in flowers and had created a large garden filled with aromatic trees and plants in the hippodrome which he had built to replace the old parade-ground of the Qara Maydan. On its western side were pavilions and belvederes overlooking a pond where he held councils of state and where, in 1510, he celebrated the Muslim New Year, when each great amir was called forward by name and presented with a rose.

Formerly an acting soldier, serving many arduous years in Syria and on the borders of Anatolia, al-Ghawri had been elected sultan as a compromise ruler after the bloody power struggles following the death of Qaitbay, and was forced to accept the throne at sword-point by the council of amirs. He was aloof and shrewd, sometimes cruel, but at the same time was a connoisseur of verse, some of which he composed himself. He enjoyed the company of poets who were invited to recite their works at the citadel, and revelled in the good life under the shade of jasmine trees, fanned by his pages.

The Venetian embassy's second audience took place in a large square, most probably the hippodrome, outside the citadel on 12 May. Troops of horses were to be seen going through their paces. Owing to the threat posed by the Ottoman Turks, an intense period of military training was initiated by al-Ghawri in order to revive the rigorous cavalry skills of the Mamluks, so vigorously promoted by the despotic Baybars. Al-Ghawri felt it of importance to display publicly the prowess of his soldiers to visiting foreign embassies. Zaccaria estimated that the sultan's garden in the hippodrome was as large as the square itself. In the middle of it there was a loggia, covered with greenery, having stone columns on each of which were attached cages of singing birds. At one side and at the back, there were awnings that gave shade from the sun.

By this time, the preliminary courtesies between the two states had been exchanged; at the third audience, in what Zaccaria called the large *maydan* (parade-ground), the sultan took off the kid gloves. On Ascension Day (20 May), al-Ghawri, dressed in white, wearing his formal head-dress and surrounded publicly by the court, ceremoniously received Domenico Trevisan with the Alexandrian consul and a company of merchants. While Domenico was loudly addressing the sultan through the interpreter, the consul for Damascus, Pietro Zen, was ushered in, dressed in scarlet. There followed an unpleasant altercation when al-Ghawri publicly accused Pietro of being involved in the correspondence detrimental to the Mamluks with Isma'il Shah. He demanded that the Venetians should kill the consul or at least banish him. The ambassador pleaded for Pietro Zen and the other merchants, maintaining that the Signoria had no knowledge of the matter and that furthermore, to placate the irate sultan, he would personally take responsibility for the offending prisoner. As an onlooker, Zaccaria was obviously distressed at Domenico's seeming lack of support for Pietro Zen, who was blatantly being used as a scapegoat: 'Thus with many other words, here in the presence of the Lord Sultan, His Excellency the Ambassador put the chains on the neck of His Excellency the Consul.' After a prolonged discussion of about three hours, the Venetians mounted their horses and left, except for the unfortunate Pietro Zen, who was led to the house of the interpreter, chained by the neck and on foot. 'What will happen to the said Consul,' Zaccaria wrote, 'I do not know, but I hope it will be well... what was done was to satisfy the Sultan, even though he [Pietro] might not have erred.' As a diversion from this disagreeable encounter, the ambassador was shown a live crocodile and a leopard, which, according to Zaccaria, belonged to Pietro Zen!

The luckless consul managed to survive this ordeal, afterwards returning to Venice, and was loaded with honours by the Republic. Subsequently he was sent to Constantinople as vice *bailo* where he remained for seven years. The Signoria must have been well satisfied with his tour of duty, since he was once more ordered back to Turkey as ambassador in 1529, but sadly perished on the voyage before he taking up his post.

On 30 June, at the fifth audience, the ambassador was taken to a gate behind the citadel, before entering the square where the first audience had taken place and through the room where the sultan had accepted his costly Venetian gifts. Having ascended a small staircase, they passed through about six bronze doors 'carved with Moorish letters and gilded', leading into a further golden room similar to the first. Al-Ghawri awaited them seated on a round crimson velvet cushion. Outside, a large pond could be seen through two adjacent bronze windows. Fountains threw up cooling jets of water, while around the pond orange trees provided shade for the windows. Inside the room there were three small divans, one of which was covered with embroidered velvet adorned with a costly gold fringe about one *braccio* long. Along the southern side of the *hawsh*, al-Ghawri had built a new palace, connected to the reception hall of the former residence of Qaitbay, overlooking the cemetery to the south of the citadel. The palace was surrounded by courtyards and gardens, with a rectangular basin filled with fresh water and small fish. As the citadel buildings expanded, the need for water increased. In 1508, al-Ghawri repaired the aqueduct of al-Nasir Muhammad and built a large intake tower with a cistern connected by a tunnel to the river.

At this point, further costly gifts were sent to the sultana in her apartments in the harem block near the kitchens in the southern enclosure, and, in order of importance, to the various court officials who oiled the wheels. Once more all details of disbursements were faithfully recorded by Zaccaria for the ever-watchful eyes of the Signoria back home.

In all, Qansuh al-Ghawri received 14 foreign embassies in the months of May and June 1512. On 15 June, the ambassador of the Ottoman sultan, surrounded by 150 horsemen, confidently swept into the city from Constantinople. He was resplendent in a golden coat *alla turchesca* and a turban ornamented on top by a bunch of feathers. Before his audience, the Turkish ambassador had sent in advance thirty hampers without handles containing cloth of gold, silk, fine carpets, bows and horse saddles. There were also eight leopards. In his company came an envoy with about 20 horses from the Christian king of Georgia, whose lands, according to Zaccaria Pagani, lay towards India 60 days' walking from Constantinople. He was dressed in gold and his cap was adorned with ermine. It was said that he had come to petition that the church of the Holy Sepulchre should be reopened, as it had been closed against the Christians for two years.

In the more relaxed atmosphere of his private apartments shaded by his peaceful garden, it seems that the sultan was persuaded of the Venetians' good faith and amid a threatening future the friendship of Venice must have seemed advantageous. Subsequently the ambassador had two more audiences at the citadel in quick succession, the first on 25 July, which lasted for two hours in 'a more beautiful place than all the others amongst gardens and fountains', and the second on 26 July once more in the *maydan*. For this final formal leave-taking, the ambassador and his party were arrayed in all their finery, Domenico once more donning his ermine-lined cloak. In his company were two consuls, though Zaccaria only mentions specifically the consul of Alexandria who came with Domenico's son Mark Antonio. In honour of the last farewell, the eight Venetian trumpeters played in the presence of the sultan and according to Zaccaria, they continued triumphantly playing in front of the ambassador as he processed back to his residence. That evening, everybody, including the company of merchants, sat down to a banquet where they were entertained by four young men who sang Domenico's praises in a short pastoral poem. On that happy day, there was further rejoicing in Cairo, as the sultan sent two of his amirs to cut the barrier into the canal from the Nile, risen to a satisfactory 20 cubits, so that the water gushed refreshingly through the waterways and replenished the pleasure lakes of the city.

Domenico Trevisan was regarded as one of the most notable Venetians of his time, and, being wise in the ways of tricky diplomacy and the playing off of one country against another, he undertook many important diplomatic missions to the principal European capitals. Zaccaria Pagani, his secretary, recorded that the ambassador's salary during the time of the Egyptian embassy was 300 ducats per month, with 1,000 ducats paid in advance. As befitting his status, when he was sent to Alexandria on 22 January 1512, he was conveyed in one of the largest galleys, *le galere bastarde*, in the Venetian fleet, 150 feet long and reserved for the transport of the most important people. His portrait as a proud illustrious patrician was painted by Titian and could be seen in the great hall of the Council. After a long and distinguished career Domenico died on 28 December 1535 and was buried in the church of San Francesco della Vigne in Venice.

Sultan al-Ghawri was only to survive four more years after

Domenico's visit. Though he was well aware of the weakness of his position, reluctantly he felt obliged to enter into a defensive war against the aggression of the Ottoman sultan Selim I, who could not be restrained from casting his eyes in the direction of Egypt. Selim, who had ascended the throne in Constantinople in 1512, was embarking on more warlike and unscrupulous policies than those of his father Bayazid, and had already received emissaries' reports regarding the outdated methods of cavalry warfare displayed in the exercises at the hippodromes of Cairo. Though al-Ghawri had rightly urged the casting of guns and the use of arqebusses, the obstinacy of the Mamluk factions in adhering to conservative ways was in stark contrast to the effectiveness of modern methods of warfare employed by the Turks. Al-Ghawri's forces were far fewer than those of the Ottomans and had already been weakened by treason and disunity. At the battle of Marj Dabiq near Aleppo in 1516, the aged sultan fell from his saddle and was said to have died of a stroke, though his body was never found. His army quickly suffered defeat: the Ottoman cannon and the arquebusses fired by the infantry took heavy toll among the Mamluk cavalry, who, however brave, had no chance against them. The Ottoman soldiers dispersed the Mamluks having killed many of them, including their commander in chief and the governors of the provinces. Al-Ghawri's huge treasure of gold and jewels, to the value of over a million dinars, which he had taken on 50 camels to the battle, was appropriated by Selim who used it to pay his own troops. Meanwhile the amirs in Cairo quickly elected the reluctant Tuman Bay, al-Ghawri's nephew, as the new sultan, who could not but know of the bleak future facing him. Having conquered Syria, Selim progressed through the north of Sinai and on 22 January 1517 reached Birkat al-Hajj, north of Cairo, where the battle of Raydaniyya sealed the sultan's fate. Tuman Bay fought bravely but was forced to flee. After a further disastrous stand at Giza on 2 April 1517 he escaped once more, only to be betrayed by a so-called ally who had sworn to hide him.

Selim lived up to his soubriquet 'the grim'. The historian Ibn Iyas who saw him in Cairo after the conquest described him as a clean-shaven, wide-nosed, wide-eyed, short man about forty years old with a hump on his back; furthermore he was bad-tempered, irascible and bloodthirsty. He had no royal etiquette and did not keep assurances of immunity.

Tuman Bay, who had been acclaimed as sultan by the people, was captured by Selim and subsequently taken from Bulaq on an old camel preceded by about 400 Ottomans and arqebusiers. He greeted the crowds on the way until they reached the Bab Zuwayla gate where he dismounted and his bonds were loosened. Surrounded by armed guards with drawn swords, when he saw he was condemned to be hanged, he asked the people to pray with him, before bidding the executioner to do his work and place the noose round his neck. It was said that the rope broke twice and he fell to the ground. At a third attempt he was hanged. When his spirit went forth the people cried with a great cry and there was much sorrow for him.

The story of Tuman Bay's death provoked much sympathy in Europe since it was a further manifestation of the hated Turkish aggression. The incident was described by the Cordelier André Thevet of Angouleme (1516–92), who visited Egypt in 1549. André, who was an illustrious royal geographer at the French court, was widely travelled and had explored countries as far off as Brazil. A friend of Sir Francis Drake, he was lauded by Ronsard, who compared him as a traveller to Jason. André wrote several works, one of which was his *Cosmographie Universelle*, published in Paris in 1584. He felt such sympathy for the unfortunate sultan that he promoted him to the ranks of the most illustrious of Muslim monarchs, the equal of Saladin and other revered rulers. His particular account of Tuman Bay included a woodcut representation of the unfortunate sultan tied on the camel on his way to Cairo, his turban carried aloft on a lance. He wrote of the sultan's torn green robe and how he was mocked while tied to a post for six days on a scaffold. André added further embroidery to the account of Ibn Iyas. He said that because the people were in a tumult, it caused Selim to be so enraged, that on 13 April 1517, Tuman Bay was taken to a butcher's shop where cattle were killed, and having dismounted from his camel he was strangled. It was known that the head was displayed on the Bab Zuwayla like a common criminal.

According to André, the victorious Ottomans killed 28,000 people in Cairo, while the women and children with the workmen threw down stones and other objects from the windows and tops of houses and the blood ran in the streets. During three days of looting the soldiers pillaged the homes of amirs, and the granaries of Old Cairo and Bulaq, until janissaries were placed around the city to stop them, The people of Cairo suffered great hardships after the conquest, not the least being the debasement of the currency and grave interference with their civil laws. After a reign of more than two and a half centuries they had become used to the Mamluks, despite their shortcomings, and they found the new regime much worse. For the next few centuries, Egypt was degraded to the status of a province ruled over by successive Turkish viceroys and their governors. As such it was a fortunate acquisition for the Ottoman sultans, since the rich land of Lower Egypt, growing wheat, sugar, rice, cotton and all kinds of fruit, together with all the lucrative taxes, became a major source of wealth which contributed to enriching the expanding capital of Constantinople.

Although the citadel remained a well-guarded fortress after the advent of the Turks, the opulent decorations disappeared. The palaces and mosques were stripped of many of their treasures as part of the spoils of the Ottoman sultan and taken away to Constantinople. At this time of turmoil many of the royal Mamluks were slain. Instead of the Mamluk sultans, a pasha made his residence in the palace of the deceased sultan al-Ghawri in the *hawsh*, which came to house thousands of government employees. A large Ottoman force of over 13,000 troops was stationed in the country, the largest and most important group of soldiers being the janissaries, slave soldiers taken from the Christian subjects of the Turks, as a slave tribute from the Balkans and elsewhere. Their jealous rivalries were nurtured by the pasha, who feared any one faction becoming too powerful. In addition to this large army, the fortifications and walls of the citadel were strengthened for defence. Meanwhile, those Mamluks who survived the onslaught retired with their men to live in fortified palaces west of al-Rumayla Square. The foremost amirs were accorded the title of Bey, and after swearing fealty to the Turkish sultan, they were given seats in the government and occupied important posts. After 1566, when the harsh Turkish rule started to relent, the Mamluks once more came to be a strong force in Egypt, continuing to perpetuate their highly disciplined private armies with the ongoing purchase of Circassian slaves. Despising the native Egyptians, they only married Caucasian slave women. Though they indulged in ferocious power struggles among themselves and against the occupying Ottomans, the Mamluks managed to maintain their powerful presence. Eventually in 1811, all but one were brutally massacred by Muhammad 'Ali Pasha as they were filing from the citadel after a banquet, to which they had been lured by their host.

Notes

General: Winter, 'Ottoman Occupation', pp. 493–503 (Tuman Bay as sultan, his defeat and death, pp. 501–504); Holt, *Age of the Crusades*, pp. 192–206; Lapidus, *Muslim Cities in the Late Middle Ages*, pp. 225–46; Garcin, 'The Regime of the Circassian Mamluks' (sultanate of Qansuh al-Ghawri, pp. 295–97); Petry, 'Late Mamluk Military Institution and Innovation' (Qansuh al-Ghawri's embassies, p. 464; methods of gaining revenue, attempts to modernise army, pp. 474–89).
Venetian embassies: Wansburgh, 'A Mamluk Ambassador to Venice in 913/1507', pp. 503–29; Prescot, *Once to Sinai*, pp. 133–37; Barozzi (ed.), *Zaccaria Pagani, Viaggio di Domenico Trevisan*, pp. 19–35; Lestringant (ed. and introd.), *Voyages en Egypte* (André Thevet's account of tribulations of 'Prinse de Tomombey' [Sultan Tuman Bay] in *Cosmographie Universelle*, II, pp. 175–77).

CHAPTER 7

Exploring the Pyramids and
Mummy Fields

Pliny the Elder (AD 23–79), whose works were universally read by the educated, wrote in withering terms that the pyramids were but vain and frivolous pieces of ostentation on the part of Egyptian monarchs (*Natural History* 36.16). But before the tide of works from classical authors permeated the libraries of European scholars, it was commonly thought that the pyramids were the granaries of the most holy Joseph, used for storing corn during the years of famine. As such, they were regarded as objects of reverence, and indulgences were awarded by the church to visiting pilgrims on a kind of points system. This pious belief, stoutly upheld by Sir John Mandeville, had almost evaporated by the end of the sixteenth century, when the structures were recognised as being the tombs of the ancient pharaohs.

Few monuments in Egypt have been surveyed and measured, for whatever reason, so often and with such care as the Great Pyramid of Cheops. In 1384, Simone Sigoli and his Tuscan friends Lionardo di Frescobaldi and Giorgio Gucci marvelled at the wisdom of Joseph in creating such immense storage for his bushels: 'the width at the base, according to what we measured with the braccia, every side is 140 braccia: and each has four sides, and the corn was placed inside: just imagine the very great amount that inside would take'. Simone did not say if he climbed to the summit or ventured into the interior, though in his time a large opening had been roughly hacked into the core a little below the original entrance. According to Muslim tradition, in the latter part of the ninth century the caliph Ma'mun, son of Harun al-Rashid, had ordered this penetration as he coveted the fabled treasure rumoured to be hidden inside. Over one hundred years after the Tuscans went there, Father Francesco Suriano from Mount Sion in Jerusalem showed himself to be more intrepid. He did not reveal the date of his visit to the pyramids, but it probably took place while he was on business in Cairo in 1498 when he became acquainted with the wily Mamluk Taghribirdi (whom he called 'Tagrebardin' or 'Tupolino') who later went to Venice as the envoy of Qansuh al-Ghawri:

> I climbed to the top of the big one, which is square and each side is a bow shot. It is shaped like a diamond, as was Noah's ark, inside, it is built with stones and lime, but outside it is covered with hard thick flagstones of three braccia square, which are joined together, like the gate of the Via Vecchia in Perugia, with marvellous art without lime, and they are so joined that from the foot to the top they form a stairway. And on the summit there is a stone that closes the whole building and it is of such a size that I wondered how it were possible to bring it to such a height, for it is seven braccia square and one cubit in thickness. To descend was more fatiguing to ascend than to ascend...
>
> You can enter this great pyramid by a small door, and then farther in there is another door which with difficulty can be entered with a light. Then there is a passage that leads to a tomb so marvellously worked of fine marble that it amazes everybody: it stands in a room encased in the finest marble of ancient work with inscriptions all around. You can go all round the tomb. For that tomb the building was raised.

Whether Francesco actually entered the big pyramid is uncertain: the marble tomb he depicts as covered all over with writing is not in fact inscribed, so probably his description came from hearsay. Many travellers of this epoch described the granite as marble.

In 1547, after spending some days in Cairo, Pierre Belon du Mans accompanied M. de Fumet together with a *sanjac* (an official under the pasha), several *spahis* (cavaliers) and 'Toute la compagnie qui le suyvoit'. The party was ferried across the Nile, partly by sail and partly by oar, passing close to the island of al-Rawda opposite Cairo.

Reaching the west bank, they proceeded along a lengthy causeway with stone arches, and small wooden bridges, culminating near the village of Busiris, where the Nile had broken the arches of a stone bridge over a dyke.

Beyond the village there was a further long causeway which terminated in the desert by the pyramids. As the inundation was high, the dyke had been breached, forming a lake. The party confronted with crossing the lake was in some difficulty; those who were well mounted could easily ford it following the guides, but pedestrians had to wait for a boat. Others, having taken off their clothes, led their mounts by the halter, wading through the water up to their armpits. When they reached dry land, some Moors in the next village showed them the path up to the pyramids. On reaching 'the first and fairest of the greater Pyramids' on a rocky hill, Pierre took its measurements, and having climbed to the summit, he saw clearly the whole city of Cairo and to the north the submerged countryside of Egypt like a great sea. To the south towards Ethiopia there was only sterile sand. Examining the

7.1 Excursion to the pyramids

northern face, he found it more damaged than the other sides and conjectured that the humidity, as well as the dews of the night from the Nile stirred up by the north winds, had greatly damaged it.

The party entered the interior through 'a lower opening'. They could only proceed one by one, each holding a lighted candle. In order to negotiate the passage it was necessary to advance flat on their stomachs, creeping like serpents and moving with discomfort. After reaching a wider part, they turned towards the right and discovered a square built gallery, well notched, which went up from bottom to top where a man could continue upright: Pierre described the gallery as an extensive and high cavity ('large espace et haute cavité') without steps for ascent, paved with large wide stones very polished and slippery ('moult polies et glissantes'). This gallery was in all probability the Grand Gallery, on each side of which are flat-topped ramps two feet high and one foot eight inches wide. Pierre said that they steadied themselves on rails at each side. They went on into a handsome square room which in his estimation measured six paces long and four wide and four to six *toises* in height (one *toise* equals just over six feet). Inside it they found a sarcophagus, described by Pierre as of black marble hewn out of one piece like a coffer, which he guessed to be twelve feet long, five feet high and as many wide, without a cover. Pierre had no hesitation in calling it the sepulchre of a king of Egypt for which the pyramid was built.

They retraced their steps down through the Grand Gallery and once outside it they had to turn to the left where they found a well almost full of stones. Pierre had read accounts of the pyramid by Greek historians such as Herodotus and Diodorus, 'as well as Pliny writing in Latin'. In particular, Pliny spoke of the depth of the well and stated that water drawn from it was used for the masonry and to refresh the workmen. Pierre encountered some large bats haunting the dark corridor, noting that they differed altogether from those in France, which had tails no longer than their wings. Those in the pyramid had tails four fingers in length.

Beyond finding the height of the entrance tunnel uncomfortable, Pierre did not express any fear of his experiences. But in 1588, Samuel Kiechel from Ulm, who had clambered round the ancient subterranean

7.2 Inside the grand gallery of the 'First and Great Pyramid'

wells of Alexandria, found the expedition unnerving. The visit had been proposed on 2 July by an old German renegade, a janissary who had lived in Egypt for 30 years. He had taken Samuel back to his lodgings where they were joined by three others. They drank a cup together and became happy and convivial. Even so, Samuel realised that it was necessary to be cautious, as too much trust could not be placed in one's acquaintances. During the course of conversation it appeared that Samuel would dearly like to see the pyramids, although he was warned of the dangers posed by the local Arabs and was told that he could not go unarmed or without companions. Privately he feared the expense of the venture, as he did not have much money in his chest to pay for three or four janissaries to accompany him. However, another of the renegades, one Michael Müller, a jeweller from Strasbourg married to a Greek Christian, who had been made to turn 'Turk' three years before, offered to accompany him alone. This was despite the fact he had been attacked by some Arabs on a previous visit to the pyramids with some German nobles. The party had come off badly; Michael had been stripped to the skin and the old janissary, Samuel's host, who had accompanied them, was badly wounded, leaving him with a paralysed arm. Because of these mishaps, the old man had no wish to repeat the journey, but by way of encouragement he bespoke a donkey man with two donkeys for the following morning, and invited Michael and Samuel to spend the night at his house.

The next day (3 July) Samuel and his companion started off in good time, as the sun rose early at that time of year. Each had taken the precaution of donning an old torn shirt, trousers and a jacket of little value. Instead of his turban, Michael Müller wore a grey pointed bonnet, since they hoped to disguise themselves as poor Christian hermits so as not to be accosted. The Nile was not yet at its height, so the friends, not faced with the problems of flooding, could walk the six miles or so to the pyramids. On the way they were hailed by some Arabs working in fields of sugar cane, inquisitive as to their route; the two companions pointed to the pyramids which were not far ahead. Michael could speak Turkish well but not Arabic; it was only later that the donkey man told them, through an interpreter, that they should not proceed, as the place was full of thieves; further, that Samuel's companion would be wise not to act as if he was a Turk, since the Arabs looked on them as the greatest of enemies, something which without doubt would cost them their lives. Samuel gave one of the Arabs some bread though he was unwilling to accept it. He was also afraid that they might be searched, although he had only ten medines on him, of which he had retained two for the return crossing of the Nile. They also might have been beaten up, since, apart from the bread, they had brought with them a large leg of pork which they were absolutely forbidden to eat. Samuel understood that the Arab wanted money because he said '*Ente flous?*' ('You are money?') and straight away Samuel put two of his medines into the man's hand. This did not satisfy, so Samuel had to give him two more, whereupon the Arab summoned two companions, each with a lance and spear, who escorted them to their destination. Samuel remained a little behind, taking the pork and burying it in the sand. Before reaching the pyramid they were forced to surrender all the provisions they had brought for themselves.

Samuel's real difficulties commenced on exploring the interior of the pyramid. While the Arabs waited for them outside, the two entered the cavity, stooping very low and carrying lighted torches. After descending for a short way, they found a further dark orifice to the right which sloped up a little and where they had to bend down even further. A large number of bats flew over Samuel's head. In this passage they missed seeing a 'marble' stone near an opening leading to another corridor (the Grand Gallery?) where it would have been easy to climb to the top, but Samuel, relying on his companion (who told him erroneously that he knew the way), was misled. They retraced their steps down the passage and continued ever lower down it. At the end, the way was so stony and dilapidated that they had to crawl flat on their stomachs for a good distance. Eventually, after a long way, the tunnel became so full of stones, sand and dust that it was impossible to proceed. On the right they found an opening, a hole so small that they could hardly stand upright. They started to climb up into the hole, which was square inside like a chimney; it rose straight up like a wall and Samuel conjectured that it had been cut into the rock. There were small niches in the sides where they could latch on with their big toes, groping from one step to the next. The friends stripped down to their shirts as it was impossible to climb wearing clothes and shoes; in two places particularly, Samuel found the chimney so narrow that his body became jammed and he could neither continue nor retreat. It was difficult to keep a hold, but they managed to continue upwards by gripping on to a niche with one foot, while supporting themselves with their backs and buttocks. The enormous labour and effort expended caused Samuel's strength to be exhausted. This was also partly due to the heat, which was very intense at that time of year, and the lack of air and light, plus the fact that the 'chimney' was full of dust and desert sand. Their difficulties were compounded because of having to hold the lighted smoking torch. Samuel, who was sure nobody had been there for countless years, was apprehensive that if the foot of the first one to climb up gave way, he could bring down his companion who followed and both of them would cascade to the bottom.

Half a century later, John Greaves, professor of astronomy at Oxford would not have had much sympathy with these haphazard meanderings. In 1639, accompanied by a Venetian, Tito Livio Burattini, 'an ingenious young man', Greaves set out from Alexandria to Grand Cairo to make a systematic, accurate survey of the interior corridors of the first pyramid. So as to inform his readers of his scientific approach, he carried with him

> [a] radius of ten feet most accurately divided besides some other instruments for the fuller discovery of truth... I shall now look inwards and lead the reader into several spaces and partitions within: of which if the Ancients have been silent, we must chiefly impute it to a reverend and awful regard, mixed with superstition, in not presuming to enter those chambers of death, which religion and devotion had consecrated to the rest and quiet of the dead.

Greaves made a diagram showing the notched sides of the shaft up which Samuel probably climbed, identifying it with the circular well mentioned by Pliny: 'the diameter exceeds three feet... the descent into it is by fastening the hands and feet in little open spaces cut in the sides within, opposite and answerable to one another, in perpendicular'. Greaves compared it to the type of access to the wells of Alexandria, of which he gave a description. Sounding the depth with a line, he estimated it as a drop of 206 feet, and threw down some combustible material which he set alight. This shaft, which Samuel and Michael Müller almost certainly climbed, may have been the one used as an escape route by the labourers after the funeral of Cheops when the Grand Gallery had been sealed.

When Samuel and his friend finally reached the top of the shaft,

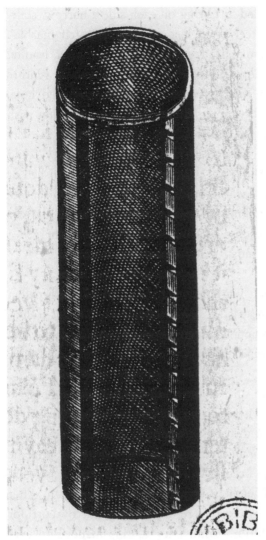

7.3 Diagram of the so-called 'well' mentioned by Pliny

they emerged through a small opening located at the bottom of a long corridor (probably the Grand Gallery). Following a further horizontal corridor, they arrived at a large dark hall like a chamber, which he said was clad all over with fine red marble. It is possible that Samuel was referring to the so-called Queen's Chamber, lying in the central axis of the pyramid, which runs up through the top of the Grand Gallery, before the antechamber passage of the King's Chamber. The smell given off by the large number of bats was so strong that it was impossible to stay there. They returned to the foot of the first long

corridor, which he described as having on each side a narrow 'staircase'; the steps were scarcely two feet wide, all of 'red marble'.
Although they could see a small staircase 'going up still higher' leading
to the tomb of the pharaoh, Samuel and Michael did not venture
beyond that point. After their experience in the constricted hole,
Samuel owned that he had got into such a fright that he did not wish
to explore further; besides, he realised Michael did not know the way
and he anticipated other passages and openings where they could
become lost and perish. Above all, the light might be extinguished or
give out, which had happened before. Samuel imagined too that he
heard the Arabs outside making wild cries. Perhaps fear played tricks
on his mind, though according to John Greaves, who discharged a
musket at the entrance, its noise made

> a long continued sound... For the sound being shut in, and carried in
> those close and smoothe passages, like in so many pipes or trunks,
> finding no issue reflects upon it selfe and causes a confused noise, and
> circulation of the aire, which by degrees vanishes as the motion ceases.

Because the climb up the claustrophobic shaft had been so
alarming, Samuel had no wish to lead the way down; above all he was
afraid of being jammed in the constricted space he had encountered
during the ascent. His companion therefore went down first while he
followed; on reaching the bottom they thanked God to be safe and
sound, although Samuel's light was extinguished once again. After
they had rested for a short while, they returned up the narrow corridor
which led up to the exterior. Samuel found this manoeuvre very
distressing; the stones cut his knees and arms and he became so
exhausted and apprehensive that he thought he would suffocate
because of the terrible heat, lack of air and light. On reaching the
wider part of the passage, just as they were about to make their
exit, they met five Arabs with lances and spears demanding money.
Samuel summoned up his only words of Arabic to tell them he had
none, and eventually the Arabs retreated, having made a lot of noise.
The friends followed them outside, thankful to breathe freely in the
fresh air.

The so-called well was notorious. In the middle of the sixteenth century, the Turkish ruler of Cairo forced a criminal who had been condemned to death to climb down it to ascertain if there was any treasure at the bottom. The cord which had been tied round the waist of the unfortunate man broke and he fell the whole way to the bottom, after which he lay bruised, without light or hope of salvation. Not knowing which way to go and after turning this way and that, he found a passage which he followed the whole of the next day. Eventually he perceived some light and soon after saw the sandy desert. Having had the good fortune to escape from this terrible ordeal, he decided to return to Cairo to inform the pasha, who forthwith granted him freedom.

Once outside, Samuel quickly regained his composure, and at once proposed to climb up the outside of the pyramid to estimate its height. Overcome by weakness and fatigue his companion could not face the effort, so he stayed at the bottom with the Arabs and the man who kept the donkeys. Samuel's guide, a young Arab, ascended the pyramid first and climbed up more quickly than Samuel, who rested several times on the way. The stones (estimated as about 230) were set like a staircase, but some were so high that he could only climb them with difficulty. Because of its enormous height he had the impression from the bottom that the pyramid was pointed, but when he reached the top he found a large space on which nearly 50 people could stand upright, one against the other. From that height he could see the pointed summit of the smaller pyramid of Khephren (which he was told was the tomb of the queen) with its slippery exterior, impossible to climb, as well as the many large and small pyramids in the vicinity. When he had seen enough, he was astonished to see the Arab leaping down daringly to the bottom from one stone to the next; but Samuel was too frightened to follow his example.

In 1577, Filippo Pigafetta from Vicenza went twice to the great pyramid. The first occasion was with Paolo Mariani, the Venetian ambassador, who had sent off orders ahead to clean out the entrance. They were accompanied by the consul, some janissaries and many other attendants. With such a large company it was unlikely that they would be attacked, though a few days before, Filippo learnt that when

some other visitors were exploring the interior, the last straggler had
been forced to stay the night because the hole had become closed by
sand and stones. He had nearly died, either from fear or because of
the nocturnal winter cold in a place where the sun never penetrated.

Filippo's second venture took place with some sailors and a few
French merchants. Nervous of the dangers, they took with them two
men armed with arquebusses, and spent a certain sum per man on
having the entrances cleaned and hiring guides and donkeys. Their
four- or five-mile journey in December along the plain must have been
very pleasant. The countryside was green and the soggy ground had
dried up, the beans were in flower and the mature ears of wheat were
being harvested. When they reached the desert and the higher ground,
Filippo noted the geographical position of the three pyramids in turn
and assessed their measurements with his customary precision. He
examined the building blocks and pondered how they were laid. He
judged that the Great Pyramid could be climbed easily at the corners
though not if one had a fear of heights. At the top he saw the names
of many people written in every language on the stones.

Inside, they carried candles that could not be extinguished by the
wind and stripped off their coats, putting on light woollen shoes so as
not to fall on the slippery stones. All the time they were affected badly
by the obnoxious smell from the unventilated atmosphere. On
reaching the King's Chamber, Filippo noted that the ceiling was not
vaulted like that of the Grand Gallery, but flat, strikingly high, made
of large fine slabs dissimilar to others in the pyramid. He was of the
opinion that the sarcophagus was made of *pietra tebaico* (granite) like
the obelisks in Rome or the red column in the piazza in Venice. Then
having measured it (ten spans of his hand long and five wide) he struck
it inside, making a sound like a bell; as it was a such a curiosity and a
rare antique, Filippo 'broke off a piece' and sent it to His Excellency
'Signor Giacomo Foscarini, Proveditor Generale nell 'Isola de Candia'.
Though he did not say so, he must have had a tool with him to cut the
hard granite. Paolo Mariani had already drawn Filippo's attention to
the fact that rain had penetrated down to the southern part of the
chamber, more rain having fallen from the sky in those days than at
any time men could ever remember. When they regained the last

passage to the exit, some Bedouin were there to take away the sand so that they could pass through the restricted space on all fours. They were covered in sweat due to the great heat, but once outside they changed their shirts, noting that a strong wind had blown up in their absence.

Filippo saw the sphinx lying to the south of the pyramid complex in a small valley. 'It has a large head beyond every belief so that an eye is as long as an ordinary man.' Crows had made their nests in its ears and there was a hole along the middle of the spine. He wondered if there was the sepulchre of the king inside it or whether it was the place where the priests hid themselves so as to reply to those who came to consult the oracle. But for whatever reason, the hole was stopped up, and nothing was to be seen except the rim filled up with sand; the main body of the sphinx was visible, although both the fore and hind legs were buried. The head, neck and chest of the colossus were complete but the nose and a piece of one eye were broken off. (He did not comment on the royal head-dress and the cobra on the forehead, though these would have been visible. As the front legs were covered, he would not have seen the large tablet of red granite between the lion paws.)

Pietro dalla Valle, an Italian traveller in Egypt during 1615–16, was born in Rome in 1586 of a famous noble family. He had been given a Catholic education which endowed him with a knowledge of the classics, Italian literature, music and letters. He was acquainted with the *Observations* of Pierre Belon du Mans, which he used as a guide book. For 12 years Pietro had been wooing Beatrice Boraccio, a lady who finally jilted him for another suitor, an event that almost drove him to suicide. But after spending some time in Naples to forget his romantic attachment, he was encouraged to satisfy his curiosity about the East by his friend Dr Mario Schapiro, a professor of medicine, who agreed to collaborate in a correspondence. Mario suggested that Pietro should write down his travel experiences in the form of letters, which Mario would subsequently amalgamate into a cohesive narrative back home. At the beginning of the correspondence, Pietro indicated that he would write in his own Roman dialect and not in elegant Tuscan, while his impressions were still fresh in his mind. It happened however that

Pietro's letters remained unedited, so that in spite of being verbose, his original descriptions remain lively and spontaneous.

As a prelude to his Egyptian journey, Pietro elected to go as a pilgrim to the Holy Land. Before departure, he was blessed at the convent of the saints Festo and Marcellino, dressed rather flamboyantly in his brown pilgrim's tunic adorned with a red cross and a little gold staff which was hung round his neck. In all, Pietro was away from Italy for 12 years, being financed by letters of credit sent by his agents in Italy. His party embarked at Venice on 8 June 1614 on the *Gran Delfino*, a galleon in which many died of the plague, bound for the Levant.

Having spent over a year in Constantinople, where he was presented to the Grand Turk, Pietro sailed for Alexandria on 25 September 1615 on a large galleon used for official business, plying between Turkey and Egypt. It carried 2,000 passengers and was owned by the Georgian pasha, Muhammad Kaymakam, the first vizier's lieutenant. In a letter of 25 January the next year to Mario Schapiro, Pietro wrote that he took with him nine persons, seven Christians and two Turks: 'The priest Fra Giulio da Monte Rubbiano commissary of the Franciscans who…wanted to go out of devotion to the Holy Land; my hermit friar Andrea, brought from Italy, Monsieur de Vernyes, a young Fleming of fine quality who had been in the service of His Excellency the French Ambassador.' The Fleming was seriously ill with fever but begged Pietro not to abandon him, saying he did not mind about dying as long as he was in Pietro's company. Against the advice of the doctor, Pietro relented and took him along. Among those from Italy were his servants Lorenzo and Tommasso and 'Giovanni my painter likewise a Fleming and of some standing in the art'. From Constantinople came 'Paulo the Greek who was then my dragoman or interpreter, a very worthy young man' who was, however, still very ill from consumptive fever. Pietro was thus hampered by two invalids, though he was persuaded to take Paulo against many people's advice because of his and his mother's prayers. His Turkish companions were Hussein Beg, a palace official of the Grand Signor, and his servant. Pietro was honoured that Hussein Beg had been chosen by the good offices of 'My Lord the Ambassador with the widest command from the Grand

Turk, ordering him to guard and take care of me and the people accompanying me during the journey'. The ambassador did Pietro the favour of telling everyone that he was his nephew (and referring to this in documents), so that his patronage might protect him from the avarice of ministers and the many difficulties imposed upon strangers in a foreign country. In short the ambassador did everything to ensure that Pietro went on his way with all the honours and safeguards possible.

Fortified with these credentials, after a week's sojourn in Alexandria, the party sailed upstream in a capacious flat-bottomed boat to Bulaq. The well trodden commercial route into Cairo appeared delightful, since the Nile had receded, leaving in its wake various grasses and herbs sprouting up among the palms. In the suburbs just before the city gate, Pietro particularly admired Ezbekiyya, which he described as a low shell-like plain fringed with houses 'as beautiful to see when the terrain is green as it must be when filled with water like a lake'. On arrival, he dismounted at the house occupied by the consul of France, on whose orders he was received by the steward in his own rooms.

On 8 December, Pietro and his retinue sailed across the Nile for the pyramids. Even though he had been forewarned by Pierre Belon in his *Observations* about the dark passages inside the Great Pyramid, Pietro found that the intense heat of the interior caused the perspiration to soak his doublet, and that the crawl along the tunnels on his stomach was very tiring. Inside the King's Chamber, the stone of the sepulchre proved so hard that he found it impossible to break off a flake with the steel hammer he had brought with him. When he struck the coffin, the sweet noise of a bell was so loud that, had they not been in an enclosed space, it would have been heard a long way off. Afterwards he climbed to the summit of the pyramid where 'above at the highest point, on the part which looks towards Italy, I took pleasure in leaving my name carved'. He asked the Turks who accompanied him to shoot a number of arrows from the top with the greatest force, but no matter how strongly they tried, the arrows always fell back on to the slope, never reaching the bottom.

Interest in ancient Egyptian mummification of the dead gained in popularity in the sixteenth century, because of its connection with the trade in ancient Egyptian corpses for medicinal purposes. Those acquainted with the accounts of the funerary practices of ancient Egypt by Herodotus and Diodorus Siculus had no reason to doubt the veracity of their source material, although it was not entirely correct. In 1553, the doctor Pierre Belon published a treatise on embalming, citing Egyptian methods and listing the best preservative materials, quoting from ancient classical authors.

The curious tradition of *mummy* as a medicament, the origins of which can be traced indirectly to the use of bitumen as a preservative in later antiquity, came down via classical and Arab medicine. Under the name *mummia* the Persian type was prized as a panacea; later it was found that the pitch-like substances in embalmed bodies were of similar virtue. Among Arab writers, *mummia* was mentioned by the physician Avicenna. He advocated its use for a number of ailments which included abscesses, eruptions, fractures, concussion, paralysis, palpitations of the heart and disorders of the spleen and liver. He prescribed it to be taken (presumably to make it palatable) in concoctions from plants such as marjoram, thyme, elder, barley, roses, lentils, saffron, cassia and parsley. Avicenna's prescription for powdered mummy was contained in *De Viribus Cordis*, which was listed in the library inventory of San Marco, Florence, in 1444. This collection of books was donated to the city by Niccolò Niccolì, the Florentine humanist, antiquarian and correspondent of Cyriaco of Ancona when he was in Egypt in 1436.

From the eleventh century, some Arab authorities had begun to ascribe the therapeutic values of *mummia* to the actual flesh of the embalmed and it was chiefly in this sense that *mummy* was understood in Europe. The use of the cadaverous flesh was mentioned by Guy de Chavillac, surgeon to Pope Clement VI, in 1363, and by the beginning of the sixteenth century it was so highly regarded that according to Pierre Belon, when the French king Francois I was on horseback, he used to carry a small leather bag containing mummy mixed with powdered rhubarb in case of accident.

The popularity of this unsavoury medicament became widespread; it was a valuable article of commerce, sold via the markets of Cairo and Alexandria and peddled in Europe for making balms, healing wounds and for use at baptisms. The Florentine merchant Francesco Pegolotti listed *mummia* in his handbook as being among 280 spices imported from Egypt. The best was generally considered to be hard and easily powdered, dark brown to black in colour, having a bitter taste and a pungent smell, the French preferring the variety known as *fille vierge*. Not all *mummia*, however, came from an authentic deceased ancient Egyptian, particularly when demand exceeded supply. On a visit to Alexandria in 1564, Guy de la Fontaine, doctor to the king of Navarre, discovered that the Jewish merchants who trafficked in cadavers had the habit of supplementing their merchandise with the bodies of executed criminals and the dead fresh from the hospitals. These were prepared in haste by filling them up with asphalt and drying them in the sun to simulate an antique appearance. Astonishing though it may seem, the so called 'white' variety was often accepted, particularly if it had been prepared from the corpse of a redhead or a witch, and the corpses of travellers who had suffocated in desert sandstorms or drowned off Egyptian shores were also used.

The necropolis of Saqqara, the antique source of this sepulchral material, lay ten miles or so up-river from Cairo on the west bank. The ancient cemeteries became a novel diversion to which some of the travellers to Cairo seeking grave goods and *mummia* went with alacrity from the sixteenth century onwards. After his visit to the pyramids, Filippo Pigafetta was conducted to a large populated village situated in the sands, the abode of Arabs who made a living digging out the ancient dead buried in the rocky caverns scattered around the desert. Among a multitude of small pyramids was a shaft cut into the stone where some steps led into the interior. Having reached the bottom, Filippo peered into a very large cavern, long and wide, with alleyways, divided into large and small rooms with openings, where an innumerable quantity of human corpses were laid. He saw that these were wrapped around with lengths of cotton wool bandages and that under the bandages the cadavers were black, their flesh solid and their limbs intact. Many had the teeth attached to their gums, likewise the hair on their heads, especially the women who had kept it very long. There were children adorned with beautiful bandages and other artefacts. The stomachs of the dead had been stuffed with bitumen brought from the Dead Sea, as was the custom of the ancient Egyptians, to conserve them for a long time. Afterwards they were wrapped round a hundred thousand times in soft bandages like small babies; among the wrappings, idols and gods adored by them had been placed, made of earth and then fired, or cut from precious stones. In addition, there were scarabs bearing many signs and strange characters. From the middle of the highest part of the chest down to the soles of the feet ran a strip of cloth painted with a multitude of animals such as bulls, crocodiles, men with horses' and wolves' heads and other such things. Having been bandaged in that way, each body had been placed in the hollowed-out trunk of a palm tree. On the outside of these containers, Filippo saw painted pictures of the man or woman dressed in the clothes of that time, and if it was a man, with a long beard, accompanied by 'many idols'. 'These mummies are the realities,' he declared, 'And not as I used to believe with many others, men found in the deserts suffocated in the sand.'

It was well known that the warrens of subterranean caverns could be dangerous, because of the torches and candles taken to illuminate them. If the least scrap of *mummia* caught fire, the balm burnt like pitch and thereafter set alight to all the other corpses, dismembered arms and feet and pieces of bandages. If an inextinguishable conflagration occurred lasting several days, all those who were inside the cave at the time would be burnt or stifled by smoke.

Egyptian antiques acquired by consular officials, merchants and other travellers soon featured among classical objects collected by Italian nobles, who were not concerned that some of their so-called Egyptian pieces were of Roman origin, or that the scarabs were sometimes Renaissance copies. Stimulated by the raising of the obelisks, the interest shown in things Egyptian went side by side with the collection of strange objects. Pirro Ligorio (b. 1513 or 1514), a Neapolitan who was a painter, antiquarian and designer, entered the service of Cardinal Ippolito d'Este in 1549, and afterwards worked as papal architect to Pope Paul IV. Subsequently he was employed as an antiquarian to Duke Alfonso d'Este at Ferrara since he was known to be an accomplished excavator and recorder of ancient objects. In 1553, he published his *Libro di Pyrrbo Ligorlo Napolitana delle Antichità di*

Roma, illustrated with his own drawings of antiques. Among them, Pirro depicted a block statue of an Egyptian scribe showing a scroll of Egyptian writing unrolled in front of him, various statuettes of cynocephali and some drawings of the squat and ugly god Bes.

But it was the Italian Pietro della Valle, with his background of classical scholarship, who was the first European to organise a somewhat primitive archaeological dig among the *pozzi profondissimi* at Saqqara, where he and his large retinue pitched their tents in 1616. In the third century BC, Saqqara and Memphis had become the focus of Greek culture when Ptolemy I introduced the hybrid god Serapis to Egypt. Thus the place once more became one of religious importance where burials took place, and where the Serapeum was a centre of pilgrimage. Pietro's enthusiasm for his rather macabre task shines through the letter sent from Cairo to his friend Mario Schapiro in Rome on 25 January 1616:

> In the morning I had not yet dressed, when I had more than fifty peasants around me, who brought me small idols, some saying they would lead me to one place, others to another: I weeded them all out and went off happily. I had with me, not counting those peasants, some twenty five or thirty men, because besides my own party and some soldiers I had brought as guards (those places not being safe) many friends from Cairo had joined me when they knew where I wanted to go, as a favourable opportunity and for safety, and I conducted them willingly. Thus we went, all armed like St. Georges so that we appeared like an army. Having reached the mummies I went about exploring the place a little and I saw it to be very large open country , similar to the other sandy places.[1]

Pietro noted that the desert was dotted with countless deep underground pits constructed of masonry, and vaulted like cisterns, where the bodies reposed buried in sand; after the interment the cavities were filled up to the top so that they could not be seen. He conjectured that a number of the tombs contained corpses belonging to the same family,

---

1   All sixteenth- and early seventeenth-century travellers called *shabti* figures *idola* (or in this case *idoletti*).

as was the burial custom in Italy. Many of the pits were empty, looted
by the peasants who were continuously searching for new material:

> I did not want to descend into some of those empty pits as others do
> and possibly Belon did, because my principal desire was to see the
> bodies as they were placed so that I could speak from sight and not
> from the hearsay of those ignorant peasants. So leaving aside the empty
> pits and having with me a quantity of skilled labourers, I wanted them
> to excavate in new places, to find some others untouched and filled up
> if that were possible. But because of being ignorant where they were,
> it was necessary to seek at random; I noted where the ground seemed
> to me to be less turned over and probed (one recognises the signs where
> the peasants have dug many times and found nothing) and there in
> different places which seemed to me more hopeful, having divided my
> workmen, dispersed them over a large part of the countryside; and to
> encourage them there I pitched my tent in the middle, with determi-
> nation and the promise that I would not depart from that place before
> I might have found something and because I alone could not be every-
> where. I put one of my men on guard over each of those pits where
> they were searching, to protect me from all fraud, and so that I might
> be called at once if a sepulchre was discovered or something beautiful.
> While I was pursuing this work energetically, one of those peasants
> who let it be known that he had, I know not what to sell me, accosted
> my interpreter and spoke to him very softly in his ear, that he had a
> very beautiful and whole mummy and that if I wanted to buy it he
> might have shown it to me; it was close by, but he did not want any
> of the other peasants to know of it, as they would want to participate
> in the price which was the custom among them; Therefore if I wanted
> to see it, it was necessary to go without them where he would guide
> me. I was happy to go at once after these words were reported to me
> by the interpreter and having left clear orders to everyone who was
> digging, I took with me Tommasso on foot, the interpreter and the
> painter and followed the peasant accompanied by two or three of his
> relatives, He made us walk more than a mile, perhaps two, seeming to
> me a long way, he pointing with his finger saying all the time 'here,
> here, quite close'.

We arrived finally in a place where near by there was an excavated pit, which I was told had been discovered by him three or four days before. Inside some sand, under which it was kept hidden, he drew out a mummy: the whole body of a dead man, being extremely well preserved and curiously adorned and laid out. It seemed to me something very beautiful and dignified. One could see that it was a man, stretched out and naked, bandaged tightly and wrapped up in a great quantity of linen cloths, embalmed with that bitumen which incorporated with the flesh is known to us as mummia and given as medicine. These wrappings and bindings at once reminded me of the story of Lazarus raised up, which one could believe might be like this. Further, there was all around the body a covering of the same cloth all painted and gilded expertly stitched and smeared I believe with pitch, and sealed on each side with many lead seals; all these things indicating that he was a person of importance. But of interest, was on the top part of the body which because of the quantity of wrapping up, came to be flat almost like the lid of a small chest, was painted an effigy of a young man, which without doubt was the portrait of the deceased; and his garment was adorned from head to foot with so many trifles, made of pictures and gold, and so many hieroglyphs and characters and similar notions, that as I said believe me, that it was the most refined thing in the world. Furthermore, curious men of learning can deduct a thousand proofs for the truth about the antiquities of those times. One can see the length of the man's garment to be from the neck to the feet; and shows that it was of linen cloth about which we have precisely in Herodotus, how the ancient Egyptians used to clothe themselves. However it can be seen that over the white of the linen, the garment of this one is strewn all over with small golden pieces, with various ornaments, jewels, and signs of unknown characters impressed on them. The head is covered as well with a gold ornament and with gems under which can be seen protruding his black crinkled hair. And likewise he has a thin curly black beard from which, together with the colour of his face and hands which is very brown, precisely the colour of the earth not dissimilar to that of the fairest Ethiopians. It seems to me that it can be believed that this man was born in some of the upper parts of Egypt and more to the south and not in the regions of the Delta where usually men are not so brown. It can be seen clearly that he is a man of importance as much from the ornaments of gold and jewels, as I have said above, as from the lead seals which hang all around the sides of the wrappings of his body showing much more than ordinary care in its preservation; and in their impression not well discerned there might be a carving of an animal. And a still further indication of the great status of this person, is the gold necklace which he is wearing round his neck, in the manner of our orders; in the centre where it hangs above the chest is attached like a jewel a large golden pendant which represents a figure of a bird, and inside cut in the middle with different unknown signs… In his right hand he is holding a gold cup full of red liquid either of wine or of blood, I myself believe it to be wine, agreeing with the sayings of Herodotus; I am certain that it denotes some libation of sacrifice. With the left (on two fingers of which, that is the index and the small, he wears a gold ring on each one, on the last knuckles near the nails) he holds something else of oval form and dark colour. The legs and feet are bare except for the black sandals which only cover the soles of the feet, having a thong, also black, passing from beneath the sole between the big toe and the next nearest to it, and then attached to two flaps behind the heel, adorning the top of the feet in an elegant bow knot.[2]

At the sight of this noble mummy, Pietro quickly paid the peasant the asking price of three piastres, even though he realised that it was too little. He asked him if he had any others and if could he see them quickly. On learning that there was another inside the pit no less beautiful, Pietro wanted to go below to see for himself how it was lying; but the peasant, eager for further payment, hurriedly sent off a companion with a rope and had it drawn up for him to see:

This one was equally beautiful and decked out in the same way; but the portrait above (and this pleased me more) was of a young woman, which without doubt must have been either the wife or sister of the

---

2   Pietro guessed the object 'of oval form and dark colour' to be an aubergine (known in Tuscany as *petronciani* or *melanza*), but it was probably a rose wreath, as found in graves of that period.

man already excavated, as the peasants told me (and I myself already saw the place) that they were lying together in the same place in the tomb one beside the other. The woman's dress is much richer with gold and jewels than that of the man. In the golden pieces which are scattered all over, besides the signs and characters, there are as well certain birds and animals carved which seem like lions and on one more in the middle, an ox or cow which must be the sign of Apis or Isis. On another [piece], on a necklace, of which she has many on her breast, is impressed with the sun. In addition, she has pendant, jewelled earrings and pairs of bracelets on her arms as well as her legs. Many rings on both hands, that of the left on each finger except the thumb and on the other, yet a further on the joint of the last finger next to the nail. On the right hand only two rings both together in the usual place on the finger which is called the ring finger. In her right hand she holds a golden vessel quite small almost in the form of those jugs used in Rome at table for water for the hands, it seems that she holds it lightly with only two fingers. In the left she holds what appears like a bunch of certain round objects but I do not know what they might be, due to showing the way in which the mummies lie buried in the sand I have not completely cleaned the sand away from this woman, but in some places have left it still there, thus at times obscuring the painting. The colour of this woman is a little less brown than that of the man; and she also has black hair rather more curly than the other, uncovered around the face; her eyes are black in the same way, and the eyebrows are thick and joined up, like they are in those countries today. Her eyes are large and wide open and the upper and lower lids a little darkened, perhaps with kohl [antimony] as is commonly worn by all Orientals today, and recounted of Jezebel in the Sacred Scriptures of old.[3]

Before the peasant even asked him, Pietro at once counted out the same money and was offered help in climbing down into the cavity. But because it was very deep and wide, perhaps fifty or sixty palms if

---

3   Both these portrait mummies of a man and a woman (of tempera and linen) date from the time of Galienus, c.250–268 BC. The small stucco ornaments were pasted on all over, giving a display of opulence. Illustrated in Dioxiadis, *The Mysterious Fayum Portraits*, nos. 9–12.

not more, Pietro was afraid that the man below might not save him breaking his neck. He therefore made Tommasso descend first with some firearms should the need arise:

> Then, tying myself up very securely with a rope on my belt, which I fastened to those above, I went down gaily, but I found in doing so, the descent was far easier than I thought so that without any help I dropped down on my own very easily and quickly. Having reached the bottom, I found the tombs all around full of dead bodies which truly, as the peasants said the pit must have been found just now. The bodies were lying buried irregularly in the sand as I told you, which as it was extremely dry had kept and conserved them from corruption; and they were lying enveloped one on top of the other exactly like macaroni between the cheese.

Pietro only saw one further body which was painted and gilded, wrapped in linen. It was not well preserved, perhaps because it had been damaged by the peasants, who found it in its wooden chest which was carved on top with the effigy of a young girl. Pietro guessed this corpse might have been the daughter of the two already found. The chest had been prised open, and on examination he saw many engraved hieroglyphs on it which pleased him so much that he had it hauled up outside:

> I made them break it in my presence, first to see how the bones with the bitumen were arranged inside the wrappings, then to get some of that substance which is medicinal and as you know it is said that of young girls and the bodies of virgins is preferred; and further to look inside amongst the bandages in case I might have found any curiosities, idols or things of that nature... I therefore broke it but found nothing inside.

The mummy had congealed into such a hard mass of mixed-up bitumen and bones that Pietro owned that in his desire to break it up it was necessary to give it some very hard blows with stones and iron implements:

Of this fractured mummy I wanted for myself the whole head and a good piece of bitumen with a handful of those wrappings; the rest, because I felt I had received more money than I had spent I left entirely to those poor peasants who usually break them up in that way and go to sell the material in Cairo to those who buy it for large profit for trade... In the same tomb I also desired a head of a woman (another maiden according to her attire) made of very thickly coated glazed material. Inside it was hollow and outside, the face and neck was gilded, having ebony eyebrows, or other kind of wood, inset; the rest was of gold and painted, particularly on the neck and shoulders very curiously with disparate little figures of Egyptian idols, altars and other mysterious hieroglyphics. And in the guise of a mask, this was used to enclose the head and neck of a body which had first been dug out by the peasants. There were no eyes and one can discern they have just been cut out; and I believe readily that they might have been of jewels or some precious metal, and therefore at the first good chance, removed by the peasants, throwing out the rest which was of no use to them. In the middle of the head above the brow across which there is a gold band all carved with unknown characters in hieroglyphs there appears to have been removed something which, whether it was a jewel or gold or some other precious substance, I feel certain that it was a representation of a falcon's head which was one of the most esteemed hieroglyphs of the Egyptians. Its wings at the sides and the rest of the body with the feet and the tail are to be seen delineated with stitches on the veil which covers the entire head of this woman, entirely concealing her hair, except for the protruding ears also gilded. On the same veil, on the part behind is painted the figure of a woman wearing black ornaments who is holding in both her hands, on either side, certain strange things with another similar, on a round plate above her head which I do not know what they could be; but I guess that they are mysterious hieroglyphic figures and the woman either Isis, or some goddess Libitina, or other such deity associated with funerary matters. I took as well a small idol of baked clay which was lying there on the ground amongst the sand, it was a head of the Apis bull. Satisfied that the excavators had everything they wanted I returned well pleased to the top. I then sent a man to the tent to fetch animals for us and for the articles we had found, as it was too far to carry them away on foot.

So, having paid off the workmen, Pietro ordered their tents to be taken up while his prizes were wrapped in palm branches to keep them safe before being securely placed in carts. Amidst some envy on the part of those who had not witnessed his exploits, Pietro progressed triumphantly to Cairo, reaching there two or three hours after nightfall: 'And do not be surprised that I arrived so soon because I had only been away three days and had not once travelled a short day's journey.' Soon after, he despatched his mummies to Italy by way of Sicily, where 'I myself passing there at least on my return, will hope to bring them with me.'

By way of a long digression in his letter written after the expedition, Pietro told Mario Schapiro that he had become fascinated by the hieroglyph letters decorating the mummies, among which he had discerned elements of Coptic. As the letters were mingled together, this led him to believe that the Coptic religion was extremely old, older than all other creeds. He surmised that the Coptic language was more ancient than Greek, and that it had been suppressed by the Arabs at the conquest:

> This Coptic or Egyptian has been lost among them and that they have it only in some sacred books, still saying Mass in that tongue. Accordingly I am taking with me a few books, including the entire book of David, the whole Gospel of St. John and some others which on return to Italy with God's grace, I will be able to show to you and read them to those who might be interested, at least keeping them to ornament my library. But among the others is one, which I was very lucky to find. It contains four authors who write in Arabic (briefly in truth but sufficient enough amongst all of them) the Grammar of this Egyptian language; and further, two dictionaries with about six thousand Egyptian words; the most important translated faithfully in olden times into Arabic. Whether in Rome, or elsewhere as well, where some understanding of the Arabic language is beginning, there could ever be found someone who could use it to translate this book of mine into Latin, I would surely make use of it diligently; and by means of printing, I might be able to disseminate it to men of letters throughout the world.

Pietro believed that though this ancient Christian church overseas had been separated from Rome for many centuries, nevertheless it had retained 'all the sacred scriptures in their language and many other things in their religion' which accorded with the Latin faith. Therefore all these things would make a strong case against the modern heretics of Europe who dissented in so many ways from the status quo. Pietro's wish was in part fulfilled, owing to the manuscripts he brought back to Italy. Based on this material, Athanius Kircher (1602–80), a scholarly Jesuit priest, professor of mathematics at the University of Rome and professed philologist, produced two publications on Coptic which contributed to the understanding of the language and laid the foundations of Coptic studies in Europe. Furthermore, Kircher was convinced that his observations on the symbolic connections between individual Egyptian hieroglyphs would lead to their eventual decipherment. Kircher's efforts marked a turning point in the history of Egyptology thanks to the contribution of Pietro della Valle

Pietro was not content to finish his travels in Egypt. He was determined to satisfy his curiosity and pursue his journey eastwards to visit Persia and India. Accordingly, in the late summer of 1616, he took the desert road to Baghdad, which he reached on 20 October. On the way he encountered some dangerous adventures, and a great misfortune when Tommasso in a fit of jealous rage knifed Lorenzo, with the result that Tommasso disappeared to Damascus. Thus Pietro lost two of his Italian servants who had accompanied him from Rome. It seems, however, that he had recovered from his 12-year love of Beatrice Boraccio, since in a long letter to Mario Schapiro dated 20–23 December 1616, he revealed that he had married a beautiful Babylonian girl, Maani Joerida. They travelled together to Isfahan and on mules amid the snows and ice of Kurdistan. While in Persia, Pietro obtained an audience with the powerful Shah 'Abbas, a man of compelling personality whose seductive powers kept him in the country for six years. When at last he was focusing his thoughts on home, misfortune struck once more when his Babylonian wife sadly died. True to his professed interest in mummification in the *pozzi profondissimi* of Saqqara, he had her body embalmed, keeping it with him in the cabin of the returning ship.

Pietro's two prized portrait mummies must have been carefully protected with their palm branches en route for Cairo, and well packed for the sea voyage to Italy, since they eventually arrived safely in Rome. In 1728, they were sold by order of the estate of Count Chigi to the Municipal Office of Dresden, and now form part of the Egyptian collection in the Dresden Art Gallery.

Notes

General: I. Edwards, *The Pyramids of Egypt* (the Gizeh Group, pp. 116–69); Petrie, *Pyramids and Temples of Gizeh*, p. 84. **Mummy (as a drug):** Harris, 'Medicine', pp. 130–35; Bates, 'Mohammedan Europe', pp. 182–239; Sauneron (ed.), *Voyage en Egypte de Pierre Belon* (Francis I carried it on horseback, p. 117a). **Mummy (as a commodity):** Heyd, *Histoire du Commerce du Levant*, II, pp. 635–36; Evans (ed.), *Francesco Pegolotti, La Practica della Mercatura*, p. 295. **The explorers, pyramids:** Sauneron (ed.), *Voyage en Egypte de Pierre Belon*, pp. 113a–17a; Bellorini and Hoade (ed. and trans.), *Francesco Suriano*, pp. 196–97; Sauneron (ed.), *Voyages en Egypte, S. Kiechel, H. Teufel*, pp. 105–20, 160–64; da Schio (introd.), *Viaggio di Filippo Pigafetta*, pp. 168–81; Greaves, *Pyramidiographia* (description of the interior of the first pyramid, pp. 85–101). **The explorers, mummy fields of Saqqara:** Sauneron (ed.), *Voyage en Egypte de Pierre Belon*, p. 117a–b; da Schio (introd.), *Viaggio di Filippo Pigafetta*, pp. 182–84; Sauneron (ed.), *Voyages en Egypte, S. Kiechel, H. Teufel* (fear of fire in mummy pits, pp. 161–62). **Pietro della Valle's excavations:** Dioxiadis, *The Mysterious Fayum Portraits* (see especially portrait mummies of a man and woman from the time of Galienus appropriated by Pietro della Valle, pp. 18–19, 122–25, Figs. 9–12); Parlasca, *Mumienporträts*, p. 18 and nn. 4, 5 (Dresden mummies illustrated in 47.3, D, 1, 2.); Whitehouse, 'Egyptology and Forgery', p. 188; Pietro della Valle, *Viaggi di Pietro della Valle* (sea voyage, pp. 19–20; journey to Cairo, pp. 304–61; excavation of mummies, pp. 372–90; Coptic manuscripts, pp. 395–98; sent mummies back to Naples via Sicily, p. 399); Bull (ed. and trans.), *The Travels of Pietro della Valle*, pp. x–xvi, 3–63. **Coptic manuscripts:** Volkoff, 'À la Recherche de Manuscrits en Egypte', pp. 45–47; Iverson, 'The Hieroglyphic Tradition', pp. 190–92; Janssen, 'Athanase Kircher Egyptologue', pp. 240–41; Whitehouse, 'Towards a Kind of Egyptology', pp. xii–xiii, 65–79.

CHAPTER 8

Pilgrims to the Monastery of St Catherine

After they had prayed in the old churches of Babylon, tasted the delights of Cairo and clambered round the pyramids, Christian pilgrims prepared for the journey through the Sinai desert to St Catherine's monastery, the supreme point of their Egyptian itinerary. It was an arduous and dangerous enterprise, taking on average about 22 days for the round trip through extremes of heat and cold. Almost everyone who wrote of his experiences made an effort to capture in words the loneliness and desolation of the peninsula. Felix Fabri, a Dominican friar from Ulm who went on pilgrimage with a group of German nobles in 1483 from Jerusalem via Gaza to St Catherine's monastery, described the great desert as follows: 'No village nor town... neither house nor dwelling, neither field nor garden, tree or grass, nothing but sandy earth burnt up by the great heat of the sun.'

But whether they were Christians making for Sinai or Muslims on the 40-day pilgrimage to Mecca, the privations were much the same. Often travelling in darkness to avoid the sun's heat, they plodded on through the silence of the night under brilliant starlight which glittered in the velvet skies. Dawns rose coldly, sometimes in the teeth of bitter winds, which at the height of noon became stiflingly hot, whipping up clouds of choking sand that shrivelled the skin, dimmed the vision and parched the throat. Sometimes furious whirlwinds blackened the skies and scattered the camp fires, shuffling the sands about like running water so that newly filled ravines became deep traps for man and beast. 'When a man finds himself there and the wind rises he can consider his journey at an end, because so great is the motion and the cloud of that sand that any man would be suffocated therein.' Cleanliness was almost impossible and vermin pervaded the body. No one, however noble, was exempt. Felix Fabri spoke from experience: 'Woe to those who wear long hair, for they carry with them a refuge and preserve of lice... and worse woe also to those who are too lazy to cleanse themselves at night, for at every moment [the lice] will multiply into enormous numbers.' But mesmerised by the stark, silent grandeur of the desert, where there were 'every day, almost hourly new landscape[s] of fresh soil and climate and mountains of fresh shape and colour', many temporarily forgot the physical hardships where the dry air banished the langour of humid heat. Felix 'felt more pleasure in the barren wilderness than I ever did in the rich and fertile land of Egypt with all its attractive beauty'.

Before departure, there were interminable negotiations with court bureaucrats. Overstaffed, lacking urgency but having care of their dignity, they stamped and sealed the necessary permits in the name of the ruler of Egypt allowing Europeans to travel through his territory. Prices for this safe conduct varied. In 1350, the Franciscan Friar Niccolò di Poggibonsi paid 20 silver dirhams. In October 1384 for his party of 20 people from Tuscany Lionardo di Frescobaldi noted a payment of 96 gold ducats demanded by the Grand Interpreter at the court of the sultan Barquq, an official who also 'wished many other things from us'. There followed the prolonged bartering for hiring sturdy camels; the city camels customarily used for porterage, picking their way through the narrow Cairo streets, were totally unsuitable for such a journey – their soft pads could not have sustained the rigours of stones and sand. On Niccolò di Poggibonsi's behalf, the Interpreter sent a Saracen into the desert to procure some camels from the Arabs who hired them out. After six days the animals arrived, 'seemingly made of iron so much hardship can they support'. The economic life of the nomadic Bedouin, travelling between unpredictable oases, was based on the supply of camels, which were best bred on the rigorous upland pastures with their strong nutritive thorns. By instinct they knew the route over pathless ground if they had been that way before, though the white bones of those servicing the caravans could be seen along the recognised routes, where large flocks of predatory vultures circled, ready to swoop down on the flagging invalids too weak to stand up. It was decreed that under the threat of imprisonment and confiscation of their animals, the Bedouin could not carry travellers or their goods into the city. Thus the authorities prevented marauders pouring through the gates to rob and pillage at will.

Niccolò found that a good camel could carry as much baggage as ten donkeys and though of great abstinence it was a very moody animal, 'but when the cameleer wants to go fast he plays some instrument or sings something and then they all go happy and content without a halt'. To most Westerners the songs resembled monotonous raucous cries and whistles, even those of frogs croaking in rhythm with the pace of the trot. Niccolò agreed a price of 60 dirhams per camel from Cairo to St Catherine's, though it was known that those who did not give extra *mangeries* and failed to share their food with their guides were hindered and insulted. By custom, the Bedouin regarded all travellers as a means of livelihood and they set their own rules as to how to obtain it.

The friar was happy that he and his companion had found seven other pilgrims in Cairo to accompany them. He did not state their names, but two were from England, one from Syria and two from Constantinople. They were fortunate in having an honest conscientious guide of whom they became very fond, who was 'a good and just man according to the law of Muhammad'. His name was Sa'id, at that time 35 years old. Sa'id was popular among the pilgrims, for in 1384, during the reign of the sultan Barquq, it was the same Sa'id who with his son acted as guide and interpreter to Lionardo di Frescobaldi's party, from Alexandria to Cairo.

At the crowded stalls of the noisy markets, Niccolò purchased cheese, mutton, salad and vinegar (also used to wash certain parts of the body) for the journey. Other travellers bought oil, honey, flour, onions, hens with a cock to wake them in the morning and chick peas, which could be roasted in a pan without water. When the French doctor Pierre Belon set off for the monastery in 1547 with the French ambassador M. du Fumet, they travelled in some style with 20 janissaries to guard them. The cavalcade was resourceful enough to prepare the mutton before leaving. They boiled a great quantity, which was cut up in pieces, the bone having been removed. Then it was cooked with the fat and some onions until all the liquid was evaporated, after which it was salted and spiced, packed into barrels and loaded onto a separate camel. Even in the desert heat the meat kept for a long time; after fifteen days when it was reheated with an extra onion it tasted like a fricassee freshly made. The Arabs made their own bread each day. They spread out their sheepskins on the ground, on which they mixed a paste of flour and water; when the dough was ready and shaped into broad flat cakes, they baked them among the ashes and charcoal, until cooked into tasty bread which they ate covered with oil. Raw meat was roasted between two sunbaked stones.

Many died from thirst, and those in extremis could be seen running through the encampments begging for even a spoonful of water 'for the love of heaven'. It was carried in a most unsavoury way, in uncured pliable goat hides, sometimes only freshly skinned and full of hairs from the animal: 'If you drink water which is in the goatskins, it is more than tepid, and there is not a body so constipated it would not move. It pleased God that we carried with us some lemon syrup, with which we often refreshed ourselves.'

The disparate equipment essential for the trek was very bulky. The burdens were laid on the camel's saddles, on the centre of the hump without fixing, loaded equally on both sides. The passengers some-times rode in a box covered over with a thick pelt to shade them from the sun or sat face to face in pairs in baskets woven from date leaves, while their possessions were placed on the other side. Extra camels were strung along carrying baskets for the invalids, but some unfor-tunates could be jettisoned and left to die on the way if too far gone, especially if the captain of the caravan considered that progress to the next waterhole was being hindered. Along the well-trodden routes, bodies of dead men could be seen mummifying, protruding from the sands, their corpses picked over by the Bedouin who gleaned from them whatever they could.

On the way to St Catherine's, many pilgrims took the opportunity to visit the garden of Matariyya which lay about four miles north of Cairo. It was revered by Christians because, according to tradition, it was the place where the Holy Family had rested on their flight into

8.1 'An Ostrich, and how to get off a camel'

Egypt. A large and ancient fig tree could be seen by the enclosure gate. It was known as the Virgin's tree and, according to legend, gave the fugitives shade on the hot journey. In its hollow trunk two lamps were always kept alight. A further legend told of water gushing out from the ground when the infant Jesus drummed on it with his heels. In time, the ground around the sacred spring was transformed into a garden where, in the inner section, the renowned balm bushes were cultivated. A little beyond the village at Heliopolis there was an obelisk (erected by the pharaoh Seti I) which seasoned travellers judged as being greater than those of Alexandria and in the Hippodrome at Constantinople. The guides' patter told of the pyramid-building pharaohs who had erected it long ago with other colossi. Situated in the fertile land on the edge of the desert, Matariyya was an attractive resort for the rich Mamluk lords such as the amir Yesh Bek, who built a domed house where he entertained his friend and master, the sultan Qaitbay. From time to time, Qaitbay pitched his own sumptuous tents near the gardens where he held lavish banquets, and he and his guests disported themselves at the imposing baths, accommodating 300 bathers in large painted rooms with belvederes overlooking the countryside. A hundred years before the time of Qaitbay, Giorgio Gucci, with his Tuscan friends Lionardo di Frescobaldi and Simone Sigoli, visited the sultan's villa, which was 'beautiful and large'. There was a garden full of palm trees and good fruit trees where the famous balm bushes were cultivated, which the sultan employed many workers and clerks to guard; the balm was a precious commodity that brought him large revenues. Georgio noticed the clerks ostentatiously recording all that was gathered.

Towards the end of the sixteenth century, the area had become pleasantly developed. The Czech traveller Christopher Harant described the ornate pleasure pavilions built by the previous rulers, as well as an inn for the pilgrims from Sinai waiting to enter Cairo:

> We first visited a chapel built in Italian style, it had been renovated and enlarged by the French consul, though it was originally constructed by the Venetian consul in 1553. As the French consul had allowed it to be done without permission and without paying the taxes, he had to pay a fine of two thousand thalers, the same sum spent, according to rumour, on the construction itself... It is thus that he escaped an even larger danger, as not only does a Christian not have a right to build, but he has none to rebuild, neither of making it bigger without payment nor without prior permission.

Inside the chapel, they drank from a square fountain made of dressed stone a few feet deep, bubbling with fresh clean water. After a period of vandalism, the irrigation wheels had been mended and the sparkling water ran freely through the conduits. They were allowed to taste the fruit of Mary's tree, laden throughout the year, but found it small and acid. Close by the gate, they spied a number of balm bushes in the garden, their branches about the thickness of the beak of a goose; the leaves resembled those of basil, only bigger. Christopher was told that the present plants had been brought to Egypt from the vicinity of Mecca in 1575, 40 ordered by the pasha in Cairo, and that every year the 'Emperor of Turkey' sent 150 ducats to the Lord of Mecca. In exchange, the Lord sent back 400 pieces of the finest Indian silk and three or four pounds of balm.

The number of people allowed into the garden at a time was strictly regulated by the gardeners, by custom Christians, who expected generous tips. As every part and product of the plant was valuable due to its proclaimed medicinal qualities, visitors were watched carefully, so that they did not snip off any of the leaves or twigs to take away. Most pilgrims compared the balm plants to vines which required pruning each year, though Christopher learnt that the branches were pruned twice a year in the presence of Turkish doctors sent by the pasha and that the juice that flowed from them was always white; after a few days the colour turned greenish like oil, then to a honey-coloured yellow. Emanuel Piloti, the Venetian merchant who exported balm to Europe among his disparate merchandise, saw the leaves torn from the plant in such a manner that the branches sweated. Afterwards the gardeners squeezed the branches with their hands, directing the moisture into costly ivory phials. Giorgio Gucci paid the large sum of two gold ducats for one very small phial which was gathered secretly, before their eyes, by four Saracens: 'When it [the shoot] is pulled off close to the thick branch it begins to drip as the vine does in March and casts off small and rare tears. And with a little compressed cotton they gather the said balsam and when the cotton is soaked they press it out into a phial.'

All parts of the plant were on sale; juice, leaves and branches were sold to the Christians in large quantities. With their keen interest in medicinal plants, both the erudite doctors, Pierre Belon du Mans and Prospero Alpini from Padua, wrote learned treatises about the balm and its properties from which educated travellers freely quoted. No wonder that with such propaganda from eminent men, the supposed Egyptian medicaments such as balm and powdered mummy were in demand. Like *mummia*, balm was a universal panacea, prescribed for ear and eye complaints, for gallstones, as a prophylactic against the plague, as an antidote to poisons and as a remedy for sterility. It was sold in pharmacies throughout Europe, even providing good business in Prague. The sale of the balm was a source of great profit to the rulers of Egypt and the prices charged were astronomical; even so, demand often exceeded supply and counterfeit liquids were added. Pilgrims heard tales of the Saracens who played many tricks and deceits, even putting saliva into it. It was all sold under the magic name of 'balm' and marketed as such to the credulous.

Christopher Harant from Prague, habitually good humoured and tolerant, was unusually critical of the frivolity of the indolent, pampered Arab and Turkish women of Cairo. With heedless extravagance, they applied the costly balm as a cosmetic during their frequent visits to the baths. In their avid desire for a pliant smooth skin, the ladies coated themselves lavishly in the liquid, lying for an hour in the dry heat so that it could penetrate the body; on their return home, they neither wet it nor wiped it off. On the third day, they returned to the baths and repeated the performance. For fifteen days, the treatment was continued in a similar fashion, after which the rejuvenated beauties were given a relaxing therapeutic massage in oil of bitter almonds, before being finally washed in a concoction of berries.

After the death of Qaitbay, the balm garden was almost destroyed on 7 August 1496, when the streets of Cairo were filled with the clash of arms, houses were wrecked and pillaged and their inmates attacked. The old sultan had ordained that his son 14-year-old son Muhammad should succeed him on the throne, but disliking the idea, the Mamluks rose up in rebellion and besieged the citadel. The teenage sultan escaped with his followers to Matariyya, where the balm bushes were destroyed, the waterwheels rotated for irrigation were vandalised and the oxen taken away. The unpopular Muhammad did not survive for long: he was murdered two years later, after which the place was neglected and nothing grew in the garden for ten years.

After leaving Suez, the route to St Catherine's monastery branched off to the south-east, at first following the narrow shores of the Red Sea on the western coast of Sinai. At the port of al-Tur it plunged eastwards into the interior through the Wadi Firan, skirting the peak of the high Jabal Firan (Banat) on the right-hand side, before finally turning south towards the higher mountain peaks and the lofty mounts of Moses and St Catherine.

Disregarding the protection of a large caravan, relying only on their guides to lead them, Lionardo di Frescobaldi and the party of Tuscans had left Cairo on 19 October 1385 in great and immeasurable heat. They suffered greatly from the rays of the sun that seemed to beat down mercilessly, appearing to shimmer spasmodically, from dawn to dusk and their skins became nearly black. They had hired 13 camels and six hardy asses with saddles and stirrups of rope, and travelled all day up to 10 o'clock at night, when they unloaded the animals and pitched 'a leather pavilion three braccia high and so long that six of us could be under it with head and shoulders covered'. They slept on small light mattresses that almost disappeared into the sand under their weight. In the morning it took about an hour and a half before they were ready to mount their beasts, eating their food as they rode along. The party cooked one of their chickens every few days, and carried with them two small barrels of wine, dried fruit, sugar, a few sweetmeats, dried almonds and rice. Sometimes they came on little valleys where they saw a few roebucks, hares and wolves, with ostriches and porcupines in plenty. There were great numbers of partridges and francolin but nobody could catch them. Since they suspected that their guide was in league with the local Arabs and regarded them as fruit ripe for picking, they had to keep a continuous eye on their belongings. It was a sharp contrast for those unaccustomed to this strange country to cross so abruptly the sudden boundary between green irrigated fields with waving palms and the abundant water of the Nile, into a different world of barren waste and parched sands.

Even though the Tuscans had decided to strike out on their own, it was always considered prudent for pilgrims travelling in small groups to accompany one of the merchant caravans at least as far as Suez. Subsequently, some of these caravans followed the northern route for Jerusalem and Damascus, or the southern road to al-Tur, on the west of the Sinai peninsula, where spices and other merchandise were landed from India. Like all the other desert travellers, those heading for St Catherine's left Cairo by filing through the stern old massive arch of the Bab al-Nasr leading to the Suez road and pitched their tents among the assembling multitude the night before departure. Henceforward they were under the overall command of a captain whose word was law for the duration of the journey. He gave the signal to start, he ordained what order they should keep and laid down the times for rest and food. Any dispute was referred to him and he had powers to mete out arbitrary punishment to those he considered in the wrong. Even if they were innocent, some unfortunates were forced to submit to the unpredictable and spiteful arrogance of the overseers, who might consider them less important than the guilty but powerful transgressors. The caravans contained a motley selection of people, some of whom joined them on the delta road north-east of Cairo. When George Sandys, an English traveller, went to Palestine from Cairo in 1611, some Jewish women of advanced age joined their company. They carried with them the bones of their parents, husbands, children and friends and came from all parts of the world to undertake the tiring journey to Jerusalem, only to die there.

Just beyond Suez, surrounded by little groves of palms, lay the so-called 'Wells of Moses', which comprised a few springs rising from the sand where depleted goatskins could be filled. Despite high expectations, the condition of the wells and quality of the water, especially if it had been recently sampled and fouled by a large caravan, provoked feelings of disappointment and disgust. Niccolò di Poggibonsi, who had set out with a great caravan of 600 camels, took five days to reach the wells. At the hour of terce they came to the water, 'where Moses by the command of God with the rod struck by order'. But in spite of the water tasting of sulphur, they filled up their skins and let the camels drink, for they had had nothing for about four days since the start of the journey.

On the shore of the Red Sea, Niccolò found time for beach-combing. His companion chanced on a 'a fish which had a head like a man's, with face mouth teeth and nose eyes hair and nose and like-wise a bit of a neck... and all the rest like those of a fish'. Other pilgrims saw strands of coral, wild ducks, gudgeon, terns and gulls, which were a great source of pleasure and surprise. The receding tide uncovered all kinds of small fish, large shells and 'sea hedgehogs' of different kinds. As for Niccolò, he chanced on many stones for rings, crystal, jasper and many other desirable objects, but more especially he discovered a precious stone:

> which I believed, and so I was told, should be [worth] more than a fat farm, and it was so charming and so well worked that no man on earth could know how to imitate it; and for the faith I had in it and the solicitude I had in guarding it, God had his revenge in the following way: for as he caused me to find it, so he caused me to lose it, for I lost it in

the desert. But I was so grieved and others with me, I am never so glad but that I grow sad; but it was so made, that the heart of man could never by hearsay imagine it, nor could tongue relate the mode or beauty of its making... I was not grieved so much for its value as for its preciousness and beauty, so fair it was!

Besides the marine novelties on the shore, the desert was a home for wildlife altogether different from the fauna of the Nile valley. Pierre Belon du Mans was in his element in this environment and worked hard at collecting information for his books. He dissected and stuffed horned vipers with wadding of different kinds, and he sketched a winged serpent and a chameleon, which he noted as being more corpulent than those he had seen near the Nile. It was coloured white underneath and speckled with red. He tracked the heart-shaped footsteps of wild goats in the sands and saw gazelles running in large herds through the hot arid plains, leaping with nervous agility to escape any would-be hunters over the rocky spurs. He was told that they rarely had need of water, something that he could well believe. And he made sketches of the spiny thorned acacia bushes and the 'rose of Jericho' thriving in the dry ground.

Though they were apprehensive of the pitiless desert, pilgrims feared the unpredictable Bedouin who, having no respect for the laws of foreign rulers, virtually controlled the territory. Though these desert Arabs were wretched and dirty, they were fiercely proud. They lived in smoky caves and tents of hair and dug wells, only known to themselves, which they guarded against unwary travellers. They were avaricious and rapacious, contemptuous of outsiders and intolerant of restraint. The women washed in the urine of camels and goats, considering the pungent smell to be attractive, and could sometimes be seen performing undulating dances while they clicked castanets in fingers and thumbs in the Spanish fashion. The men anointed their moustaches and beards with the residue of oil left in their cups after a meal. By way of defence, some pilgrim groups armed themselves with a variety of weapons: bows, swords and daggers as well as guns. At night they gathered their tents and baggage in the middle of the camp, round which lay the camels and asses with their drivers. It was prudent for one of the party to keep a watch and be on patrol while the rest slept, since the camel and ass drivers took every opportunity to rip open their sacks to steal their biscuits, pilfer eggs from the baskets and wine from the bottles. In the morning petty tricks were played, the camels were loaded slowly and unwillingly and many things were left behind, only to be restored after demands were satisfied for more money or biscuits. It became a tiresome wearying routine, particularly as the pilgrims could not communicate with their persecutors except through an interpreter.

While the silken sand dunes of northern Sinai are formed by the winds into long changing shapes with sharp crests, the country to the south of the peninsula bordering the west coast is an area of chalk and limestone. The interior of the peninsula rises to the forbidding massif known as al-Tih, a desiccated gravel and limestone plateau, deeply incised with broad wadis, many of which fill up with rain for several days after an unpredictable flash flood. The groundwater appears in the form of springs where wells can be dug (though in 1972 a large deep subterranean reservoir of brackish water was found, from which deep wells were bored by the Israelis for irrigation purposes). Towards the south, the landscape becomes one of spectacular beauty, with mountain peaks reaching to altitudes of between 750 and 2,500 metres. The rock strata run at every angle, tinted with a multitude of glittering colours which lighten or deepen according to the sunlight. Granite in hues of shining pink, yellow and grey is mixed with igneous rock of deep azure blue, limestones of white and ochre are interspersed with brown clay deposits, giving a striped appearance to many of the hills. Southern Sinai is not entirely barren, as some of the stony beds of the wadis are covered with intermittent vegetation and at certain times of the year, manna in the form of flat white sticky cakes, tasting sweet like honey, erupts on the bushes, caused by the dew. It was in these isolated mountains, oases and scrubby valleys that large numbers of Christian ascetics from the Byzantine Empire, including Egypt and Syria, found refuge. Among these Christian hermits, there arose the tradition that in this wild untamed area were located the biblical sites of the burning bush and the mountain where Moses received the laws. This tradition was perpetuated by the pilgrims who followed them.

With seemingly endless peaks and valleys unfolding before them, without compasses and entirely reliant on their guides, it was easy for the pilgrims to suffer feelings of deep insecurity and even panic in the baffling landscape. It was difficult to judge the distance when a mountain appearing close at hand in a shaft of light would then recede into a false horizon. Only the shining star of St Catherine above them, which they were told pointed the way to the monastery, gave them hope and reassurance.

After finding some water in one of the valleys, Niccolò di Poggibonsi and his friends, much to their consternation, were accosted by some Saracens who seized Sa'id, their well-loved interpreter, and led him off for questioning to a small nearby fortress. Despite the sultan's letter of safe conduct, their attackers took them for spies, asserting that they had never before seen pilgrims on that route. Finally they kept Sa'id prisoner and threatened to take him to the sultan, though they allowed Niccolò's party to continue their way with only the Arabs from whom they had hired the camels for company: 'We proceeded thus in tribulation, without a shepherd, for we had been deprived of our interpreter, who was our guide, without whom we could not but experience evil.' They lamented bitterly that the Arabs understood nothing of their tongue, nor did the pilgrims understand any Arabic: 'so that when we asked a thing, they did the very opposite: and so in distress we continued for two days in the desert without a guide, ever recommending ourselves to St Catherine with many tears that she send help for evil was in store for us'.

Niccolò, who had managed to survive the perilous storms and attacks by pirates that beset his sea voyage to Egypt, must have felt mortified to contemplate the frustration of his hopes comparatively near to his goal. On the second day there was a further occasion for fear when they saw a Saracen about a mile away from them, ever running ahead so as to cross their path, after which he waited for them to approach. To their great astonishment, on drawing near, they could not believe that before their very eyes was their devoted interpreter Sa'id: 'We ran towards him and we made great glee and delight, and we gave him well to eat, for he had great need of it; and he told us that the Saracens had taken from him his sword and bow, because he would not agree to our being ransomed from them.' And so with promises of restitution of all he had lost, they continued on their way with uplifted hearts, until on the thirteenth day they came to a plain amid a range of mountains. On the day following, they beheld from afar the precious Mt Sinai and joyfully fell to the ground on their knees with many tears, chanting 'Salve Regina'.

Times of journeys were a matter of chance. Lionardo di Frescobaldi and his party arrived at St Catherine's on 29 October, ten days after leaving Cairo, having travelled between 22 and 26 miles each day without mishap. This was in contrast to the wanderings endured by Niccolò di Poggobonsi and his companions, who in addition to the attack on their guide had lost one of their companions. The man had wandered off into the desert, and despite a search party sent out to look for him 'even unto the Red Sea shore', he was never seen again. In 1576, Filippo Pigafetta from Vicenza took just nine and a half days without delays from Cairo to St Catherine's, almost a record. Having turned east after al-Tur, Pigafetta's party rode for about three miles over a pass fashioned naturally by the waters which had cut away the

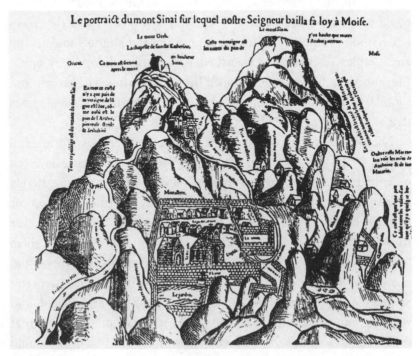

8.2 Woodcut of St Catherine's monastery, and the twin peaks of Mount Sinai

stone, through high sheer rocks through the mountains. He said the night was immensely cold and from their camp site, the walk to the monastery took about three hours.

After the monastery valley was colonised by the hermits fleeing from persecution, in AD 337, the Empress Helena, mother of Constantine, ordered a sanctuary to be built around the alleged site of the burning bush. Because of its vulnerability to attack by nomadic tribes, in c.562, Justinian (d. 548) fortified the enclosure and built the Basilica of the Transfiguration, dedicated to the Virgin, in memory of his wife Theodora. It provided shelter for several hundred anchorites. In about the ninth century, as a further claim to fame, it was alleged that the body of St Catherine had been flown from Alexandria by holy angels who had deposited it whole and entire on the summit of Mt Catherine, and that some monks, who had been alerted of this event in a dream, had found the corpse and carried it down to be interred within the Basilica. From then onwards the monastery became a focus of pilgrimage to pay tribute to this popular saint whose cult was so closely followed in Europe.

Following the Arab conquest of Egypt in AD 640, St Catherine's monastery became an isolated outpost of Christianity in a Muslim world. According to tradition, in 625 some of the monks made a journey to Muhammad to seek protection from marauders. Allegedly the Prophet visited the monastery where he was given hospitality, in return for which he granted them a charter known as the Covenant of the Prophet, certified by his closest companions who were mentioned by name. The covenant (part of a copy is in the monastery library) affirms that Muslims should not change the status of the monks or coerce Christian communities, that they should not move a bishop from his diocese, a priest from his religion or a monk from his cell; furthermore that the Prophet would be their protector and he who did not conform to this would be going against God's law and that of his Prophet. This admonition was observed by successive Mamluk and Turkish rulers in Egypt. In the middle of the ninth century, the church became a separate bishopric, the monastery was restored and the mosque within its walls, comprising a square tower capped by a dome and minaret, may have been built.

The period of the Crusades attracted many Europeans in Palestine to go on pilgrimage to St Catherine's, some of whom described large communities of monks living nearby, among whom were Ethiopians, Copts, Armenians and Georgians. After the fall of the Crusader kingdom at Acre in 1291, the monks remained within the jurisdiction of the Latin patriarch in Jerusalem, though remaining in close touch with the see of Constantinople and the Catholic popes in Rome. During the fourteenth to sixteenth centuries, the fortunes of the monastery were erratic and the devout lives of the monks were harassed in varying degrees by the lawless Bedouin tribes of the district, who clamoured for extortionate daily tribute, as of right, in the form of food, while besieging the entrance. Their incursions became so severe that the gates were fortified with iron doors and at times the only access was by rope and pulley from above, by which the monks hauled up visitors and provisions in a large basket.

Even today, no tourist tamely travelling by car through the peninsula along a tarmac road, or disturbing the peaceful sanctuary by landing by plane on the newly constructed airstrip, can remain unmoved by the sight of the walled monastery, with its dark green cypress trees, which silently nestles at the head of the narrow valley overshadowed by the tall mountains of Jabal Magafa, the Ra's Safsafa, and Jabal Musa. To arrive in the silence of the sharp exhilarating air, as the rising sun illuminates the multicoloured rocks, which range from dark red to bluey-purple, is a haunting, unforgettable experience. For earlier travellers, who had stoically suffered days of toil over treacherous paths, hungry and thirsty, harried and hindered, the attainment of their longed-for goal fulfilled their wildest hopes.

On the twenty-second day after leaving Cairo, Friar Niccolò di Poggibonsi and his companions finally reached the monastery at the hour of vespers. When they had caught their first glimpse of it from far off, they felt they had risen from the dead, 'so tired we had grown'. Many of the monks came out to meet them and they all embraced 'with great love'. Having unloaded their camels, the monks went to seek permission to permit them to enter, and returned quickly to lead them to a separate house where the pilgrims rested, 'for the need was great'.

The monks, clad in long grey cloaks with a black embroidered

8.3 Monks of St Catherine hauling up visitors by the hoist

scapular, followed the rule of the great St Basil of Caesarea. Living in the fourth century, he was the first to change the eremitical way of the desert into an organised coenobitic life henceforward governed by a set of monastic laws. The community was customarily woken by 33 rings of the bell, representing the age at which Christ died. After spending an hour at matins in the Basilica, they occupied themselves in their tasks up to dinner at 1.30, taken communally in the refectory.

At three in the afternoon the bell rang three times for Vespers, after which supper was eaten in the cells. The monks lived very poorly, never eating meat, though occasionally dining on unpalatable dried fish and desiccated cheese. Such commodities as flour, rice and peas had to be brought on camels from Cairo; prolonged delays of the caravans caused great hardship as produce from the gardens was only seasonal. In August and September the monks augmented their meagre diet by gathering manna resembling newly made wax, which was sweet and pleasant and melted in the mouth.

In 1350, the area round the monastery, as in the rest of the sultan's domains, must have been fairly peaceful, as Niccolò said there were further monks who could live in the surrounding area and for 'greater penance, never go to the monastery, except for certain feasts of the year'. It was not always so. From time to time extreme violence erupted and the monastery was attacked by the Bedouin, who ruled the countryside. On arrival in 1494, Francesco Suriano, the Father Guardian of Mount Sion in Jerusalem, found many armed Arabs who had just killed the abbot (Macarius III), but, despite their weeping, the monks received the Guardian's party with great love and charity and blessed God for their coming.

So that it could be better understood by those at home, Niccolò laboured hard in writing down a detailed description of the monastery, recorded on the spot on his pair of gypsum tablets carried by his side. In front of the mountain he saw 'a big beautiful garden with many arbours and olive, pomegranate, almond and date trees'. Through it, in due season, ran a large stream, while at the foot of the garden were several fountains of good water. All his fears and fatigue evaporated in his uncritical appreciation of the warmth of the welcome by the brethren and with his love of nature, he took true and simple delight in the beauty and holiness of the surroundings.

The Dominican monk, Felix Fabri from Ulm, used wax tablets as notebooks carried in his girdle and transcribed his jottings into a book, afterwards rubbing out the wax so that he could write on the tablets afresh. A rather severe cleric, he did not hesitate to condemn the Greek orthodox monks, who set certain restrictions on Western pilgrims as to where they could celebrate Mass within the monastery. If a Latin pilgrim died on the premises he was buried outside in the asses' grave-yard. They were considered heretics, excommunicated and cursed.

After they had received their warm welcome, Niccolò di Poggibonsi passed through an iron door facing north-east:

> In this place are the houses where the pilgrims lodge, when they go there. As you enter the door you ascend to the right [some] stone stairs and reach a terrace of earth where there are many rooms where pilgrims lodge; beside [them] is an oven. The first iron door where certain monks keep guard is very dark; and near to this is the other door. Being within the monastery there are two doors, one to the right leads to a chapel, the other to the church of St Catherine. The church of St Catherine is covered on top with lead and the facade is intagli-ated. The entrance of the church rises in VII stone steps; the door is large and vaulted; the wood of the door is cypress, all carved. In front of the door hangs a black curtain; this door faces north. Within the church is a kind of porch five feet in width; and there is another big door, which does not open. Above this door St. Mary with her Son in her arms is represented in mosaic; on the one hand stands that precious St Catherine and on the other Moses, in front of these figures above the door always burn three silver lamps and one is as big as a bushel of corn. Three paces on either side of the door there is a small door, each with a black curtain before it; and by these doors you enter the church.

On average, the majority of pilgrims remained at St Catherine's for three days only, but Niccolò, who wanted to see as much as possible, had ample time to describe it, as his party remained for a week. Wisely they had hired camels for the outward journey only. Those who had paid for both directions in advance were continually harassed to return by the Arabs. In the comparatively peaceful conditions of the mid-four-teenth century, the community numbered between 40 and 60 monks, some of whom Niccolò said were 'old with long beards, looking lean and pale'. Living in the utmost austerity, they slept dressed in their clothes on mats on the ground in cells of woven reeds plastered over with mud, which were set in a warren of passages and stairs 'all made alike', so that it was difficult for strangers to find their way. In spite of their poverty, the monks dispensed generous hospitality and honoured the guests with all they had:

> All who go there have to eat and drink, such as pure water and good bread and much meat, every morning and evening; and once a week wine is served, not so much as to harm you, being a small glass each. And when people leave, they get XII loaves a person, a loaf is big enough to last a person a day; the same for big and little, and if a man were a count or a knight he would receive no more than others.

Over thirty years later, on 29 October 1385, Lionardo di Frescobaldi and his Tuscan companions found some 200 monks in residence. He said that they were 'accustomed to wear round their necks a crucifix of black wood', one of which he managed to obtain. The members of the community darned their home-made heavy woollen garments in their spare time and subsisted on alms donated from pilgrim visitors and money brought as gifts from the great lords of Europe. Two great fourteenth-century benefactors were Queen Joanna of Naples (d. 1381) and Galeotta Malatesta, Lord of Ancona. The community was ruled by an archbishop who had been appointed by the Patriarchs of Alexandria and Cairo, an office confirmed by the sultan. The archbishop granted the Tuscans several audiences, though conversation could only be conducted in Latin through the interpreter, one John of Candia from Crete. They perceived that the archbishop was a venerable man of wisdom and experience, honoured and revered by all. The pilgrims were hospitably entertained; initially they had been taken directly to 'a good and beautiful room', and each one was served with half a glass of wine, bread and plenty of salt fish from the Red Sea.

Over two centuries later, when Christopher Harant and his brother-in-law from Prague arrived at St Catherine's in October 1598, affairs had taken a turn for the worse. After they had dismounted and knocked for admittance, the monks scrutinised the travellers from the top of the walls and interrogated them as to their credentials. They feared to open up the gates because of marauders and even as they talked, the pilgrims were surrounded by a crowd of vociferous Arabs. A short time before, the community had suffered a serious raid by lawless tribes which had only been thwarted by the strong locks on the solid double doors, which the attackers had tried to burn down. It was not until evening, after the mob had been bribed to disperse by two of their leaders, that the strong gates were finally opened and Christopher's party welcomed inside. Because of the severe attacks, the monks were forced to use the strong hoist and pulley, which they operated from a room on the top of the walls. By means of this, they lowered down a basket to haul up visitors and provisions and also to let down whatever food or necessities (even to a needle and thread) they could spare to propitiate the hostile Arabs who habitually camped by the gates.

After the hardship of the desert journey, Christopher and his brother-in-law were allotted cells furnished with bare stone benches without a mattress or even straw to lie on. Tired, hungry and thirsty, they were promised supper, but when at last it came, the meal consisted of a little black bread, a dish of raw beans like the fodder the Moors fed to their horses, and some raw dried fish from the Red Sea. Christopher, who was afraid of breaking his teeth on the unpalatable food, asked for some cheese, only to find that it tasted of soap, and 'for dessert, instead of fruit, there was conversation'. After supper, however, they were welcomed kindly by the archbishop, who gave them a small jug of his date wine. It was a period of tribulation for the persecuted community, painfully short of life's necessities.

The refectory was a rectangular room with vaulted roof to the south-west of the basilica. In the fourteenth century it seems to have been used as a dormitory for visiting Latin pilgrims. A small apse at the east end contained an altar where Mass according to the Latin rite could be celebrated. A mural in the alcove (painted in 1573) depicted three angels visiting the Patriarch Abraham. A much larger one above it showed the Second Coming of Christ on Judgment Day. Over the years, the great names and arms of famous Crusader knights and those of later medieval pilgrims had been carved along the architraves of the doors and the stones of the roof arches. The refectory was probably used as a dining hall in the sixteenth century, since Filippo Pigafetta

8.4 Plan of St Catherine's monastery

saw the dining tables without tablecloths, lying along the sides of the room. The archbishop sat apart at a high table covered with a cloth, by the wall at the head of the chamber, whence he could survey the assembled diners. Above him was a cross and a lamp.

Originally called 'St Mary at Bush' in honour of the Virgin, the basilica dominating the monastery complex became known as St Catherine's after the legendary translation of her body to Sinai. Built of large solid granite blocks, it lay at an angle within the fortified walls; the pointed roof was entirely covered by lead, something that had impressed Friar Niccolò of Poggibonsi. There was no belfry, but instead of bells there was an iron rod on which hung brazen rings. The sacristan beat on the rings with hammers 'in a certain order and measure so that one could dance to the sound'. Behind the wall of the high altar, the Chapel of the Burning Bush was the first sanctuary of the area, marking the place where traditionally God appeared to Moses (Exodus 11.5). In medieval times the chapel became incorporated within the main church.

Although there have been alterations to the interior, several features as described in 1350 by Niccolò di Poggibonsi can still be seen today. These include the magnificent eleventh-century Fatimid carved wooden doors giving access to the narrow transverse narthex, as well as the sixth-century interior double folding doors (leading into the church), with a wooden portal beautifully decorated by a stylised vine. The deeply inset carved door panels of rare beauty have patterns of plants, animals, fish and birds. Most pilgrims, however, would probably have entered the church by one of the two small entrances on either side of the main narthex door.

Inside the building, the high central nave rises as a clerestory with rectangular windows above the two side aisles. On each side of the nave, there are six monolithic pillars surmounted by large carved capitals; each of the twelve has a *kalendar* icon depicting the saint whose festival falls within a particular month. Besides a number of side chapels, Niccolò saw the sanctuary screen 'with one door Greek fashion', where 'behind the wall is a big and beautiful altar', and the 'painting of the Saviour', the mosaic in the semi-dome of the apse. This glorious sixth-century work of the Transfiguration of Christ surrounded by a nimbus is flanked by the main figures of Moses and St James on the right, and Elias and St John on the left, all set against a gold background; rightly admired by many pilgrims (though rather obscured today), it was possibly executed by one of the artists from the Imperial school at the height of its powers in Constantinople. The interior of the church was lit by glittering oil lamps suspended from the ceiling, with each monk having one before his seat. Niccolò often tried to count them, 'but there were so many that I could never finish the count; but from what I could understand and from what the monks told me, there were over one thousand five hundred lamps, many of gold and silver'.

To the right of the apse, Niccolò wrote of a small wall perhaps six paces from the ground where lay the tomb of St Catherine, 'made of white marble with a cross on one side' and covered by a beautiful gold cloth. He measured the tomb, finding it to be five palms long and almost two wide. The interior was divided in two, the part by the altar containing the relics of the saint with the head turned downwards, so that the mouth dripped 'holy manna' into a gold cup with a silver spout, through which the liquid flowed 'like oil' throughout the compartment. In 1384, Lionardo di Frescobaldi described the saint's head as 'not adorned in any way', though retaining its black skin.

Francesco Suriano, the Guardian of Mount Sion, was perhaps soured by the negative outcome of the Council of Florence, convened in 1439 in an attempt to settle the schism between the Latin and Orthodox churches. Despite their hospitality, he severely criticised the Greek monks as being heretics and not worthy to be the guardians of the precious body. He made no mention of 'the entire head of the Saint, covered by a golden crown adorned by many gems' as described by the Dominican monk Felix Fabri in 1483, merely noting:

> although they show some of her relics and bones yet truly they have nothing of St Catherine but the hands, white as milk with the fingers which are long and covered with rings, although some of the joints are missing and not one of them is entire; these I touched and kissed with unspeakable devotion.

Over a period of time, sections of the body had been given away to emperors and kings in return for gifts, or stolen by pilgrims eager to snatch pieces of bone and relics, attributed with miraculous powers by the credulous, for display in their local churches. Therefore the monks, though happy to be the recipients of the rich offerings brought to the shrine, tried to ensure that nothing further was removed. Felix Fabri and his party of German aristocrats were conducted to the tomb by the archbishop, accompanied with all due solemnity by a procession of monks carrying lighted candles. He perceived that the sacristan could not open the sarcophagus, as both the locks and their keys were completely covered with rust. It was only with the help of other brethren they opened it with great force and labour and exposed the body. As some of Felix's party were rich noblemen, carrying with them jewels of gold and silver, they gave them to Felix to put into the coffin, which he did, first touching them to the noble virgin's sacred head. While he was occupied, the Father of the monastery stood close by, never taking his eyes off him, and watched his hands most carefully, lest any of the relics should be carried off. The holy limbs, coloured by the oil in the coffin, were wrapped in silk pieces which were dipped into the lamps of the church and distributed to pilgrims as souvenirs.

Close to the church there was a small mosque built by order of Abu al-Mansur Anuchtakim, the minister of the caliph al-Amir (1101–30). Tolerated by the Greek community, it served the Arabs who were the servants of the monastery and other visiting Saracens who venerated Moses. Latin pilgrims were quick to criticise its use for such an abominable religion, disliking the calls to prayer from the minaret. Some even went inside but found it disappointingly plain, except for a carved wooden *minbar*.

Although in 1480 the Greek community numbered as few as 30 and their fortunes were at an ebb, on the evening before Felix Fabri's departure two monks sent by the archbishop courteously offered his party a tray covered with twisted loaves of bread made with spices, like honey cake or gingerbread, and with dates and figs and raisins. They received the gifts respectfully and gave the bearers a little money.

The following day, while they were collecting up the camels and asses before leaving, they were importuned by the Arabs outside, who continually clamoured for extra money. There was further unpleasantness when the archbishop sent a message complaining that one of the pilgrims had chipped off a piece of St Catherine's coffin with an iron tool. Moreover, if the piece was not returned immediately of their own accord, the pilgrims would be forced to comply by the Arabs, into whose hands he would put the matter. Finding it was as he said, the party was afraid and ashamed, each cursing the man who had done it. As no one would confess, their guide Calinus declared that the culprit must give him the broken piece secretly and he would smooth over the matter without disclosure. Thus it was done. Felix lamented that the group had suffered similar tribulation and disgrace throughout the pilgrimage owing to the foolish desires of some of their party to acquire souvenirs from holy places. But in spite of their culpable theft at the shrine, he grumbled at the monks and officers of St Catherine's who, when all was settled, 'came and shamelessly asked us for money as a "vale" or parting gift, which we gave them, although they had not deserved it'.

The tiny Chapel of the Burning Bush behind the main altar was reached either through the side chapel of St John the Baptist (today that of the Saints and Martyrs) or that of St James. Here all pilgrims sat down at the bidding of the sacristan to take off their shoes in obedience to the scriptures referring to the holy ground on which they trod. Passing through a low doorway, they entered the chapel where Felix Fabri found the pavement 'strewn with costly carpets, the walls covered with precious polished slabs of marble'. It was lit by many lamps and in the pavement beneath the small altar resting on four colonnettes (where the bush was said to have grown) he noted 'a brazen plate, whereon is carved the figure of the burning bush and of Moses taking off his shoes'.

At the death of a monk, his burial took place in one of the few allotted graves dug in the sparse, stony ground in the small cemetery. As was the practice since the founding of the monastery, when the flesh had disappeared, the body was exhumed and the bones placed in the monastery charnel house in the garden. To the left of the door, in a crouching position, sat (as it does today) the cadaver of St Stephanos the porter, a holy monk of the sixth century arrayed in hooded purple robes, holding a staff in his skeletal hand. For many years of his life, he had sat at a gateway in the plain of cypresses on the way up to Mt Sinai hearing confessions from pilgrim travellers during their arduous climb to the summit. In AD 560, the saint was found dead, still seated on his chair. Inside the ossuary, the pilgrims were confronted (as they are today) with the sight of separate mounds of skulls, limbs, hands and feet, carefully and neatly arranged in order, while opposite, set apart, the bones of archbishops and martyrs were exposed in open coffins.

With his love of nature, Niccolò di Poggibonsi delighted in the refreshing peaceful monastery garden full of green leaves, flowers and fruit. Above it at the foot of the mountains the monks had dug deep cisterns to trap the water from the winter snows. From there it flowed through pipes from one well to another until the network of channels permeated the whole garden, where the monks cultivated herbs, salads, grass and grain. There were more than 3,000 olive trees, many fig trees, pomegranates and almond trees. In this way, the convent produced enough olive oil to light the church lamps, as well as for the kitchen. Every year, jars were filled from the fruits of the garden and sent through the Sinai desert to the sultan in Cairo in return for patronage and protection.

No pilgrimage to St Catherine's was thought complete without the stony climb of Mt Sinai. The mountain can be described as having one base, headed by two peaks, that of Mt Moses (7,500 feet) and the higher Mt Catherine (8,700 feet). The whole sanctified area was venerated by both Christians and Saracens because of its legendary associations with prophets of the Old Testament and the biblical stories of Moses. Medieval travellers punctuated their accounts of the ascent with liberal quotations from the scriptures and stories of miracles said to be associated with particular shrines on the way. Always in their minds was the fabulous story of the discovery of the whole body of St Catherine, so ardently believed to have been deposited on the summit of Mt Catherine by holy angels.

Niccolò di Poggibonsi and a companion set off for their climb in the early morning, accompanied by an Arab and a monk from the community. They took the steep stony road above the monastery towards the west and for two miles they ascended it vertically 'as if mounting a ladder'. Known as the 'Pilgrims' Staircase', the path took the form of 3,000 high granite steps to the top of Mt Moses, and had been laboriously cut by the first monks living in the monastery. Progress was slow and difficult, sometimes hindered by falling rocks; the way led through a narrow gorge and under two strong narrow stone arches, described by Niccolò as about a bowshot apart. This was the place where the monk Stephanos had sat so long before, hearing confessions of pilgrim travellers.

Niccolò left graphic descriptions of the mountain shrines and the best route to take, since he wrote them down on his gypsum tablets. He mentioned the beautiful church of St Mary of the Apparition, where, it was said, the Virgin caused a miraculous delivery of supplies to the starving community. According to legend, the monks had been plagued by rats and on the point of evacuating the monastery because of their plight, but they turned back because the Virgin appeared and spoke words of comfort. Having passed through two arches, Niccolò found the chapel of Elijah the prophet surrounded by many buildings, and having three trees as a landmark. A further legend asserted that this was the place where the Lord had appeared to Elijah amid fire and brimstone. Having at last attained the summit of Mt Moses, Niccolò described a small stone church (originally erected by Justinian), facing east, where according to tradition Moses had received the stone tablets of Law written by the hand of God. It was partitioned by a small wall on which was a painted board showing how Moses had divided the Red Sea with rod in hand to enable the Children of Israel to escape the army of pharaoh. Eight paces from the church there was a mosque for the Saracens with two underground cells.

The views from the peak in the clear air encompassed the whole peninsula, with the Red Sea coast beyond. But those who were anxious

8.5 The chapels on the way to the summit of Mount Sinai

to ascend before dusk the higher peak of St Catherine, with a more spectacular panorama, did not linger. Niccolò's advice about the path was touchingly solicitous for would-be mountaineers:

> If you wish to go to the Mount of St Catherine, this is the way, you descend the mount by the northeast and you make a rapid descent; and hold fast as it will be very necessary for you; for the descent was so rapid that we put our staves in front of us and we came after. During this descent you find a wild pear tree, and as you continue the descent, hold tight I say.

About halfway down the path lay the monastery known as the 'Forty Saints' belonging to the community of St Catherine, where Niccolò and his friend rested under the care of eight brethren. The church was large and surrounded by buildings, with an extensive garden containing many kinds of apple trees, through which in season ran a stream. On the lower, fertile slopes of St Catherine's mountain the monks could grow olives and vegetables similar to those grown at the monastery itself. On the stony ground of the upper reaches, there were collectable fossils with curious imprints of plants, flowers and trees.

Leaving the monastery of the Forty Saints they walked along a small plateau and entered a valley to the west. Having climbed about halfway up, they arrived on the top of a ridge to their left. Descending a little, for 'about two bowshots' there followed a steeper ascent and here Niccolò once more exhorted his readers to 'hold tight, as you need to very much; for the mount is very difficult to climb'. At last, after crawling their way over high crags to the steep summit, they found the place so small that barely twelve people could stand together at a time. A dry stone wall had been built around the edge for safety, to stop pilgrims from becoming dizzy when they looked down. In the centre of the area an impression in the rock could be seen where the saint's body had lain. Felix Fabri's party measured the length of the hollow with their own bodies, not 'out of curiosity but piety', and concluded that she must have been tall of stature.

As Niccolò and his party had climbed both peaks in one day and the hour was late, it had become fiercely cold and they felt very hungry.

They rested again at the monastery of the Forty Saints, as they could scarcely stand upright after the gruelling descent. Overcome by weariness, their feet, their shins and their knees were extremely painful. The monks hospitably gave them food and drink, but although they slept partly under cover, only the stony ground served as their mattress. Niccolò did not mention the state of their footwear. Felix Fabri was fortunate to be able to leave his old worn-out shoes in his room before starting off. He had been lent a new 'grey or blue grey' pair purchased in Jerusalem by a knight thought to be too sick to attempt the ascent. With their leather soles torn to ribbons, many of his noble countrymen returned barefoot after the climb and remained in the same unhappy state until they reached Cairo.

Niccolò's pilgrimage ended on the Friday after their descent from the mountain 'at the hour of terce'. They sorrowfully loaded their camels and parted in tears from their most beloved monastery of St Catherine, to head for the road to Gaza. Their return through the desert was again punctuated by unwelcome attentions from the nomadic Arabs, but being poor men without obvious wealth they did not suffer much harm. After a short stay at Gaza, they hastened on to the port of Damietta (Dumyat), a place of plenty with beautiful gardens, where they were freely entertained by a Latin merchant for 23 days. Eventually they found a brigantine heading for Cyprus, which took them on the first leg of their homeward journey.

Niccolò did not return to Tuscany until the following spring. Having sailed from Damietta, they arrived at Famagusta in Cyprus. But after leaving the shelter of Famagusta, he found himself buffeted in a tempest of such magnitude that their cockboat was like an infirm man who tried to walk when his feet would not carry him. On All Saints' Day they fought off a piratical attack. Even then his tribulations did not cease, as a further storm drove them ashore off Sclavonia, where some frightening experiences on land delayed his arrival at Venice until Christmas. From Venice he left by boat for Chioggia, then to the port of Francolino, where they transferred to a cart with two horses en route for 'the blessed and gentle city' of Ferrara, where he rested. He departed once more for Bologna, travelling over the Apennines and at length came home to Poggibonsi via Florence. At the end of all his eventful travels he was able to record: 'Jesus Christ has brought us safe... for from all these travels I alone with one companion escaped and out of seven friars I had for companions all died on the way, save one who preceded me home.'

Christopher Harant and his brother-in-law were ceremoniously given a certificate as a souvenir by the archbishop on the day of departure, testifying they had completed their pilgrimage to the monastery and the peaks of the holy mountains. Subsequently they left the monastery for Cairo on Monday 19 October 1598 at about three or four in the afternoon. Just as they were leaving, they were accosted by an Arab riding a dromedary who asked if he could accompany them, promising that he would show them the best route. But shortly afterwards, choosing his moment, he announced his intention of riding off for a little distance, to meet some friends on business in the mountains, and having told their interpreter where to camp for the night he promised to catch up with them. Night soon came, so having pitched camp, the travellers fell asleep on the sand between some rocks. Around three in the morning, Christopher was suddenly wakened by the voice of their guide, who customarily slept with the camels, calling out to someone. Thinking it might be the Arab who had rejoined them, he was soon disabused of this on hearing the sound of loud voices. Having woken his brother-in-law and their interpreter, they demanded to know what was happening, only to be told by the guide that they must trust to destiny as they were being attacked. It did not avail that the Moor besought the robbers to do them no harm, as very shortly the travellers perceived their attackers by the light of the moon and before they had time to exchange many words, they too were discovered by a party of eight raiders armed with lances, bows and long Turkish cutlasses shaped like sabres. Their chief kept the victims covered with a long gun. Very soon they were encircled, and being unarmed the four felt they were as sheep ready for slaughter. Christopher found himself surrounded by four of the miscreants who held him by his shoulders, their cutlasses ready to cut his throat.

When the robbers saw that their prisoners were unarmed and could not defend themselves, they began to riffle through their belongings for money and to search their clothes from top to toe. Thinking to fob them off, Christopher took a purse with a leather thong from his pocket containing a gold sequin and a few medines, which he offered up as a sop. This merely served to whet their appetites: Christopher compared it to throwing a grain of wheat into the throat of a famished lion. Full of rage they started to take off Christopher's clothes, two of them on either side, forcibly pulling his sleeves as if they wished to tear him to pieces. They finished by removing his tunic and though they saw that he was only dressed in humble linen, they persisted in their search and forced him to sit down. Without unlacing his shoes they tore both of them off his feet by force, dragging him over the stony, sandy ground in the process. At length he was almost undressed except for his shirt which his assailants endeavoured to drag over his head. This delayed them, as it was attached securely by the band around his neck. But he suffered so much from the tugging, and the blows raining down from left and right on his bare body, that he thought his last hour had come. With great presence of mind, even while the robbers were doing their worst, Christopher remembered that he must at all costs take off the cloth belt round his left shoulder in which he had hidden 22 sequins. In the scuffle, he managed to undo it with his right hand and keep it firmly closed in his palm. Scarcely had he done this, when his tormentors finally tore off his shirt, leaving him completely naked. Seeing that he had nothing on him, they turned aside to examine his clothes, so, seizing his advantage, Christopher threw his money belt on the ground and buried it in the sand, marking the spot with a stone, taking good care to move away from it.

Their guide, who was watching his misfortunes, came over to cover his charge with a kind of white headscarf. His brother-in-law and the interpreter, who had been left clothed in their shirts and pants, were fortunate not to have been dragged over the stones like their friend. Together they watched the thieves amass all their belongings into one heap together with their provisions, biscuits, dried fish etc. The Arabs were so famished that they seemed to be as avid for food as for the money they were seeking. M. Cernin took an opportunity to find out if Christopher had been robbed of everything including the money hidden in his belt. Christopher said all had gone. In a state of shock, his brother-in-law informed the interpreter, who immediately

8.6 Portrait of Christopher Harant

besought the thieves to return at least some of it or they would never be able to get back home. On hearing this, the robbers immediately got up and ran towards their prisoners, demanding to whom the money had belonged. When they learned that it was Christopher's he was once more surrounded and he realised that his hoax had been an error. Teasingly he showed them his leg, to make them think he had tied the money to it. One after the other they examined his leg in the hope that they might somehow discover where it was. Soon they returned to the place where they had dragged their victim over the ground, while Christopher waited in fear that they might recover the purse from the sand. By the grace of God, they did not find it; instead they started to quarrel among themselves, each suspecting the others. Their chief gathered them together and grilled each one as to who was secreting the money, but on drawing a blank, returned to Christopher to ascertain what kind of money it was before he resumed the interrogation of his associates. Meanwhile Christopher made a great pretence of searching the ground in the wrong place to show his innocence. At length, the chief issued an ultimatum that if the travellers did not disclose the whereabouts of the cash, since his followers had sworn to a man they did not have it, their fate would be certain death. Realising that it was no longer a question of a game, Christopher decided to ask their pardon, giving them to understand that he had been misunderstood, and gave his word that the only money he had possessed was the gift they had received in the first place. With this fabrication they appeared to be satisfied.

Their Arab guide besought the robbers to give back the clothes and some food, pleading that his charges were poor Christians having to pay heavy taxes to the Turkish emperor. Their tunics were returned and Christopher recovered his pants, but all the rest, including their blankets, was retained. Some bread and a few biscuits were granted to them to last for a day or two. While these exchanges were carried out, their interpreter persisted in kissing the hands and foreheads of their assailants with expressions of humility and friendship, but had it not been for the faithful guide who had secreted a little flour, they would have surely perished. As a parting shot, the robbers made them swear not to return and complain of them to St Catherine's, nor to inform the authorities of the robbery on their return to Cairo. It had become clear to Christopher and his brother-in-law that the Arabs had come from the monastery, and that the man who had initially accompanied them was their informant, although he had not taken part in the raid.

Three hours had passed by the time their assailants finally departed, and the pilgrims, thankful that their lives had been spared, made haste to continue their journey, though they were shaken up by their experiences and apprehensive about further attacks. Thanks to the flour, resourcefully eked out by their guide, who made it into flat cakes with such herbs as he could find, and cooked them between the hot stones in the sand, they managed to subsist somehow until they reached Suez. So demoralised were they that on being accosted by some mounted Turkish soldiers they weakly fell to their knees, begging them not to attack. The Turks, perceiving their ragged, emaciated state, did not molest them and on hearing of their misfortunes even roundly condemned their mistreatment by the lawless Arabs. Christopher sent their guides into Suez, where one sequin purchased only a little bread and cheese; but even if the cheese tasted as soapy as that offered up at St Catherine's, they were somewhat revived.

Towards evening, they caught up with a caravan of about 50 camels composed of Turks, Moors and Arabs about to depart for Cairo. As Christopher's camel was suffering from fatigue, he asked his guide to find out if he could hire a camel just for the night. It was thus that an old scoundrel of a Moor agreed to let him ride one of his on payment of six medines. Perhaps because of the travellers' wild, uncouth appearance they were made unwelcome by the rapacious dealers and it was only after extortionate payments they were permitted to accompany them. The camel was the tallest of the scoundrel's herd and Christopher was forced to ride next to its owner while his companions rode at the tail of the caravan. Though he felt isolated and afraid, Christopher started to doze. Suddenly he was roused by the 'old dog', who gave him a blow on the back with a gourd which almost felled him to the ground. He could only surmise that the reason for this attack was that he was riding with one of his legs a little more to one side than the other and that he might be causing fatigue to his mount.

At dawn, when the caravan halted, Christopher managed to join up with his friends for an hour's sleep. The cavalcade resumed its journey, bearing with it the old scoundrel, whom Christopher wished would go 'a casa del diavolo e tre miglia piu in la' ('to the house of the devil and three miles further away'). Soon they too departed, but were forced to hold their noses since they suffered from the pungent smell of the fresh droppings strewn along the way from the camels ahead.

Shortly afterwards, their party was joined by a group of three Arabs from Mecca, who were transporting the corpse of a rich merchant whose widow was taking it back for burial in Cairo. The dead man was visible as the coffin was open to the skies. But though the body was exposed to the blazing sun throughout the day, it did not stink. It gave out an agreeable odour since it had been embalmed before leaving.

The party travelled all day and four hours into the night, making good time to the outskirts of Cairo. At the encampment of their Arab guide, Christopher slept with a sense of security for the first time since they had left Sinai. On the morning of 26 October, they woke with the dawn and as their tired camels could no longer carry them, they elected to walk into Cairo, taking their guide with them. Despite the dangers and privations since the beginning of the journey on 8 October, they reached their lodging in good health at about three in the afternoon, where the consul and his household joyfully welcomed them. Without delay their host served up an ample repast, and in the absence of wine, the water of the Nile tasted as good to them as the best vintage after the brackish springs of the desert. Before returning to his camp, their guide shared their meal with expressions of pleasure and faithfully returned the purse of sequins, which had been confided to his care after the robbery. That their desert journey had taken only 18 days was a source of astonishment to the consul and his friends. They could not remember anyone who had made the pilgrimage in such a short time during the hot weather.

Shortly afterwards, on 31 October, Christopher and his brother-in-law set sail from Bulaq with a flotilla of eleven boats, some of which were transporting impressed Egyptian soldiers to fight in a campaign in Hungary for the Turkish army against the Christians. The mercenaries were lured to the flag in groups by Turkish officers, preceded by a small drummer who beat a rhythm with one hand while he played a fife that he held in the other. Those who wished to enrol joined the procession, though their payment was only a few medines. Any who could write put a quill in their turbans to indicate a higher status. But there were only a few who let themselves be tempted and it seemed the hearts of those who joined up were heavy. During the preceding years, crowds of soldiers had left for Hungary but scarcely one in 15 had returned home. They had expected to find that the war would take the form of merely a harassment or pillage, as at home, instead of dangerous attacks or the conquest of fortresses. Those who came from a hot climate could not sustain the rigours of the cold winter and intensely hard work. Thus throughout the whole country and the great city of Cairo there were only a handful of volunteers. They had lost their enthusiasm for military life.

Christopher's Nile voyage terminated at the busy mercantile port of Rosetta, and from there the party hired donkeys to ride along the coastal road to Alexandria, where the deep sandy path forced them to wade through the waves of the sea. At length they reached the city gates on 5 November. The noise of their arrival at the *fondaco* joyfully alerted their friends who had accompanied them on pilgrimage to Jerusalem and were now awaiting a boat to return home. As all intending travellers were anxious to set sail from Alexandria before 15 November, when most of the fleet departed before the onset of the winter winds, the *fondaco* was packed with merchants waiting for transport.

On the following day, Christopher hastened to greet the French vice-consul, who, as was his custom, had gone to Mass in the fine, spacious chapel of the *fondaco*. They were received affably, and promised help in finding berths on a suitable boat heading for Malta or Sicily. Subsequently they rowed out to three Venetian vessels at anchor near the fort, since the harbour was too shallow to accommodate them, and managed to book places for Thursday 12 November on the *Balbania*, the largest, which was due to depart first. The vice-consul had advised them that Venetian ships enjoyed better protection at that time of year from the pirates waiting to raid the laden cargo vessels. On the evening of the eleventh, they took leave of their host with joyful hearts and although they had no choice but to accept the poor, cramped accommodation allotted by the *Balbania*'s captain, they were all in good health. When they had been rowed out to the open sea the next afternoon, the sails filled in a light wind and on losing sight of Alexandria, they left Egypt behind them.

Notes

Preparations and journey: Bellorini and Hoade (ed. and trans.), *Frescobaldi, Gucci and Sigoli*, pp. 53–57, 177, 178; *Fra Niccolò of Poggibonsi*, pp. 96–104; Sauneron (ed.), *Voyage en Egypte de Pierre Belon*, pp. 120b–26b; Stewart (ed. and trans.), *The Wanderings of Brother Felix Fabri*, pp. 526–46. **The Garden of Balm, general:** Meinhardus, *The Holy Family in Egypt*, pp. 35–40. **Pilgrims' descriptions of balm and its uses:** Alpinus, *De Balsamo Dialogus*; Dopp (ed.), *Le traité d'Emmanuele Piloti*, pp. 32–34; Sauneron (ed.), *Voyage en Egypte de Pierre Belon*, pp. 110 b–12 b; Bellorini and Hoade (ed. and trans.), *Frescobaldi, Gucci and Sigoli*, pp. 106–108, 177–78; Brejnik and Brejnik (ed. and trans.), *Voyage de Christophe Harant*, pp. 82–94. **Monastery, general:** Kamil, *The Monastery of St Catherine in Sinai*; Papaioannu, *The Monastery of St Catherine Sinai*. **The pilgrims:** Stewart (ed. and trans.), *The Wanderings of Brother Felix Fabri* (St Catherine's Mount, pp. 570–71; legend of monks retrieving her body, pp. 604–607; state of shoes, p. 582; at tomb of St Catherine, bones, jewels, pp. 599–603; chapel of Burning Bush, pp. 607–608; lodgings and monks' hospitality, p. 611; dislike of monks, pp. 616–23; troubles on departure, pp. 624–25); Bellorini and Hoade (ed. and trans.), *Fra Niccolò of Poggibonsi*, pp. 98–120; *Francesco Suriano*, pp. 186–89; Sauneron (ed.), *Voyage en Egypte de Pierre Belon*, pp. 121a–133b; Brejnik and Brejnik (ed. and trans.), *Voyage de Christophe Harant*, pp. 98–172; da Schio (introd.), *Viaggio di Filippo Pigafetta*, pp. 225–65; Wolff, 'Two Pilgrims at Saint Catherine's Monastery', pp. 33–58.

CHAPTER 9

Adventures with the Mecca Caravan

Despite the recognised dangers, a few intrepid Europeans risked the desert journey to accompany the great company of Muslims on the yearly *hajj*, the pilgrimage to Mecca. In 1586 or thereabouts, 20 days after Ramadan, an anonymous Englishman joined the caravan from Cairo for the 40-day journey on the well-trodden route to 'Aqaba across the northern Sinai desert. It was a brave venture, since if any Christian had been discovered in the Muslim holy places, he would undoubtedly have been summarily executed:

> The Captain of the caravan and all his retinue and officers resort unto the castle (that is the citadel) of Cairo before the Pasha who gives every man a garment, and that of the Captain is wrought with gold, and the others are served according to their degree. Moreover he delivers unto him ye Chisva Talnabi [Kiswat al-Nabi] which signifies in the Arabian tongue 'the garment of the Prophet'... This garment is made of purpose to cover from top to bottom a little house in Mecca standing in the midst of the Xesqita, the which house they say, was builded by Abraham or by his son Ishmael. After this he delivers to him a gate made of purpose for the aforesaid house, wrought all with fine gold and being of excellent workmanship and it is a thing of great value. Besides he delivers unto him a covering of green velvet made in the manner of a pyramid, about nine palms high, and artificially wrought with most fine gold, and this is to cover the tomb of their prophet within Medina. These precious objects are carried from the Pasha's residence on the Citadel to a mosque near the Bab al-Nasr. They are stored in this mosque until the pilgrim caravan begins to form at Birca.

'Birca' (Birkat al-Hajj) lay near Matariyya about four miles from Cairo. The so-called 'Chisva Talnabi', also known as the *kiswa*, the curtain veiling the exterior of the Ka'ba, was by tradition manufactured in Egypt.

For the journey to Arabia, such caravans set out with well-harnessed horses, mules, camels with footmen and were sometimes accompanied by women and children in hooded litters. The anonymous traveller said that the 50,000 people in their procession were accompanied by 40,000 mules and camels. Merchants placed themselves at the head of the caravan, selling their goods of coral, silk, grain and rice on the way, while the pilgrims followed behind them. There was no quarter for the dying. Sultan al-Nasir Muhammad made pilgrimages in 1313, 1320 and 1332. He travelled in comfort, sustained by access to his portable vegetable garden carried on frames on the backs of his camels.

During his visit to Cairo, on 12 December 1576, Filippo Pigafetta from Vicenza was among the crowd to watch the motley pageant file past in the dusty street The parade had first assembled in the large square by the citadel, before proceeding for about three miles along the route to the al-Hakim mosque close by the Bab al-Nasr, via the main road which led through the bazaar. The prominent al-Hakim mosque by the city walls received large revenues of money and grain to pay for the *muezzin*, the priests, the craftsmen, lighting and ornamentation and alms for the poor. From the hour of dawn, crescendos of noise erupted from the vast gathering of the inhabitants of Cairo lining the sides of the road and cramming into the booths of the bazaars. Filippo saw a multitude of people leaning down from upper windows, stretching out their arms to call down a thousand blessings, and to touch the fine sturdy camel, led by hand, setting the pace at the head of the procession. It was caparisoned in a silk cloth embroidered with gold; on its saddle rested its precious burden, the *mahmal*, which took the form of a four-sided pyramid, covered over with silk material to which were attached small bells, decreasing in size, that tinkled with harmonious sounds. After touching the camel, the onlookers placed their hands on their eyes and beards, venerating the animal as a saint, wishing it *bon voyage* while invoking God and Muhammad.

In its train came a bevy of barefoot ragged wretches, jumping and singing, begging in the name of God from the crowd who indulged them, believing that these vagabonds were holy men. They held in their hands curved hooks, decorated at the top by a half moon, while multicoloured ragged strips of woollen cloth fluttered down from the bottom.

A retinue of dervishes followed, self-confessed saints by profession, close-shaved and bareheaded. They drew the respectful attention of the crowds by swallowing the impossible, such as skewers and snakes, and indulged in all kinds of chicanery. But however bizarre they may have seemed, they lived comfortably in their own establishments where their affairs were well organised. The Moroccan globe trotter Ibn Battuta regarded the dervishes as men of good education and adepts

9.1 The camel carrying the *mahmal*

in the mystical doctrines. In the grip of a frenzy, they leapt and twirled in the air among the noisy throngs, uttering raucous cries, beating their heads, their antics orchestrated by their leaders who bade them stop and start.

A procession of bearers with rich presents came into view. They carried 27 pieces of velvet cloth and materials of silk and damask of different colours about two spans wide, beautifully worked with Arabic letters embroidered in gold. On show was the black velvet cover worked in gold for the tomb of Muhammad. These gifts were spread out like tablecloths on the shields of men on foot, who rested from time to time so that the crowd below could touch them. Those watching from the top floor ruffled the hair of the crowd as they dangled down various pieces of cloth to caress the gifts, afterwards reverently touching their eyes and beards with the material with great shows of humility. Amid the raucous noise, there was a real danger of being killed or ill-treated by the excited mob increasingly worked up to fever pitch by their religious fervour. Some of the janissaries who were posted along the way to keep order indiscriminately beat anyone who did not stay behind them and, in particular, any foreigners or Christian Copts wearing black turbans.

After a kaleidoscope of court officials and an innumerable train of baggage camels had wound past, there came a number of litters each carried by two camels covered in brightly coloured material, containing important men and women with their children going on pilgrimage. Some palanquins followed bearing poets and those who sang hymns, all in their best array. In the rearguard of the procession were six small pieces of artillery of 6 cm calibre, each drawn by two horses with a rider, followed by their camels carrying the ammunition and impedimenta for the guns. Finally, amid due pomp and ceremony came the *sanjac* responsible for conducting the caravan and the splendid presents to Mecca. He was accompanied by all the other *sanjacs* of Cairo riding beautiful horses, attended by their retinues with all the dignity they could muster. Filippo waited until the whole procession had passed by; it culminated with a military escort of about one hundred janissaries carrying arquebusses, mounted 'on the fleetest of dromedaries, well saddled and harnessed'.

9.2 Janissary going to war wearing a plumed helmet

The Victorian orientalist, E.W. Lane, described the *mahmal* as

a square skeleton frame of wood, with a pyramidal top; and has a covering of black brocade, richly worked with inscriptions and ornamental embroidery in gold, in some parts upon a ground of green or red silk and bordered with a fringe of silk, with tassels surmounted by silver balls... it contains nothing; but has two mus-hafs (or copies of the Kur-an), one on a small scroll, and the other in the usual form of a book, also small, each enclosed in a case of gilt silver attached externally at the top.

It was in 1266, during the reign of the sultan Baybars, that the *mahmal* first accompanied the Egyptian caravan and thereafter it was

sent annually by the Mamluk sultans and their successors in Egypt up
to the reign of King Fu'ad in 1926. It came to be regarded as the essential token of Egyptian sovereignty over Mecca and showed Egypt's
superiority as the religious centre of Islam. The fine tall camel chosen
to bear the *mahmal*, which walked before the procession and set the
pace, was generally exempted from every form of labour for the rest
of its life.

Ludovico di Varthema, a Venetian 'seeking places to visit little
known to his countrymen', travelled to Mecca with the pilgrimage
which left from Damascus on 8 April 1503, during the reign of the
sultan Qansuh al-Ghawri. Not much is known of Ludovico, except
that he was intent on travelling the world, was the son of a physician,
was married and had fathered a family. Like the Cairenes, the people
of Damascus delighted in pageantry, which the Mamluk rulers took
pains to satisfy in their Syrian capital. The citizens loved to watch the
sultans, shaded by parasols and preceded by banners, ride out of the
citadel for prayers to the great Umayyad mosque. The yearly
pilgrimage to Mecca surged out of the city in a tide of ten thousand
camels, taking with them an old revered Qur'an (the *mahmal* uniquely
went from Cairo) on a richly caparisoned camel behind drums and
trumpets, horses and camels swathed in gold, accompanied by pilgrims
from the far reaches of the Islamic world.

But without the friendship of the Mamluk captain of the caravan,
who was a Christian renegade, Ludovico could not have succeeded in
his desire. The Mamluk treated him well throughout the journey,
clothed him like a Mamluk, gave him a good horse and placed him in
the company of other Mamluks. Ludovico owned however that the
journey could not have been accomplished without the money and
other gifts he gave him. As was the custom when they rode out to war,
the Mamluk soldiers were furnished with a formidable array of arms.
Curved iron swords encased in wooden scabbards covered with fine
leather, damask, velvet or metal hung from a waist band or from the
shoulder. Sometimes they had bows slung around their bodies and
carried long lances with iron tips. Their round convex shields were
fashioned from wood or metal and the mace, a popular weapon used
for crushing helmets, was carried under the knee. The soldiers were

protected by coats of mail, and on their heads wore tallish pointed helmets, lined with fibre to cushion the blows, having ear and neck guards made of one plate of metal each. On occasions, fine lacy chains dripped on to their shoulders. Ludovico wrote: 'We sixty Mamluks were sufficient defence against 40,000 or 50,000 Arabs; for pagans, there are no better people than are the Mamluks with arms in their hands. You must know I had excellent experiences of these Mamluks during the journey.'

The commanders of the caravans, known as the amirs of the *hajj*, were government officials having under them various officials to whom they delegated duties in the running of the complex organisation. They had responsibility for the overall security, which entailed overseeing the militia who guarded the pilgrims and the variety of merchants who had business in Arabia. Under Turkish rule, the military escort was composed of professional soldiers who held land from the government in return for this service, as well as the janissaries from the garrison who strutted about in high boots and tall hats decorated with long drooping feathers. Organising the *hajj* was not a simple operation, and sometimes the government found it expedient to hire extra soldiers for reinforcement. The caravan commanders had considerable powers over everyone under their direct supervision. They became rich, for besides receiving purses of gold from the Ottoman sultan, they traded in their own right, besides acquiring substantial fees in Mecca, Cairo and Damascus. Guides went before the procession, experienced in the route, and at night followed the stars like mariners at sea. Sometimes a secondary caravan was despatched from Cairo three or four months before the main *hajj* cortège to allow pilgrims to spend longer in the holy cities if they wished to perform optional liturgical acts at their leisure.

In 1606, after the German slave Johann Wild had served his master for about six months, the Persian left Cairo for Mecca, taking Johann with him. As the time of the *hajj* was a great opportunity for trade, the merchant went yearly to promote his affairs as well as for the good of his soul, thus satisfying himself with a blend of profit and piety. Though Johann admitted that he took part in some of the Muslim religious rites, such as ablutions and other practices, he owned that his heart was not in them. For this journey, the pasha sent about one hundred Mamluks and six cannon to defend the caravan from attacks by the predatory Moors, who optimistically lay in wait for expected plunder. The amir of the *hajj*, who had pitched his tent with those of other dignitaries near Matariyya eight days beforehand, announced formally to the assembly the evening before departure that all who wished to go to Mecca with them should prepare to leave early next morning en route for 'Aqaba, the first leg of their journey. At this news, great feasting and rejoicing took place 'with castles and other infinite devices of fireworks, the Janissaries always standing about the tent of the Captain with such shouting and joy that on every side the earth resounds'.

At sunrise after the trumpets had sounded, Johann and his master made ready amid the roaring of 20,000 camels grumbling at their loads and the enormous, jostling, shouting crowd of fellow travellers. The amir ordered the cavalcade to be arranged in an orderly file, one after another, so that they would not career about pell mell like animals. Vendors from Cairo increased the throng, their camels loaded with fat, oil, honey, bread, flour, beans, vinegar, grain and onions which they cooked for sale on the way. But the rich Turks brought with them all they required for the three months there and back.

After three days of desert travel, they arrived at Suez, where the company rested and watered the animals. The custom of all caravans was to travel much and tarry little, starting in the misty cold at two in the morning and continuing till sunrise. All rested in the heat before travelling again till nightfall. On the third day, having crossed the plains after Suez, they arrived at the notorious countryside near 'Aqaba with its rocky mountain ranges and desert valleys. Faced with negotiating a high mountain, the vast company without exception, men and women, healthy and the complaining sick, were forced to descend from their camels and climb it on foot. One after the other, the animals had to be led over by hand. If they stumbled and fell on the downward path, not only could they be injured, but their unsecured burdens might slide over their necks with sudden swiftness and roll down the mountainside. It was said that the Turkish sultan Selim I, who had defeated the Mamluks in 1517, had cut the mountain road through to 'Aqaba;

Johann noticed a small wall and pillar engraved with Turkish letters raised up in his memory on the path.

About 50 Mamluk soldiers employed by the pasha were stationed at 'Aqaba, to guard the town's reservoirs which dammed the rain-water, as it pleased the Moors to raid them, swooping down from their hideouts in the mountain. The evening after arrival, after Johann had washed his master's soiled clothes, there was a general call to arms as a warning that the Moors were attacking the town. Each man took up his gun and the cannon were fired, but after three salvoes, the marauders turned tail, though not before making off with some camels at pasture belonging to the amir of the *hajj*.

After some months of toil in Arabia along the desert roads to Mecca, Mt 'Arafat, back to Mecca, thence to Medina, the burial place of the Prophet, and a visit to the Yemen to trade with Indian merchants, the Persian finally completed his business. At last they turned their backs on the arid mountains of the interior, to return to the lucrative markets of Cairo. At Jedda on the west coast, they were fortunate to find a boat due to sail north up to the port of Suez. Among the exchange of news, the captain of the vessel relayed to the assem-bled merchants the welcome report that many traders had arrived in the Egyptian capital from Constantinople, and were waiting to buy their goods.

It was dangerous sailing among the rocks and shallows of the Red Sea; the sudden treacherous winds whipping up the waves could wreak havoc among the infamous reefs and shoals, as testified by the grave-yard of wrecks along the shores. Johann owned that they were more afraid during that watery stretch of the journey than in all their nine months away in the blinding desert heat: 'I cannot say how terrible it is to sail there'. The captain and sailors exhorted the passengers on the vessel to pray for safety: 'how zealous were the Turks in their prayers as I had never heard them before. They vowed before God that they would make a sacrifice when they arrived on dry land.'

Indeed, on landing at Suez each one sacrificed two or three sheep and distributed them among the poor. The beggars of the district walked barefoot, without head-coverings and without shelter in winter or summer, sleeping in the fields under the stars, or retreating into the mosques. They found sporadic work looking after the merchants' camels near the water, taking every opportunity to steal, though if caught in the act they were severely beaten or executed. Such thank-offerings from the relieved passengers were manna from heaven.

Master and slave lodged in the town until the ship's holds were opened; each boat had a certain measure of loading, not too much and not too little. If too heavily loaded, the vessel could not navigate without danger among the unpredictable winds and dangerous rocks lining the narrow waterway of the Red Sea. If too light, it could completely turn over. The larger ships had two or three holds, one above the other, so that the goods were secure from damage by water. Should any of the merchandise become wet or spoilt, the captain of the boat had to pay recompense to the owner.

When the Persian's wares were unloaded on the quay for inspection, he learnt that someone had informed against him to the effect that he had secreted precious stones and pearls in his sacks of pepper to evade taxes. When the chief of the customs saw the stamp of the Persian on the bales, he asked to whom they belonged and what they contained. The Persian replied that they were his and they contained pepper. In spite of this, the officer in disbelief ordered him to cut open the bales. 'Sir, if there are precious stones or pearls inside I will give you a present of all that I have', replied Johann's master. But these words fell on stony ground: the bales were ordered to be cut open and the contents emptied out on the ground. As the officer had doubted him, the Persian became angry and threatened to plead his case before the pasha, something the officer assured him would be useless. But as the sacks had been emptied in front of all the onlookers and no precious stones were to be seen, the man became the subject of mockery: 'His Lordship has sought for precious stones and pearls but has found dirt on his nose.' When Johann's master pursued his claim before the *qadi* who administered the town, it was found that one of the sailors with them had denounced him to the customs, and when questioned, he owned that he wished to play a trick on the chief officer, as he knew that he was greedy for large sums of money and perks. As a punishment the *qadi* ordered his servants the janissaries to give the sailor 300 strokes of the cane. As for the chief customs officer, he had to pay the judge six gold ducats as forfeit and under threat of losing his post he had to replace the pepper into the bales exactly as they were before. As a watchful bystander, Johann considered that the Turkish method of confronting an adversary with a false witness was justified and the fact that he who was guilty was punished openly, in front of everyone, was to be commended.

The sandy country around Suez was a rocky sterile place with nothing to commend it. Much of the water, provisions and wood for the small population had to be transported by camels, while dried camel dung was used for fuel for cooking. But all this porterage was well worth the trouble, as the small village served as a port for boats carrying goods from the Indies and Portugal as well as Mecca. Thousands of ducats were collected in revenue from customs duty, which the chief officer remitted to the pasha in Cairo. In 1547, the doctor Pierre Belon du Mans counted about 30 or 40 Turkish boats drawn up onto the shore, since the port was at the mercy of every winter wind. The vessels had been brought from Constantinople via the Nile up to Cairo, where they were taken apart and carried piece by piece by camels and carts to Suez to be reconstructed. In 1516 the town of Zabid in the Yemen had been captured by the Turks, and Pierre noted that a punitive expedition was being prepared against the people who had rebelled against them.

Johann Wild and his Persian master spent about eight days in Suez by the time all taxes had been paid, and the number of camels required by the company of merchants had arrived from Cairo. With the disturbing news that some hundreds of Arabs were lying in wait for the caravan on the last lap of the journey to the Nile, the hundred or so merchants, armed with guns, commended themselves to the grace of God and set off with 3,000 loaded camels. They were guarded by some 200 armed soldiers, half on foot and half on horseback. Fresh and alert after their enforced rest, the company took care to cover over their precious merchandise with carpets and baskets so that it could not be seen. In spite of the threatened dangers, they were happy to be going home and to be on land, having escaped from the roaring threatening sea; some sang, some jumped, while another told diverting stories to pass the time. On the second day, after they had ridden for about four hours and the sun was becoming hot, an urgent message was received from the horsemen who had gone ahead, warning the company to arm and be ready for an attack in force. At this the merchants took fright, though nothing could be done except trust to chance. After the camels were gathered up and crowded together, the merchants stood fast, having divided themselves into two equal groups at the front and rear, ready for the combat. Scarcely a quarter of an hour went by before they were quickly surrounded on all sides by about a thousand shouting Arab horsemen attacking them with hails of arrows.

The amir of the caravan rode up and down exhorting everyone under fear of losing their lives not to let themselves be separated and to keep the camels together. Where they were attacked most strongly he told them where to aim their fire. The amir divided the cavalry into two groups, placing one in front and the other at the rear. When midday came they made the camels kneel to feed, while the company contented themselves with bread and cheese. Some of the merchants, including the Persian, had been wounded, and two of his camels had been shot by arrows, one in the neck, the second in the flank. Meanwhile, the Arabs, who had been stalled by the gunfire, withdrew to parley, and subsequently sent an envoy to demand 3,000 ducats from the amir as payment for the caravan's unhindered progress. As this request was condemned out of hand, all feared the renewal of attack, but though the Arabs made attempts to harass them during the resumption of the journey, they accomplished nothing.

That night, the fortuitous light of the moon enabled the caravan to press on well before resting, as all longed for the life-giving river ahead. They were tired and the camels suffered from their heavy loads and lack of water. The Persian grumbled a great deal about the arrow wound in his arm but his slave Johann owned that he 'would not empty his eyes' to cry for him. Early the next day they continued in silence for three or four hours, until just as the sun was rising high in the sky, a few leagues from Cairo, some two hundred splendid horsemen were seen approaching, bringing camels loaded with melons, cucumbers, fresh figs, oranges and dates. Johann ran towards them with the others, and to his delight he recognised a friend in the crowd, a fellow German, one Abraham Simon de Krems. Abraham had also been sold as a slave in Cairo, but in contrast to Johann he had found a kind master, Mahmud Shawush, who was one of the pasha's men at arms. Abraham offered Johann a large and beautiful water melon, two oranges, some fresh figs and a small round loaf of freshly cooked white bread. After that he gave him a draught of sorbet to drink. Johann thanked him warmly; such gifts were worth more to him than several gold ducats.

When he returned to his master, Johann gave him an orange, some of the figs and a piece of the water melon; but after the Persian had consumed them voraciously, he became quarrelsome and made as if to hit him, demanding why he had not been given the whole water melon to eat. Johann replied that his master should thank God that he had been given so much, and that his friend had done him a kindness which he was glad to receive. But the Persian became so angry at this reply that he drew out his sabre to strike him. Johann avoided the blow and was stung into rudeness. 'I asked him if he took me for a dog or a donkey who does not know what is right and what is not. If I was not pleasing him he should sell me again.' When Johann told his friend of the Persian's ungratefulness, Abraham led him to Mahmud his master, who, having enquired as to the nationality of Johann's owner, declared that he had never heard anything good of any Persian. Both Mahmud and Abraham mounted their horses and accompanied Johann back to the Persian, whereupon Mahmud proceeded to upbraid him about his behaviour towards his slave. He warned him to fear God on high, and that should he wish to sell Johann, he would buy him himself. From fear, the Persian did not know how to reply; nevertheless he repudiated the allegations and denied that he wanted the sale. After these heated exchanges Johann feared that he would be treated more badly than ever, but nothing came of it and they set off once more.

With shouts of happiness, sounds of singing and the beating of drums, a large crowd, including vendors of food and women on donkeys emitting cries of joy, poured out of Cairo along the dusty road to meet the returning caravan. Not all homecomings were happy, and joy could quickly turn to wailing when news spread of the death of relatives on the journey, or at the sight of emaciated dehydrated travellers almost too weak to stand. But on this occasion, among the general gaiety, Johann forgot his own misery and even the Persian, who was happy that he had bought back so much for sale, treated him very kindly. They took up residence once more in the bazaar of the Khan al-Khalili among the affluent traders who sold the best quality merchandise. From the outset, the Persian quickly found good opportunities of doing business with some Venetians who happened to be in the city. For some years the Turkish sultans had made trading agreements with the French, to the detriment of the Venetians who were forbidden to stay in Cairo for more than three months.without permanent residence. The Venetians bought all his pepper and musk for cash and in particular he made a good sum on the pepper, as the price was very high. He had accomplished everything in two months and his trip had netted a profit of 2,000 ducats. Although the journey had been long, fraught with dangers and difficulties, the Persian was lucky not to have lost his precious goods on the way and had been well recompensed for his trouble. On the whole the merchant community was a sober group: the traders took care not to gorge themselves on food and wine and to avoid getting into debt. In the land of the Turks if anyone owed anything and could not pay, he was immediately put to the oar in a galley and there he stayed.

Later, the Persian made further journeys to Damascus and Jerusalem. On return to Cairo when all the business transactions were completed, Johann was sent to deliver the goods to the buyers, who customarily gave him good tips. But a certain Turkish merchant, who had bought some embroidered satin, refused to reward him. Instead, he informed the Persian that Johann had taken the opportunity to consort with the Christians at the Greek convent when they were in Jerusalem. Enraged at the Turk's words, the Persian searched Johann's clothes and on discovering a letter from the Greek Patriarch, stuffed it into Johann's mouth. Had it not been for the intervention of the Turk, who realised that he had gone too far, Johann would have been severely beaten. Eventually the Persian tore up the letter into small pieces and declared that he would no longer keep him.

At last Johann's fortunes changed for the better. When once more he was paraded through the streets for resale, an old and dignified

Turk came forward to ask the reason for the sale and his nationality. After he learnt that Johann was German, of his trading journeys on land and sea, and of his many sufferings, he intimated that if Johann behaved honourably and promised to serve him faithfully, he would buy him. Moreover, he would have no cause for complaint since both his two sons had died and in their memory, he had vowed to buy a prisoner, who, if he behaved well, would be released after one year. Islamic law under the Ottomans regarded the manumission of slaves as a meritorious act and one encouraged by the Islamic religion. Overjoyed, Johann swore to comply and after some haggling he was purchased for 100 ducats from the Persian, the same price as before.

The Turk was rich and distinguished, a colonel over some hundreds of janissaries. He owned a large property and governed a religious foundation in Bulaq. Besides caring for his new master, Johann had to oversee and collect the rents from the agricultural villages in the Turk's ownership. By way of a perk he was given four fields to cultivate for himself, and after six months he was rewarded with a suit of fine clothes and a magnificent horse. Well pleased, his master told him that he would be treated as his son and that he would make of him a gentleman. In 1609, after the harvest had been gathered and the grain collected in sacks, some 100 Arabs swooped down from the hills for plunder while the overseers were dispersed in the villages. Johann and the Turk tried to fend them off, but the old man had to ride off for help because there were so many. Soon, however, he was surrounded by five Arabs in a ravine and on hearing his cries Johann and a friend arrived at the gallop. In the melée Johann fought bravely and the assailants were vanquished, but he was so badly wounded by a lance in the side that the blood soaked through his trousers. Had it not been for the care of his grateful master he would have lost his life. It was after this, while weakened by his wound, that Johann contracted the bubonic plague.

Although he had become content in Egypt, Johann pined for his native land, and, wishing to broach the subject of his liberation, he took his chance during a banquet when the Turk was entertaining some friends, among whom was a local judge. On hearing of his wish the judge promised to speak for Johann to his master. The old Turk called Johann to him and told the company how his slave had saved his life and that he had looked upon him as a son, but true to his word, he asked the judge to act as witness to Johann's liberation. The next day, the judge brought a letter, written in Arabic and stamped with his seal, making Johann a free man after four long years of slavery. In response to his old master's offers of gifts of land should he stay, Johann gave him his heartfelt thanks, but persisted in his desire to make the homeward journey. He had saved up some money, as well as owning his horse and his fine clothes, which he proceeded to turn into cash. Thus he obtained 100 ducats to buy goods to sell in Constantinople while keeping 30 for himself. Having gained some experience of trading while serving the Persian, Johann was able to buy merchandise in Cairo, where he met some merchants with whom he had sailed in the Red Sea. They were astonished to hear of his good fortune and agreed that he should accompany them on the Nile to Damietta, where they intended to buy rice to sell in the markets of the Ottoman capital. They found good lodgings in the green and pleasant port with its luxurious orchards, and eventually had their goods loaded in the holds of an awaiting vessel. These had to be ferried out in small boats, since the sandbank at the mouth of the port prevented seagoing ships negotiating it while they were heavily loaded.

Alas, once more Johann's luck changed for the worse. After two days at sea, a violent tempest arose in the night and the ship foundered on some rocks. Many of the passengers lost their lives, but Johann, who had seized hold of two planks, managed to keep afloat and was rescued at first light by a passing foreign ship. All his goods, so carefully purchased out of his savings, sank without trace. He was put down at Limassol, then sailed via Paphos to Antalya where he was ill for one month. Eventually he found work as a servant on a ship bound for Alexandria, whence he returned to Cairo, where he sought the house of his old master. Overjoyed to see him once more, the old Turk agreed to take him on for a further year's employment.

Having earned enough money for his second departure, Johann found a vessel at Alexandria bound for Constantinople, for which journey he paid the captain three florins. Though the voyage had its dangers he arrived safely and found lodgings near the embassy of King

Matthew of Hungary. He travelled via Poland on his return to Germany. The rest is silence.

Notes

General: Burton, *Narrative of a Pilgrimage*, pp. 128–487; E.W. Lane, *The Modern Egyptians* (the return of the *mahmal* procession in Cairo, pp. 439–62); Peters, *The Hajj*, pp. 70–96, 145–49, 162–71. **European pilgrims:** di Varthema, *Travels in Egypt, Syria and Arabia*, pp. 16–19; Hakluyt (ed.), Anon., 'A Description of the Yearley Voyage', pp. 167–97; da Schio (introd.), *Viaggio di Filippo Pigafetta*, pp. 160–97; Volkoff (ed.), *Le voyage de Johann Wild*, pp. 23–62.

CHAPTER 10

To the South

A year after the Spanish Armada had suffered defeat and shipwreck on the shores of Britain, an anonymous Venetian fulfilled his desire to explore the southern provinces of Egypt. On 7 August 1589 he departed from Cairo with a crew of Nubian boatmen. For some years he had wanted to make that journey 'for no profit whatsoever, but only to see the many splendid buildings, churches, statues, colossi, obelisks and columns and also to see the place where the above mentioned columns were dug out. In order to look at these excavations I had to journey further than I thought.'

He did not, as he says, travel there for profit; he was neither a pilgrim nor a missionary, and he did not pepper his account with quotations from classical authors like many of his contemporaries. Hardly anything is known of this Venetian except that he could speak Arabic, and had resided in Cairo for some time, though he did not say why he lived there. He did not mention the government, though in 1589 Egypt was ruled by the Turkish viceroy, 'Uways Pasha, whose palace in the citadel had been sacked in a violent uprising by mutinous soldiers dissatisfied by their rates of pay. This traveller's rather truncated account, written in his native dialect, revealed that he was a practical man who cast an experienced eye over the mixture of building materials and ancient monuments he so carefully measured. The suspicious Mamluk rulers had always frowned on the Franks who struck off on their own, away from prescribed routes, and the Turks followed their example. So perhaps the Venetian who had lived in Cairo for many years was trusted by the authorities, who put no obstacles in his way.

Before setting off, he had been warned by well-meaning friends about the unknown dangers he could encounter and that he might not even return alive. But overcome by his great desire to see the rumoured splendours of Luxor and Karnak and the quarries where the obelisks were extracted, he brushed all their objections aside. On his return he belittled the sufferings and tribulations of the journey, caused by both the great heat and the lack of food, sometimes not having even an onion to eat, one of the staple foods of the local population. 'But everything is easy when you return safely, suffering is something ordinary and he who does not want to suffer may he stay at home!' At a time when the cult of antiquity had become popular in Italy, this Venetian wanted to encourage other more cowardly and easily frightened travellers to learn from his first-hand experiences:

Although I was away long enough, I did not see any building among all that I looked at which was worthy of admiration, with one exception: the place which is called by the Moors, Ochsur [Luxor]. It takes ten days from Cairo in a good wind. Note that I estimate the days at fifty miles a day and no more because of the fast current. And as I said this superb construction can be compared to all those the Ancients could build; the pyramids which are so renowned and unique, I consider little in comparison with this.

The Venetian had no European companions with him, so had to rely a great deal on his own resources. He shared with the Nubian boatmen the absorbing panorama of the river, where flocks of cranes, ibis, hoopoes and herons of all kinds waded and fished in the shallow waters and fed among the clumps of grasses, the flashing kingfishers that hovered and darted among the reeds, and the white egrets standing sharply defined against the muddy shores. As they sailed slowly up-river, he watched occasional mud brick villages go by, their curved walls decorated with pots, and white doves fluttering around the oval pigeon cotes. They passed country women with graceful carriage who carried tall jars on their heads, and children ever watchful over the dark brown cattle, prodding the donkeys almost hidden under the weight of their loads. As the Venetian and his crew tied up at dusk, just as the sun like a ball of fire sank swiftly in the west, they would have experienced the brief afterglow in the sky which sharply defined the darkening grey-green palm trees.

Having assumed that the countryside south of Cairo was universally green and fertile, similar to the delta, the traveller found much of the land along the river to be surprisingly arid, backed by bare flat-topped limestone hills which rarely rose above 200 feet. There were no towns of merit, only the mud brick villages, whose inhabitants, he thought, must have been ignorant of the easily worked building stone obtained from the nearby hills. Crops were more abundant in the fields on the plains of the west bank, stretching up to the mountain range. Random landing places dotted the shores where craft in large numbers gathered twice or three times a year to load up the ripe corn, sugar, vegetables, flax and other produce. After leaving the pyramids and the plain of the mummies the boat sailed past a number of such peasant villages:

> I will not tire myself to speak of them in detail because it would be too long. I will start only to tell you about the city of Tenssani, and of some buildings... On August 10, four days distance from Cairo I saw on the left bank of the river a celebrated and noble town called 'Tenssani' by the Moors and named Thebes by the Ancients; it was one of the principal towns of the Greek Empire. Today it can be recognised by the multitude of columns to be found there and the numbers of letters inscribed on some of the bases... At first sight along the river can be seen at some seventy steps, each of five feet, a triumphal arch of hard stone where there are three gates, one large and two small; all these gates are arched; above the middle gate there is a big arched window; above the other smaller ones, a square one over each. At each side there is a gate arched as well. This resembles the arch of Septimus or Constantine, but on the Egyptian [one] there are no historical figures like those on the former; on the contrary it is completely bare.

'Tenssani' (Antinopulis) was often confused with the site of pharaonic Thebes by early European travellers because of the classical ruins situated in the middle of a 'vast plain' about three miles from the

10.1 Triumphal arch in the ruins of Antinoë

mountains. Having passed through the arch, the Venetian perceived a road measuring about 400 hundred steps long and eight wide which led towards the mountain; on each side of it there was a long line of small broken columns about three steps apart. In the middle of the road, a little outside the line of columns, there were four larger ones of great beauty and of the same stone, with what he termed 'doric capitals of a pure style'. Each stood on a high base, positioned at each angle of a square. One of the plinths was copiously inscribed, and though he could not read the writing, he copied down the first line of script cut in large letters as a reference. At the end of the road was a further road crossing it, flanked by a similar file of columns, large and small and inscribed with the same letters. The Venetian guessed that originally the roads must have been covered over, and that four of the higher columns upheld the dome of a church. Wandering around the site, he assumed (correctly) that some of the pillars had been plundered from the area to underpin the porticos of the grand mosques in the capital.

After eight days of navigation from Cairo (about 400 miles) they came to Girga, capital of the province of Sa'id south of Sohag. From Sohag a track led west to the White Monastery of St Shenoute, founded

in AD 440, and the nearby smaller red-brick Red Monastery, founded
by St Bishoi. Although the Venetian did not mention them, these foundations gave peaceful hospitality at that time to Ethiopian monks on
their journeys to and from Alexandria and Jerusalem. Girga was a
largish town in the sixteenth century, without walls or monuments,
built of crude mud bricks and thatched roofs:

> I expected to see some fine things there according to tales I had heard
> from many people, but I saw nothing artistic not even handicrafts; very
> few shops, for the most part some weavers making coarse cloth, no
> fine textiles; some shoemakers, and a few other shops with things to
> eat. There were no other kinds of trades as is normal and necessary for
> a man's life; and you find three or four barbers with much difficulty
> and only two baths, two things as needful to the place as bread. This
> large village or town as one might call it, produces bread in great abun-
> dance as all the grain which is gathered from Girga to the south is
> brought there. As well, the town is surrounded by beautiful country,
> and is reasonably provided with livestock and poultry, the river
> supplies good fish at a very cheap price. But there is no wine neither
> here nor in any other place in Sa'id, except that some make it artifi-
> cially with raisins or 'zibib'. With this same 'zibib' they also make
> spirits. The Christians around the countryside make great use of these
> two drinks, as well as the Turks who are garrisoned there; and no week
> goes by without the arrival of some Turks coming from north or south;
> by north I mean Cairo and by South the Sa'id frontier and the land of
> Nubia.

Girga lay about half a mile away from the west bank of the Nile
and the August inundation currently flooding the land reached up to
the houses. An Arab sheikh who ruled the province lived there for four
to six months of the year. The rest of the time he camped outside the
town in the fields near the river, just at the end of the collection point
for the agricultural produce. He was overseen by a *sanjac*, the representative of the Turkish government, who ruled the militia, and the
local *qadi*, who dispensed justice.

Continuing south after Girga, the Nile takes a U-turn to make a great sweep to the north-east. At this point the mountain spurs come down sharply to the shore and it can be difficult for a sailing boat to proceed against the current when the north wind blows across the river. The Venetian had been told by the Moors that the mountains in the province were riddled with ancient pagan sepulchres, now the homes of tens of thousands of Christians. But the present inhabitants maintained that the sepulchres had been refuges for the Holy Fathers who had retreated there to do penance, something which the practical Venetian found hard to believe. How was it possible to withdraw from the world, even given their godliness, to live in a place where there was neither grass nor roots and nothing except stones? Convinced that the rock caves had merely been tombs, he explored seven of the most typical. Each had a small entrance two and a half cubits high and one and a half wide. Inside at ground level, he found a hole like the mouth of an oven, one cubit wide and almost as deep, in the centre of the rectangular floor. A number of steps descended perpendicularly from the hole, though the Venetian realised that of the seven steps he could see with the light of a candle, he could only go down four or five because the cavity was filled with rubble.

They resumed their journey to Qena on the curve of the river, where they slept the night in the boat, fearing the enormous numbers of deadly scorpions said to flourish in the area. The traveller did not disembark on the opposite bank to visit the temple of Hathor at Dendera (now on a desert ridge about five kilometres from the river) with its backdrop of yellow mountains. He decided that there was nothing to see of note or beauty. Today the temple is not visible from the Nile, though the traveller claimed to have perceived the ruins of a very well-known site 'rich in diverse monuments which the Moors called "Dendale"'. Perhaps he wanted to make haste to Luxor, perhaps in August 1589 the land towards the temple was flooded, or his curiosity was curbed by lethargy caused by one of the indefinable illnesses of the Nile valley, or he was deterred by the quantity of crocodiles said to be lurking among the slippery mud banks and shallows. The Moors told legends about the Christians who used to inscribe exorcisms on stone tablets many centuries ago, and throw them into the water, which they insisted curtailed attacks by the reptiles. The

Venetian conceded that these and many other things could have taken place by the power of God, through intercessions and prayers by the Holy Fathers who lived in the arid desert.

A short sail up-river brought them to Qus, where merchants took the road for the port of al-Qusayr on the Red Sea. Once the caravans had reached the limit of the green cultivation lining the Nile valley, they faced the parched earth of the eastern desert, where the blue sky shone in a shimmering line, and the ground glistened and dazzled the eye with flakes of flint, cornelian, quartz and alabaster. Nearing the coast, the camel tracks threaded through gorges between pink and dark blue rocky mountains. Scarce water of poor quality was available in a few brackish wells on the four- or five-day journey, during which caravans were often attacked by the Bedouin. Sailing vessels from al-Qusayr set off to the south along the coast to Ethiopia or to Suakin, governed by a Moorish sultan in South Arabia.

A further caravan route from Qus led to the port of 'Aydhab, to the south down the Red Sea coast. It was indicated on a fifteenth-century map, the *Egyptus Novelo*, drawn by the Florentine Pietro Massajio in 1456 for Alfonso I (the Magnanimous) of Aragon (ruled 1443–58). In medieval times, the Nile port of Qus, strategically placed on the eastern spice route, was second only to Cairo in size and importance, though it had declined after the discovery of the Portuguese sea route via the Cape of Good Hope to India. The town lay a good mile from the river, surrounded by fertile farmland, but in August craft could reach it by canal.

After the Venetian's party had sailed south for 58 kilometres, the flat-topped Theban mountains, set back from the green cultivation, appeared to the west. In spectacular dawns they reflect the fiery red light of sunrise, changing to a pinkish ochre hue by day when the waters of the river mirror the aquamarine blue of the sky. At sunset, the colour turns to a hard metallic blue before plunging suddenly into darkness. In the sixteenth century, although the Turk was master in name, stationed so far from Cairo he did not have the upper hand. The wild bands of local Arabs kept up a running fight with their enemy and would kill any prisoner they managed to capture. Whenever the Turks attempted retaliation, the Arabs strategically withdrew to their strongholds in the safety of the hills. They would agree to the taxes imposed on them only through negotiations with their chief, which they felt ensured some measure of independence.

The Venetian was unable to examine the 'large stretch of ground filled with ancient ruins' on the western plain stretched out before the mountain ridge, as it was flooded by the high August Nile. His boatmen were also afraid of attack by the Arabs. Though he was unable to examine and measure the two enormous colossi which caught his eye, he dismissed the mendacious tales of the Moors, who tried to convince him that among the fallen stones there was another Luxor, raised by a brother of the one who had built the first.

At last, the Venetian arrived at the ruins of the great temple complex of Luxor, dramatically situated on the east bank of the river. He was so impressed by this stupendous site that his description covered two pages of his manuscript. Possibly he alighted from the boat at the quay 'made of very large stones', which he said served as protection against the encroachment of the water. Starting his visit at 'a little temple' (the sanctuary?) he saw on each side a row of stone columns half a step in distance one from another:

> All these columns as well as others I will describe to you are in white stone, none are made of a single block, but contrary to many, these are very well assembled, they are very well worked and have most beautiful capitals. The columns which are visible number seventy, the others are buried under ground. You must know that this little temple as well as all those about which I am going to tell you has a flat roof and not in the form of a cupola, made of very large stones which go across from one column to the other; and in the interior, all the part going from the wall up to the roof was painted and sculpted with endless whimsicalities; under the roof a beautiful dark blue can be seen, with a number of gold stars.

He entered a second temple of the same type but taller and wider, which led to a third having only two rows of ten very thick columns. As there was no roof he thought it had not been finished: 'After the above columns, that is to say at the end of the two lines, are situated two high walls built like ramparts which I firmly believe were their sepulchres' (he refers to the Luxor temple pylons). He paced out the measurements visible above ground and guessed what could not be seen below:

> Of these walls the part opposite is sloping, the other is perpendicular. In the corners, there is the lintel which crosses [the wall] one pace below the summit, this summit is made like a lip turned upside down. In each of the walls four windows are visible, inside there are some rooms one above the other, crossed by a single length of stones, each of three paces; they are thick and wide. The summit of the ramparts is reached via some steps laid out in different ways, as soon as one reaches the ground the steps descend underground six or seven paces; in the basement another room can be seen which was I think at one time above the level of the ground. Then there is a passage of numerous steps which descends steeply... At the end of this are their tombs, that is to say sepulchres. A little in front of the two pylons at only one foot are placed two large statues of a stone which looks like black marble...

10.2 The pylons of Luxor temple

These statues emerge from the ground just about two and a half steps, but they are sunk in deeply, and I would like to tell you how they are made: their hands are clasped and they wear on the head material without a fold like a hat – I do not know with what to compare it but that matters little – At nearly three steps, can be seen two incomparable obelisks unblemished on all sides; today the part which protrude above the earth is exactly eleven palms, but the part below ground is very much larger. Neither Rome nor Alexandria nor all Egypt have ever possessed obelisks to compare with these two. Those of Rome and Alexandria, I have seen, seen again and measured. These two only surpass all the others in size. They are without fault and make a pair. They are standing and you can observe the rare beauty of mixed granite very pleasing to the eye, and then an infinite number of signs, more than I have ever been able to see, and so well carved that they appear to have been newly worked. My words will never be enough to describe their perfection. Ah, how it would be an extraordinary thing to see them placed in the middle of a beautiful square like that of Venice which is without equal in the whole world! Because infinite numbers of people would flock to see such trophies.

The Venetian had already surveyed the obelisks engraved with hieroglyphs which had lain prostrate for so long in the sepulchre of ruined monuments lying around in Rome. After they were resurrected, they eventually provided focal points of the master plan of the city carried out by the architect Domenico Fontana, according to the wishes of Pope Sixtus V (in office 1585–90). It became fashionable among sixteenth-century Italian painters to include such obelisks in their paintings of landscapes and in the decoration of stage sets, particularly when they wanted to emphasise a grand dramatic scene. Affluent Venice, so meticulously governed, her buildings decorated and gilded, her garnished squares and alleys well swept and clean, possessed no such coveted rarities.

So as not to tarry, I will project myself a good mile further away towards the mountain where things can be seen which are almost in the realm of the impossible; I will tell you exactly what I saw. Know that to the right of the two obelisks, at a good mile distant towards the east can be seen a large monument built in the form of a square; each side of the square is 250 feet of which the perimeter is just equal to a mile; you enter it through eight gates of blended stone... nowadays you only see five in all; each gateway lies between two pylons like those of which I spoke. Of these there are few. Before going inside I espied something astonishing: on each side of the two gates which face towards the direction of the obelisks [i.e. Luxor] there is a most beautiful pathway which I think used to join up with the temple of which I told you lying by the river, where today are the two obelisks. This can be identified, as the pathways which can be seen for a great distance, are decorated by a large number of stone lions [these are in fact ram-headed sphinxes] – I rightly say stone –, their chests facing towards the path, they are arranged in a row in a straight line, one and a half steps apart from one another, nowadays all these lions are without heads, they are twice as big as a horse. Each of them is placed on a large pedestal, which is twenty palms long and a half in height, and the lion is two palms less... the pedestal and the lion is made of one single block. In one pathway I counted one hundred and sixty in two rows, and in the other two hundred and forty. Each one [path] is seven steps wide exactly, and I am sure that this row of lions used to continue up to the other temple, as I told you.

On the farther side of the Karnak complex, outside a gate in the centre of one of the pathways, the Venetian noted about 30 further 'lions' – all were yellow-beige in colour with large paws, similar to the others, though the figures were only half as large. Painstakingly he counted and measured the statues, columns and pathways, undeterred by the searing heat of August, when the temperature reaches 34°C and the stones burn the feet. All the pylons (which he called gates) of the complex were of wonderful workmanship; the Venetian observed that they were built sloping with a reversed lip on the top like those of Luxor. He found that they were a good height, measuring up to twelve steps and seven in width. He thought the pylon facing towards the obelisks was the most attractive of all. It was beautifully decorated, incised all over, inside and out, in front and behind:

10.3 One of the rams on its pedestal lining the path at Luxor

I counted two hundred figures having a human shape; all are in low relief, even painted and all of them having different motifs, some with human face, some with that of a dog, of a deer and other similar animals and strange whimsicalities. All have a human body, some nude and others clothed. Among the great many figures is interspersed an endless number of writings and Egyptian letters so that there is no part which is not inscribed. In the square over the gateway at the top can be seen at an interval of nearly two steps, a pair of large, expanded wings just in the middle, also sculptured in low relief; in the centre of these wings is a circle, at the ends of which – I should say on each side – there is a short fat serpent. It is not only this gateway which has such a decoration but all the gates on different monuments that I saw, and I saw a good number of them; all have the circle, the wings and the serpent similar to that one. And this appears to have been a common sign to all the people of those times.

When the Venetian first penetrated the complex of the gigantic ruined Karnak temples, he found several small temples, like those of

Luxor except that they were larger and roofed with stones, painted blue inside with yellow stars. An infinite number of different pictures of men, animals and other 'whimsicalities' painted in good colours unfolded before his eyes. In one place he noticed figures of saints, with some small Greek letters which indicated that the Christians had used the location as a church.

For an area of about a mile, the entire ground appeared to be covered by enormous sandstone or granite blocks. Colossal statues lay broken on the ground; their arms measured fifteen palms from the shoulder to the index finger of the hand. Giant pieces of pitifully ruined obelisks were scattered around; only two of them stood intact. At the principal temple near the river there were two large pylons similar to those of Luxor. When the Venetian stepped inside the temple he thought he was dreaming, as there was such a number of columns of immense thickness all in the form of trees. All the columns (which inevitably the Venetian measured and counted) formed an elegant square (in fact a rectangle) and according to his calculations there were six rows, each of 16 columns, ranging the length of the temple. The middle pathway, measuring three steps, was higher and wider than the others. One of the stone slabs, which he estimated must have measured more than four steps, covered over the pathway from side to side forming a roof, which was painted blue. The Venetian was struck by the beauty of the capitals, coloured and engraved with figures. Lying on the capital of each column was a large stone which connected one column to the next; he assumed that these made the foundation of the roof, though in many places the place was open to the sky. The most astonishing sight of all was of two ruined columns, which, in falling down together with all the weight they supported, were resting against the others, something the Venetian (with his evident knowledge of building structures) found very frightening to see. 'I do not believe that a painter could contrive to paint a ruin as monstrous as the one that I have just described to you.'

Having passed through the forest of columns, he found a further incised gateway like the first he described, only ruined. Among the broken colossi in front of it were four obelisks, two standing, with two others lying at their feet. Having measured the point of one of the fallen

obelisks, the Venetian guessed that it made a pair with the largest of
the two still erect, those standing being dissimilar. The largest was
'quite beautiful, of a plain granite with a lot of white'. According to
the ruins he had seen, the Venetian assumed (wrongly) that each of the
Karnak 'gateways' must have been furnished with similar colossi and
obelisks:

> Consider if this awesome monument is not superior to the seven
> wonders of the world, of which one still exists, that is to say one of
> the pyramids of pharaoh which in comparison to this great work is a
> small thing. And I do not send the man who wants to see this monu-
> ment to the end of the world, as it is only ten days from Cairo; one can
> be conveyed there at little cost.

It is hard to know how much was left standing among the ruins of
the Luxor and Karnak temples in 1589, and though the Venetian noted
the Christian inscriptions (in the temple of Tutmosis III on the eastern
side of the great temple of Amun) he failed to mention any later Arab
settlements. There are no sixteenth-century pictorial records and the
Venetian's account of the site appears to be unique among Europeans
of his time. Besides using his hands and feet for measuring (an Italian
palma of that period denoted a hand's breadth) he did not say if he
had brought measuring instruments with him. In any case, he made an
extraordinarily detailed appraisal of the complexity of the temples and
enclosures in the time at his disposal. After careful examination of the
painted decorations he became more critical and started to compare
the different workmanship on the various buildings. Having entered
a small granite temple without a column, through a large tall gate, with
two other gates on each side of 'hardest black stone', he saw that all
the ground, the walls and the ceiling were covered with the usual
figures, signs and inscriptions and that everything was painted in finest
colours. 'But it can be seen here that the craftsmen have worked with
more care than in other places.'

To clamber over the temple complexes of Luxor and Karnak and
to make a survey of the sunbaked ruins in so short a time must have
taxed the Venetian's energy. Even the modern tourist who is directed

around this bewildering collection of buildings by on-site guides, keen to inform their flocks of the lengthy chronology of the pharaohs and their religious practices, would understand the confusion and exhaustion brought on by the pleasures of ruins. However, this indefatigable sixteenth-century Venetian did not mention tiredness: 'If I was able to remember everything that I saw in this place,' he wrote, 'I would have much to tell. But I will finish with your good grace.'

A day's journey up-river brought them to Esna on the west bank where river craft moored at the village to stock up with food, which was scarce and expensive further south in Nubia. It was a place where the crews bought flour and baked quantities of flat round loaves in the village ovens. They carried them on board, stacked high in locally woven baskets almost identical to those of pharaonic times. Kneading the dough sometimes took all night; it was prepared by the local women in a special basket, and the bread usually kept for some days.

In 1877, the intrepid Egyptologist Amelia Edwards had difficulty in locating the Ptolemaic temple in the town. She looked round in vain for any sign of pylon or portico: its stupendous mass of yellow limestone masonry was quite hidden by dilapidated wooden gateways recessed between neighbouring houses. Eventually she came upon a temple neither ruined nor defaced but buried to the chin in the accumulated rubbish of a score of centuries. Three hundred years earlier, the Venetian described it as being very ancient, standing in the middle of the town. Perhaps much more was uncovered in his time, for he described it as being supported by 24 columns in a row, 'twenty five palms in circumference'. He found the temple entirely perfect, lacking nothing; it was used as a store for wheat, and both the interior and exterior walls, columns and roof were carved all over with the usual signs. One frieze showed some small ram-headed figures two palms long on a capital, holding an offering; opposite was 'a falcon having one folded wing and the other spread out'. He sketched a cartouche containing 'the god or the king' and noted a 'great many men with sheep's beards holding a baton in their hands, and certain others who were holding things of extravagance, so much so that my brain cannot bring to mind all that I saw of different shapes and in numbers of places'. Having looked at so much Egyptian writing, by now he was able to recognise that the hieroglyphs covering the earlier buildings at Karnak and Luxor differed from the Ptolemaic letters on the later temple of Esna.

On the following day they arrived at the temple of Horus at Edfu on the west bank, dominating a site above the broad surrounding valley. The Venetian was particularly impressed by the pylons, resembling those of Luxor, the most intact and highest part of the temple. He found a gateway leading to a court containing 50 standing columns, at the end of which was the temple entrance; nearby there were other buildings, though he said they were broken down and ruined. Further upstream low hills rose up on the east bank and the temple of Kom Ombo appeared, situated on an elevated promontory. The diligent traveller copied down three lines of Greek letters written on the frieze over the door. As before, he took time to count the columns, noting their position, and a wall covered over with figures and signs.

By now they were sailing far to the south, to the limit of the province of Sa'id up to Qasr Ibrin in Nubia, 'where the people with white skin disappear'. Approaching Aswan the Venetian was at once aware of the abrupt change of scenery, as limestone rock gave way to red and

10.4 A group of Nubians

black granite and the first boulders were seen jutting out from the Nile. Initially the traveller was impressed by the town, which was spread out in the shape of a half moon on the bank of the river, the houses behind elevated one above the other like rows in a theatre; but he soon realised that they were only ruined shells, open to the sky. Inside the town there was not a living soul. Beyond the surrounding walls, the Venetian saw the low hills of variously coloured granite shimmering in the sun in hues of pink, black and silver, from which a 'large number of obelisks and columns were hewn that are found in different parts of the world'. In the quarries, he discerned ancient marks cut by the tools of pharaonic workmen while they were prising out the mono-lithic blocks. (Afterwards they were rolled down to the river and floated downstream on flotillas of rafts.) The Venetian surmised that if there had been no granite in Aswan (only to the south of it) the obelisks could not have been transported down the river because of the cataracts lying above the town:

> Having arrived at Assouan, every boat wishing to go to Ebrin has to discharge all the merchandise it is carrying; this is transported on camel back for a distance of seven miles. For each camel you give seven or even eight medins. At the end of these seven miles the merchandise and the owners wait for the boats which are rapidly brought by the wind when the Nile is high – but there must be a north wind, otherwise if there is not a strong wind, they are held back by the force of the current and they cannot go forward... afterwards they are pulled by men with stout ropes against the force of the current, and in this way they take the whole day to arrive at their goal. Now I will tell you why there must be so much supervision in this place. Above Assouan or rather opposite, one sees 150 rocks among which there are some large ones like small islands, three of them are up to five miles in circumference. All these small islands are of mixed stone [granite] and three of them are so high that they resemble mountains. These small islands which are low in certain places and where there is a little piece of workable land are nine in number; and each one is inhabited by one or two fami-lies. The rest comprise only large and small rocks which stretch over a distance of seven miles; the river in this part is only a mile wide. The

reason why there is a violent current in this part is on account of so many rocks to be found. This rocky place is called Seilal by the inhabitants and neighbouring people.

In fact the first cataract was a succession of rapids in a rocky basin extending about two thirds of the way between Elephantine and Philae. Before the construction of the first Aswan dam (opened 1902), boats were hauled up the inclines of foaming water, divided into three or four headlong torrents, by gangs of workmen overseen by the 'Sheikh of the cataract' who exacted fixed payment for each boat. Of its spectacular aspect Amelia Edwards wrote:

> The scenery of the First Cataract is like nothing else in the world – except the scenery of the second. It is altogether new, strange and beautiful. It is incomprehensible that travellers should have written of it in general with so little admiration. They seem to have been impressed by the wildness of the waters, by the quaint forms of the rocks, by the desolation and grandeur of the landscape as a whole; but scarcely at all by its beauty which is paramount.

When Amelia entered the cataract, she described it as 'a fairy archipelago', comprising countless islands interspersed with red, purple and black granite rocks. A few of the larger islands were crowned with clumps of palms; and were covered in gum trees, acacias, date palms and feathery tamarisks 'all festooned together under a hanging canopy of yellow blossomed creepers'.

Although the Venetian originally intended to sail only to the boundaries of the province of Sa'id, perhaps he was encouraged by the Nubian crew to explore further sites in their native country. As they proceeded up-river, be found the high granite mountains that encroached onto the banks 'very frightening to see'. In certain places where the mountains receded, any good ground was sown with millet. Of necessity the fields were long and narrow and were irrigated by engines that worked day and night. The country was sparsely peopled, there was no town or city, apart from two fortresses occupied by the Turks. Although he thought it very poor and wretched country, in spite of the poverty the

Venetian felt secure, since they could sleep peacefully everywhere the
boats tied up. This was in contrast to the landing places to the north,
where it was necessary to be always on the watch for raiders.

After the first cataract, while they waited for the boats to be hauled
over the rapids, he explored the island of Philae and the temple of Isis
where, according to legend, the goddess had found the heart of her
husband Osiris:

> on one side appear some very large stones; quite near there is built a
> temple similar to the others but this one is small; and I will tell you
> how it is built. You see two of those high walls like ramparts, but here
> they are not very high; they must be some ten feet in height; in the
> middle of the said ramparts there is a door which opens on to a court,
> and then another which leads into a temple, less high than the
> ramparts, from there you go into another, lower, and into another very
> low, which is very funereal and dark. In the first two I saw that the
> building is supported on the columns, like the others; it is completely
> finished, so well that it lacks nothing; and in this temple many things
> are depicted... A man who is holding by the hair thirty small kneeling
> figures, their hands folded; near to him you can see the king who is
> seated in majesty with a large butcher's knife in his hand... Elsewhere
> there is a person kneeling who is offering a baboon in a basin to the
> king; another is wounding a tortoise with a spear; some men as big as
> giants who seem in different ways to be striking; some falcons who
> have a large ring in their talons; a lot of men who are sitting, who are
> standing, who are sleeping, who are dancing and who are playing
> music; and many others with griffon's heads [possibly these were on
> the columns of the Temple of Hathor]. Outside the temple on the oppo-
> site side where there are the two pylons, there are two others at the
> end of the court and these are a little higher; in the middle, there is a
> gate through which you go into a court eighty steps long and fifteen
> wide. And lengthways, you see a porch which stretches from one end
> to the other, built on some columns two steps high and fourteen palms
> in circumference, it is covered over with great stones laid flat: and along
> the side of the wall there are a lot of big windows which overhang the
> water; the same arrangement is found in one of the extremities of the

court overlooking the river... Near these buildings there is another which from afar has a fair aspect but it is nothing but a collection of fourteen columns, which make a room closed on every side and open to the sky above... on one of the walls I saw a sculptured cross.

The following day they left Philae, then one of the most scenic places in Egypt, and sailed for one and a half days, seeing nothing except the lowering mountains ranged along the banks of the Nile. At the village of Taifa, there were some small houses along the east bank and a few fields, irrigated by some creaking *sakiehs* working overtime. The Venetian saw 'about thirty sepulchres with one door in the front, certain of them having three. On the lintels over the doors there were the spheres in the form of a globe in the middle of the wings, as well as the two serpents as I described before.' A little further on, the land bordering the banks became little wider than a towing path and the Nile became extremely narrow, the current ran strongly and the water was very deep. Emerging from the gorge, the river became wider, and coursed through a small cataract which was easily negotiated. In the middle of it the Venetian counted 25 large and small rocks; four or five of them had buildings on top which he thought were small ruined churches, though he was told they might have been hermitages for some of the Holy Fathers. Further on, the river bank became sandy and unsuitable for cultivation, and the granite mountains merged into ones of white stone, like those of Sa'id.

At this point, the traveller's enthusiasm for ancient temples waned, as he owned that he did not trouble himself to see 'one of those monuments built in the same manner which I described at "Isne" and "Itofu"'. This was the Ptolemaic temple of Kalabsha, in fact the largest free-standing Nubian temple, built of sandstone blocks. It was dismantled in 1962–63 and its 13,000 blocks were transferred and rebuilt in the vicinity of the High Dam built by the Russians in the time of President Nasser.

Sailing onwards for two hours into the night, the Venetian's attention was suddenly captured at the sight of 'a magnificent sepulchre cut into the mountain'. In fact, it was the speos temple of Rameses II dedicated to Ptah at Girf Husayn, lying opposite a small, fortified, ruined village that the Venetian called 'Sabbagora'. From far off, the Venetian saw the entrance, which inevitably afterwards he went to measure, finding it to be three steps high, one and a half steps wide and one step deep in the centre. Inside there was a spacious room eight paces square and four high:

> This hall is built in such a way that it cannot collapse for the reason there are three naves; in the central nave which is a little wider than the others, there are three pillars on each side, on each of which is carved a tall statue two good steps high, the stance of these statues leads you to believe that they are holding up all the weight.[1]

On the sculptured walls of the hall, in the other naves, there were 28 other life-size figures in high relief 'connected to the wall by their backs in similar fashion... All these statues have human form except some which have heads of animals; all are standing in different attitudes; they are painted.' The Venetian described the plan of the temple with great precision: it contained the hypostyle hall with Osiris pillars, the vestibule and the sanctuary. Inside some of the dark funereal rooms, they were assailed by an 'infinite number of bats' whose excrement produced an offensive acrid smell. A glimmer of daylight from the entrance enabled the Venetian to discern a niche cut into the end wall of the central hall, where he saw four large statues seated in majesty. On the ground in front of them was a small altar. Outside, in a large open-air court, there were some tall sculptured figures resting on plinths, cut in the same manner as those inside. But the massive Ramesside statues were not to the Venetian's taste: 'To tell the truth they are not figures of good style, but you can see that it is a very fine piece of work'. (This temple has now fallen victim to progress and has disappeared under the waters of Lake Nasser.)

After sailing ever to the south, into the middle of the night, they tied up at a small place known as Aqaba on the east bank, where there were three houses at the foot of the mountain, 'the highest of all those

---

1 The statues in high relief consist of two groups: both depict Rameses II flanked by divinities.

of the region'. The Nubians told the Venetian that the road through the mountains led into the desert and to the land of the Funj, ruled by a black king from his capital in Sennar. They reassured him that after only seven days, a wayfarer could rejoin the river and had only to follow it to reach Ethiopia to the south-east. The journey need not be feared, as no robbers or murderers would waylay and food could be found everywhere for men and their camels.

Half a day upstream, the Venetian arrived at a village where a fortress, the residence of the governor and his family, lay in a strip of land about three or four miles long and two hundred steps wide. It was an important post, having a garrison of about 200 foot soldiers and horsemen living in reed huts outside it. The village was sizeable, containing 500 Nubian houses, although the nearby fields grew nothing except millet and a few onions and cucumbers. About one hundred steps away from the fortress, he saw a further sepulchre cut in the low limestone mountain. On the interior walls, among the number of strange figures, he described a scene depicting a dead body carried by ten people amid strange melodies from various instruments, dancers and songs. This he thought portrayed the people of those times rejoicing at a funeral. During the ten days they moored at the village, the Venetian was told that several years before, the Turks had wanted to annex Dongola down-river to the south, in the land of the Funj (now part of the Sudan), home of a number of Nubian tribes. Accordingly they had set sail to attack it, but God was with the natives, since the Turks were foiled by the cataract about two days further on. Only one boat returned intact; all the others were broken up on the rocks.

The frontier of the kingdom of the Funj was the limit of the anonymous traveller's journey of discovery. Even though the caravan route ahead was well charted, he was not tempted to proceed and once more he leaves us in the dark. His tale finishes abruptly in Nubia and there is no description of the return journey, though he admitted that he was dissuaded from continuing further because of his health.

Who was this anonymous traveller? Over the centuries, the Venetian Council of Ten had discussed the possibility of broaching with the sultans of Egypt the subject of constructing a canal from the Mediterranean to the Red Sea. It never materialised. The question erupted once more when the Portuguese started their trade route to India, but with the defeat of the Mamluks by the Ottomans, the idea appeared to lapse. It seems, however, that it was the Ottomans themselves who once more revived the subject, since they were obliged to construct their ships at Suez in order to fend off attacks by the Portuguese in the Red Sea. But once more nothing came of it. It was considered too dangerous an undertaking, since it was feared that the inundation pouring in from the Red Sea would pollute the Nile with salt water. But could the Venetian have been sent to do a feasibility study? At this time, too, Venice was enjoying a period of construction. There arose such buildings as the Scuola di San Rocco, finished in 1549, Sansovino's library, which transformed the Piazza di San Marco, Palladio's masterpiece, the church of S. Giorgio Maggiore, designed in 1565, and the erection of the stone bridge at the Rialto by Antonio da Ponte, paid for after the cancellation of the public debt in the 1580s and 1590s. All these works would have required the skills of a prodigious number of surveyors and master craftsmen. Venice had always enjoyed important trading relations with Egypt, so was this author, so obviously fascinated with ancient buildings, one of the versatile citizens of the Serenissima who had been sent to Cairo to research a construction project?

* * *

Because of the difficulties of travelling freely through Egypt, few Europeans had gained the fastnesses of Ethiopia, a name that alternated in their accounts with that of Abyssinia or Abassia. The Mamluk sultans feared the semi-mythical Christian Ethiopian emperor who ruled beyond the lands of Islam, known to Europeans by his title of 'Prester John'. It was thought that he could make the Nile (which, it was said, rose in Ethiopia from a cavern guarded by two large towers) flow in another direction. The reason the ruler did not do so was because all the Christians in Egypt would starve. Nevertheless, travellers were told that the sultans paid annual tribute to propitiate their southern neighbour, and further of the rather dubious 'fact' that Christians in Jerusalem were excused from paying taxes.

Maps of the region were drawn from first-hand accounts brought back to Italy by Ethiopian monks who went to Jerusalem, Rome, and Florence. Alessandro Zorzi (b. Venice 1470), a Venetian traveller, collected up several of these itineraries in Venice between 1519 and 1524 and compared the information about the choice of routes taken through Egypt to Axum and Barara, the chief cities of the emperor. Besides the caravan route from Qos on the Nile, frequently used by Ethiopian patriarchs to the port of al-Qusayr on the Red Sea, Ethiopian monks followed other river and overland passages to and from Egypt, which they recorded.

In 1439, during the reign of the sultan al-Zahir Jaqmaq, two Ethiopian monks from Jerusalem went to attend the ecclesiastical Council of Florence, set up by the Pope with the Coptic Patriarch of Alexandria and Nicodemus, Superior of the Jerusalem community. It was convened to try to unify the differing sects of the Christian church with Rome, an attempt that ended in failure. While in Florence, the Ethiopian delegates were questioned particularly about their country. Their answers provided important information that was subsequently used by contemporary mapmakers. Both the *Egyptus Novelo*, made for Alfonso of Aragon, and Fra Mauro's beautiful round map, drawn at Brother Niccolò's house in S. Michele di Murano, included such Ethiopian material. The medieval opinions originating from Ptolemy showed that many of the earlier concepts of the region were erroneous and should be amended. Ethiopian monks from Jerusalem travelled to Rome and met others who had risked the long journey from their native country to set up a community in the Holy City. This community was attached to Santo Stefano de' Mori, behind St Peter's, and afterwards became a centre of Ethiopic studies.

It seems that the Vatican was not content with the outcome of the Council of Florence. Francesco Suriano of the Franciscan convent at Mount Sion in Jerusalem recounted that in 1480, the Guardian of the community despatched two of their number, Friar Francis Sagara, a Spaniard, and Friar John of Calabria, as nuncios from the Holy See, as well as a layman, Battista of Imola, to the court of the 'Christian King popularly known as Prester John'. These missionaries were sent in order to make known to the king his errors and to convert him to the Roman Catholic faith. Besides doctrinal differences, the Vatican took great exception to the loose behaviour of the king, said to be descended from Solomon and Sheba, because he had many wives, all considered legitimate, besides a number of concubines. This missionary endeavour was not the first attempted by the Latin church. In 1316 eight Dominicans sent by Pope John XXII arrived in Abyssinia and made a number of converts to Catholicism. Some Abyssinians even entered the Dominican order.

Having left the friars in Ethiopia, Battista returned to Mount Sion in 1483, where, curious to learn the details of the journey, Francisco Suriano summoned Battista to his cell. Battista related that they left Cairo for the court of Prester John in January 1481. They sailed up the Nile for about 30 days through Egypt until they 'reached a town of the Sultan of Cairo called Nachada and paid one ducat each for freight'. They remained there for a whole month as the roads were unsafe, after which they crossed to the east side of the Nile and walked all day. In the evening they reached a town called 'Acherman' (probably Qena) and struck off east through the desert to al-Qusayr where they sailed southwards along the coast to Ethiopia. Their journey from Jerusalem took 11 months, entailing many hardships. Francesco's account of it was relayed back to Italy to satisfy the curiosity of his sister, Sister Sixta, and the community of Poor Clares of the monastery of Santa Lucia at Foligno. He introduced Sister Sixta as being an interrogator whose questions he answered in the form of long explanations. His sister asked why the Vatican did not send their own legates, as was the custom to such a great lord. Francesco did not hesitate to reply bluntly:

> From hesitation and fear that the great Sultan of Cairo, as piously believed, would have impeded the journey on account of what might easily happen to him, namely, that if the Church came to an agreement with Prester John, in a short time they would take all their dominions. And also because the legates travel with such worldly pomp and are not apt to undergo what they would meet in those countries, many discomforts. But on our Friars, used to suffering and penance, it was convenient to impose this burden.

Having reached al-Qusayr, Battista related that they paid three ducats each for freight and half a sack of flour, as was customary for the sea voyage. After a journey of 35 days, sailing about fifty miles a day in a favourable wind, they eventually reached Suakin, a town on an island half a mile from the continent, inhabited by Arabs. 'To the lord of which, according to custom we gave a multi coloured cloth, a burnous and five pieces of soap.' Five hundred miles further on they came to Decan, a mercantile port owned by the Saracens (though controlled by the Christian emperor Prester John). They sailed past many large islands but not finding a sea passage they decided to strike out overland from Massawa, hiring a good guide and buying two camels for eight ducats. Though descriptions of distances are misleading, their overland journey to Prester John's court took them 125 days including stops, with a combination of riding on camels and mules as well as walking on foot. During this time they were treated hospitably by the various lords through whose lands they crossed. Eventually they came to 'Gennata Giryorgis', where lay the King's Church and where the last king had lately been interred.[2] It contained a large ornate organ 'made in the Italian fashion', which greatly surprised them. Continuing along their way, they were delayed for thirty days by bad weather and a river (which they mistook for the Nile) in spate from the rains; at length after a further ten days they arrived at the court of Prester John in a place called Barara. According to one Brother Zorgi, who supplied the Venetian, Alessandro Zorzi, with information about the region, Barara, where the air was temperate, was one of the principal cities of the Ethiopian king, who lived for a part of the time in a castle on the mountain. A Franciscan, one Brother Raphael, who left Jerusalem in 1518, also described his journey from Barara to Cairo for Alessandro Zorzi. He related that besides Barara, Prester John lived in the great city of Axum, which had a hot climate. Moreover, around the city could be found all kinds of fruits, herbs, roses and countless milk animals. Silk, cotton and wool were among the crops from which the people made their clothes and

---

2 It was customary for each Ethiopian ruler to build a stone church for himself. Such a church was commonly referred to by travellers as 'the King's Church'.

there was iron in great quantity. The men and women were fine and wore their hair long.

Battista Imola and the two friars found ten Italians of good repute at the court of Prester John, some of whom had been living there for 25 years. He asked the men why they had gone to that strange country:

> They replied that their intention was to seek jewels and precious stones. But since the king did not allow them to return, they were all discontented though they were all according to his grade, well rewarded and supplied by the king who was pleased by their political and civil conversation.

10.5 Prester John depicted as being king of both Egypt and Ethiopia

Evidently the king found the company of Europeans congenial: one Gregorio Bicini, a Venetian who had left his wife and familiy back home in Venice, became his secretary, was given an estate and acted as the king's partner at chess and cards each night.

Among the Italians living there was Niccolò Brancaleone, a Venetian architect and painter who had been employed for over 40 years decorating churches for the emperor. Brother Raphael saw the colouring materials that were used for the pictures in religious buildings dug up in large quantities near Axum. He related that the Ethiopian temples, palaces and forts were vaulted and covered with lead. This architecture resembled medieval European and Middle Eastern military architecture with features such as domed angle towers, barrel vaulting and decorated stone arches. It was employed in both palaces and churches for the dwellings and burial places of Ethiopian kings until the middle of the eighteenth century, when those Christian monarchs could no longer afford such constructions on a grand scale. The Portuguese Franciscan envoy Francesco Alvarez, who had been received favourably by the Ethiopian emperor Claudius (son of Lebna Dengel), met Niccolò Brancaleone, who was still there 40 years later. Francesco related that he had seen Niccolò's paintings in the church of St George, originally built by the emperor Za'ra Ya'kob (ruled 1434–68) as his burial place. (Za'ra Ya'kob had sent the Ethiopian monks to the Council of Florence in 1439.)

In 1487, shortly after the visit of the Franciscan friars, the king of Portugal thought it expedient to seek a friendship with Prester John. He also wished to verify that he was in fact the Ethiopian emperor and not the fabled ruler said to live in India, as many had thought. After paying two visits to India, his envoy, Pedro de Covilham, eventually arrived at the court in 1490. Though he sent many reports back to Portugal, in his turn Pedro became yet another European to be ensnared in the royal web. Wound round in its filmy embrace, he was never allowed to depart.

On Battista Imola's return via Egypt, Francesco Suriano questioned him closely about the condition of Ethiopia and its inhabitants. He was told that the king kept his treasury in a grotto with a good guard:

their habitations were made of thin reeds daubed inside and outside with mud. There was no stone building except that of every king, who when he was enthroned must build a church in which to be buried... The country has gold without limit: it has little wheat and no wine; it has meat enough, has a dense population of ugly coarse and witless people. They have no arms to fight, their arrows and lances are of reeds. The king would never go to battle with less than two or three hundred thousand. Each year he fights for the faith. He does not pay his warriors but feeds them, and they are exempt from every royal exaction. And all these fighting men are chosen, registered and branded with fire on the arm with a royal sign. Nobody wears woolens which they have not, but linen. Men and women are naked from the navel upwards and are bare footed; they are ever full of lice. A weak kneed people of little strength and stamina, but they are proud. They are zealous in the faith and more fervent in spirit than all other Christians.

Among the miscellaneous information both true and fanciful, Francesco was told that the air and water in Abyssinia nurtured worms in the human body, that the Abyssinians had their own language and letters, and that they circumcised and baptised with water. Francesco was already acquainted with the Abyssinian community, the 'vassals of Prester John' who lived in the church of the Holy Sepulchre in Jerusalem, and in spite of his prejudices (he asserted that they were 'heretics of the worst kind, who adhered to the Jacobites following the heresies of James, Patriarch of Alexandria'), he conceded that the religious led a very austere life:

they are very vigilant at night in singing the psalms. They jump in the fervour of the spirit while chanting and clap their hands. They are far more fervent in the faith than any other Christian nation, On the night of the principal feasts of the year, they read the whole Gospels, and do not sleep that night, but spend it all in spiritual canticles.

According to accounts, the all-powerful emperor Prester John lived in opulent style: his rich empire was large, comprising several king-

10.6 Prester John as the legendary Christian ruler of Ethiopia

doms and provinces. Europeans had come to believe that the name 'Prester John' was common to all the rulers of the land of Ethiopia, as 'pharaoh' was to the kings of Egypt. 'Prester' may have stood for 'Priest' or 'Presbyter', because of the cross which was carried aloft in front of him. His surname was David, as the emperors of Rome were called Caesar. On guard over his person there were 50,000 trumpeters. When he went to war, he had before him two crosses, one of gold and the other of precious stones, to show how much greater he was than other kings. His handsome gilded bed from China was decorated with rich hangings surrounded by beautiful screens given to him by the Patriarch of Alexandria. The coverlets and blankets came from India and China, while precious carpets of silk and skins adorned his rooms. When the court came to dine, they sat on carpets, their food was consumed at low tables with no napkins or tablecloths, the wine was mild, made of honey, barley and water. The viceroys and nobles were dressed in the Turkish style; round their necks they wore gold chains like skeins with many turns of yarn wound round them, and on their arms were matching bracelets. Their girdles were of very big pieces of gold, their swords large, sheathed in silver scabbards.

The Portuguese had thought it expedient to be on friendly terms with the kings of Ethiopia because the country lay in a strategic position close to their trading route to India. After the arrival of Pedro de Covilham in 1490, the further delegation sent in 1520 under Francesco Alvarez and Dom Roderigo da Lima spent five years in the suite of Prester John. As a result of this sojourn, a compilation of works was made entitled *The History, Manners and Customs of Ethiopia*, which shed much light on this relatively unknown land.

Odoardo Lopez, a Portuguese, a further visitor to the opulent court of the emperor, described 'his courtiers and Lordes apparelled with cloth of silk, and adorned with golde and sundry jewelles'. Odoardo witnessed the feast day of Our Lady in August when all the kings and principal lords assembled in the city together with people from all parts on pilgrimage:

> They have a very solemne procession, and out of the church, from whence they walke, they carry with them an Image of the Blessed Virgin the Mother of God, which is as big as any common person, and all of Gold. This Image hath for the eyes two very rich and great Rubies, all the rest of the bodie is garnished and adorned with jewels and curious works: and it is carried on a frame made of Golde, of a wonderful and admiral workmanshippe. In this procession also there cometh abroade in publike shew Prete Gianni himselfe eyther upon a Chariot of Gold, or els upon an Elephant, all garnished and trimmed with jewelles and such rare and precios thinges, and covered all over with cloth of Golde. The multitude of people that runneth to see this Image is so great, that many are stifled in the presse and die thereupon.

The friars despatched from Mount Sion in Jerusalem, Francis Sagara and John of Calabria, evidently had a frustrating time in Ethiopia. Battista of Imola the layman brought back letters to Jerusalem saying that although the friars had remained there for eight months, they had failed even to get an audience. It seemed that the king had recently died and that as his son Alexander who succeeded him was a minor aged 12, there were 'certain lords who ruled' who did not like their mission and therefore prevented it.

Matters in Jerusalem had not run smoothly either. When two Ethiopian clerics who had been sent as ambassadors to Sixtus IV in Rome had returned from the Holy City, one of them renounced his faith to become a Muslim. It was assumed that Anthony, the second monk, would then proceed to Abyssinia carrying the papacy's exhortations to the king to renounce his heresies. Instead, Anthony tarried two years in Jerusalem and, having spent all the money given him by the Vatican for the journey, did not dare to return to Ethiopia, making excuses about the difficulties of travel. All of which, as the Guardian of Mount Sion, Friar Paul of Chaneto, explained, 'defrauded the holy See of its intention' towards the emperor.

Frustrated by this delay, and learning of the difficulties of his friars at the emperor's court, the Father Guardian Friar Paul dictated a letter to Francesco Suriano addressed to 'The King of Ethiopia called Prester John'. He pointed out to the young ruler (Alexander, ruled 1478–94) the error of his ways and exhorted him to receive Friar John of Calabria, who had patiently endured so many perils to visit him (his companion Francis Sagara had been delayed on the way because of illness):

> Give ready ear to the said messenger Friar John: send to him your wise men, your scholars, your bishops, your religious, that they may come to the light of the Holy Roman Church... Expedite, sweep, make haste, decide, don't spare gold, send men worthy of your Regal Majesty, do not procrastinate for in delay is danger. And though a youth in years, show yourself grey haired and old in thought: see that the facts correspond to the reports of your ambassadors.

Father Paul expressed his grief that the monk Anthony 'still holds the paternal and amicable letters, the presents as signs of love, the picture of the Supreme Pontiff himself, the ring from his own finger, sent by him to your excellency in proof of his good faith... all of which I cannot mention without tears'.

So ardent was the desire to bring the young emperor and his people to salvation that the community of Mount Sion decided that the luckless Battista of Imola should be sent yet again on the long, perilous journey to the Ethiopian court with their Guardian's letter. Francesco Suriano did not mention the outcome of this further expedition, but judging by later descriptions of the Abyssinian court by the Portuguese travellers, it would appear that once more, the fervent missionary zeal of the papacy was frustrated and their exhortations fell on deaf ears.

* * *

We will never know how many anonymous Europeans died during their Egyptian travels. Those who lived to tell the tale faced up to their hardships with heroism, stemming from optimism and sturdy common sense. While pilgrims were uplifted by their Christian faith, traders were buoyed up by the expectation of satisfying European markets ever eager for Eastern luxuries and by the hope of profits, however precarious they might have been. All travellers to Egypt became experienced in ways of life very different from their own. In this respect they had an advantage over the Muslims at this time, who did not usually travel to Europe, where they too would have benefited from their increased understanding of Frankish customs. Catalogues of grumbles and self-pity about the discomforts and dangers faced by these early visitors to Egypt only occasionally intruded into their accounts. Not until the nineteenth century, with advances in technology and transport, were the difficulties and dangers of desert travel and sea journeys somewhat ameliorated. The accounts of these earlier travellers, graphically related in a variety of Frankish languages, provide a panorama of dramatic, often dangerous journeys, following the same routes and using the same modes of transport as their predecessors over many centuries. After their return home, when they became a focus of attention, travellers could be excused if they were occasionally tempted to embroider their tales. There was a common saying in sixteenth-century Italy: 'Se non è vero è molto ben trovato'

('If it is not true it is a happy invention'). On the whole, though, exaggerations were few, and do not detract from the truly heroic achievements depicted in these travellers' tales.

Notes

General: Sauneron (ed.), *Voyage du Vénitien Anonyme*, pp. 30(31)–152(153) (even pages in old Venetian dialect); A. Edwards, *A Thousand Miles Up the Nile*, pp. 107–46; for the modern traveller to follow the Venetian's journey see Seton-Williams and Stocks (eds.), *Blue Guide Egypt*, pp. 483–650; for a discussion of the Venetian Senate's proposal to dig a Suez canal see Fulin, 'Il Canale di Suez e la Repubblica di Venezia', pp. 175–99; Monneret de Villard, 'La prima esplorazione archeologica dell'alto Egitto', pp. 19–48. **Ethiopia:** Beckingham and Hungerford (eds.), *Some Records of Ethiopia 1593–1646* (title of Prester John, pp. 3–7; emperor's style of living, pp. 57–60); for a discussion of the identity of Prester John see Denison Ross, 'Prester John and the Kingdom of Ethiopia', pp. 180–94; Crawford (ed.), *Ethiopian Itineraries* (various journeys of ecclesiastics to and from Jerusalem and Italy); Rey, *The Romance of the Portuguese in Abyssinia* (general); Lopez, *A Report of the Kingdome of Congo*, pp. 207–17; Cerulli, 'Eugenio IV egli Ethiopi al consiglio di Firenze del 1441', pp. 347–68; Bellorini and Hoade (ed. and trans.), *Francesco Suriano* (journey of Franciscan friars from Jerusalem, pp. 94–100).

APPENDIX 1

Europeans in Egypt in the Reigns of the Mamluk Sultans up to 1517

Date arrived in Egypt	Details of travellers	Reigning sultan
1324	Symon Semeonis and Hugo from Ireland	Al-Nasir Muhammad I, third reign (1310–1341)
1350	Fra Niccolò, Franciscan friar from Poggibonsì	Al-Nasir al-Husan, first reign (1347–1351)
1384	Lionardo di Niccolò di Frescobaldi, Giorgio Gucci and Simone Sigoli from Tuscany	Al-Zahir Barquq deposed (1382–1389)
End of 14th century	Bertrando de Mignanelli, Damascus merchant from Siena	Al-Zahir Barquq restored (1390–1399)
1396	Emanuel Piloti, Venetian merchant from Crete	Al-Zahir Barquq restored (1390–1399)
1398	Nicolas de Martoni, notary from Carinola near Naples	Al-Zahir Barquq restored (1390–1399)
c. 1398	Cyriaco de'Pizzicoli, merchant and antiquarian from Ancona	Al-Mu'ayyad Shaykh (1412–1421)
1480	Brother Felix Fabri, pilgrim monk from Ulm	Al-Ashraf Qaitbay (1468–1496)
1480	Santo Brasca, nobleman from Milan	Al-Ashraf Qaitbay (1468–1496)
End of 15th century	Francesco Suriano, Franciscan friar of Mt Sion in Jerusalem	Al-Ashraf Qaitbay (1468–1496)
1503	Ludovico di Varthema, Venetian, son of a physician	Al-Ashraf Qansuh II al-Ghawri (1501–1516)
1512	Domenico Trevisan, ambassador from Venice, with his secretary Zaccaria Pagani	Al-Ashraf Qansuh II al-Ghawri (1501–1516)

APPENDIX 2

Europeans in Egypt in the Reigns of the Ottoman Sultans after 1517

Date arrived in Egypt	Details of travellers	Reigning sultan
1547	Pierre Belon du Mans, doctor and naturalist	Suleyman the Magnificent (1520–1566)
c. 1575	Anonymous Englishman, traveller with the Mecca caravan	Murad III (1574–1595)
1577	Filippo Pigafetta from Vicenza	Murad III (1574–1595)
1582	Prospero Alpini, doctor and naturalist from Padua	Murad III (1574–1595)
1588	Samuel Kiechel, German traveller from Ulm	Murad III (1574–1595)
1588	Baron Hans Christoph Teufel from Austria	Murad III (1574–1595)
1589	Voyage of the anonymous Venetian up the Nile	Murad III (1574–1595)
1589	Christopher Harant, nobleman from Prague	Murad III (1574–1595)
1604	Pietro della Valle, pilgrim from Rome	Ahmed III (1603–1617)
1606	Johann Wild, slave from Nuremberg	Ahmed III (1603–1617)
1639	John Greaves, Professor of Astronomy from Oxford	Murad IV (1623–1640)

Bibliography

Manuscripts and Works Published before 1800

Alpinus, P., *Historiae Naturalis Aegypti*, 1590

— *De Medicina Aegyptiorum*, Venice, 1592

— *De Balsamo Dialogus*, Venice, 1592

— *De Plantis Aegypti*, Venice, 1592

— *Rerum Aegiptiorum*, Leiden, 1735

Anon. (but thought to be D. Mellini), *Le dieci mascherate delle bufole mandate in Firenze il giorno di carnevale l'anno 1565*, Florence, Giunti, 1565

Belon, P., *De Arboris Coniferis Resiniferis, Alliis*, 4 vols, Paris, G. Caullet, 1553 (vol. II entitled *De Medicato Funere*)

— *De admirabilis operum antiquorum et rerum suspiciendarum praestantia*, Paris, 1553

— *Portraits d'Oyseaux, Animeaux, Serpens, Herbes, Arbres. Hommes et Femmes d'Arabie*, Paris, 1557

Brasca, Santo, *Viaggio alla sanctissima cita di Ierusalem*, Milan, P. Leonardus, U. Seinceler, 1481

Cyriaco of Ancona, Ms. Ashburnam, 1174 Florence, Biblioteca Med. Laurenziana

— Ms. Can. Lat. Misc. 2801 Oxford, Bodleian

Giovio, P., *Le iscrittione poste sotto le vere imagini de gli houmani famosi...*, Florence, 1557

— *Musaei Ioviani Imagines...*, Basel, 1557 (this edition has woodcuts by Theobald Mueller; No. 50 is of 'Magnus Caytbeius Memphicus Sultanus')

— *Gli elogi e vite brevemente scritte d'huomani illustri di guerra antichi e moderni...*, Florence, 1552

Greaves, J., *Pyramidiographia, or a Description of the Pyramids of Aegypt*, London, G. Badger, 1646

Hermes Trismegisti: Liber de Potestate et Sapienti Dei a graeco in Latinium traductus a M. Ficinus, dedicated to Cosimo de' Medici, Treviso, G. de Lise, 1471

Kircher, A., *Prodomus Coptus sive Aegyptiacus*, Rome, Congregazione de propoganda Fide, 1636

— *Lingua Aegyptiaca Restituta*, Rome, 1644

Leo Joannes Africanus, *Primo Volume delle Navigationi et Viaggi nel qual su Contiene la Descrittione dell'Africa et del Paese del Prete Ianni*, Venice, 1550

Lopez, O., *A Report of the Kingdome of Congo, a Region of Africa, Drawen Out of the Writings and Discourses of Odoardo Lopez by Filippo Pigafetta*, London, John Wolfe, 1597

Mandeville, J., *Tractato de le più Cose Meravigliose*, Milan, P. de Corneno, 1480

Mehus, L., *Kyriaco Anconitani Itinerarium*, Florence, 1742

Mercati, M., *De Gli obelischi di Roma*, Rome, D. Basa, 1589

Nicolay, N. de, *Les Navigations, Peregrinations et Voyages faictes en la Turquie...* Anvers, 1576

Pigafetta, F., *Relatione diReame di Congo et delle Circonvicine Contrade Tratta dalle Scritti et Ragionamaenti di Odoardo Lopez Portoghese con Disegni Vari di Geografia, di Piante, d'Habit, i d'Animali, et Altro*, Rome, Grassi, 1591

Ptolemaeus, Claudius, *Cosmographia*, Vicenza, 1475

Ramusio, G.B., *La descrittione dell' Africa di Giovan Lioni Africanus. Delle navigatioui et Viaggi*, 3 vols, Venice, L. Giunti, 1554–59

Sandys, G., *A Relation of a Journey Began Anno Domini 1616*, London, W. Barratt, 1615

Sigoli, S., *Viaggio di Terra Santa*, Florence, Bib. Riccardiana, ms. 1998 (no date)

Torcellus Sanutus, Marinus, *Liber Secretum Fidelium Crucis*, Florence, Bib. Riccardiana, ms. 237

Valle, P. della, *Viaggi di Pietro della Valle il Pellegrino...divisi in tre parti, cioè La Turchia, La Persia, e l'India*, 3 vols, Rome, Vitale Mascardi, 1650

Works Published after 1800

Almagia, R., *Il Mappamondo di Fra Mauro*, Rome, Istituto Poligrafico dello Stato, Libreria dello Stato, 1956

al-Maqrizi, *Histoire des sultans mamlouks de l'Egypte écrite en arabe par Takieddin-Ahmed-Katerizi*, trans. Etienne Quatremère, 2 vols, Paris, 1837–45

Ashmole, B., 'Cyriac of Ancona', *Proceedings of the British Academy*, 45, 1959, pp. 25–41

Ashtor, E., 'Le Coût de la Vie dans l'Egypte Medievale', *JESHO*, 6, 1960, pp. 59–72

— 'Volume of Levantine Trade in the Later Middle Ages 1370–1498', *JEEH*, 4, 1975, pp. 573–612

— *A Social and Economic History of the Near East in the Middle Ages*, London, Collins, 1976

— 'Spice Prices in the Near East in the 15th Century', *JRAS*, 1976, pp. 28–41

— *Studies in the Levantine Trade in the Later Middle Ages*, London, Variorum Reprints, 1978. See especially 'The Venetian Supremacy in Levantine Trade: Monopoly or Pre-Colonialism?', pp. 5–53

Atiya, A.S., 'An Unpublished XIVth Century *Fatwa* on the Status of Foreigners in Mamluke Egypt and Syria', in *Studien zur Geschichte und Kultur des Nahen und Fernen Ostens, Paol Kayle*, Leiden, E.J. Brill, 1935, pp. 55–68

Ayalon, D., 'The Plague and its Effects upon the Mamluk Army', *JRAS*, 1946, pp. 67–73

— *The Mamluk Military Society*, collected studies, London, Variorum Reprints,

1979
— 'Furusyya Exercises and Games in the Mamluk Sultanate', in *The Mamluk Military Society*, pp. 45–57
— *L'Esclavage du Mamelouk*, Oriental Notes and Studies 1, Jerusalem, 1951
— Studies in al-Jabarti 1, 'Notes on the Transformation of Mamluk Society in Egypt under the Ottomans', *JESHO*, 1960, pp. 148–74; 275–325
Babinger, F., 'Lorenzo de' Medici e la corte ottomana', in *Archivio Storico Italiana*, XXI, Florence, Olschi, 1963
Badia, I. del (ed.), *Luca Landucci: A Florentine Diary from 1455–1516*, London, 1927
Bagrow, L., and R.A. Skelton, *A History of Cartography*, London, 1964
Baines, J., and J. Malek, *Atlas of Ancient Egypt*, Oxford, Phaidon, 1980
Ball, J., *Egypt in the Classical Geographers*, Cairo, Government Publication, 1942
Balog, P., 'The Coinage of the Mamluk Sultans of Egypt and Syria', in *Numismatic Studies*, XII, New York, American Numismatic Society, 1964
Barozzi, N. (ed.), *Zaccaria Pagani, Viaggio di Domenico Trevisan Ambasciatore Veneto al Gran Sultano del Cairo nell'anno 1512*, Venice, 1875
Bates, E.S., 'Mohammedan Europe', in *Touring in 1600* (introd. G. Bull), London, Century, 1987, pp. 183–239
Beckingham, C.F., *Between Islam and Christendom: Travellers, Facts and Legends in the Middle Ages*, London, Variorum Reprints, 1983
Beckingham, C.F, and G. Hungerford (eds.), *Some Records of Ethiopia 1593–1646: Extracts from the History of High Ethiopia or Abassia by M. de Almeida, Together with Bahrey's History of the Galla*, Series 2, London, Hakluyt, 1954
Bellorini, T., and E. Hoade (ed. and trans.), *Fra Niccolò of Poggibonsi: A Voyage Beyond the Seas, 1346–50*, Jerusalem, Publications Studium Biblicum Franciscanum, 4, 1948
— *Visit to the Holy Places of Egypt, Sinai, Palestine and Syria in 1384, by Frescobaldi, Gucci and Sigoli*, Jerusalem, Publications Studium Biblicum Franciscanum, 6, 1948
— *Francesco Suriano, Treatise on the Holy Land*, Jerusalem, Publications Studium Biblicum Franciscanum, 8, 1983
Beer, R., 'The Development of the Guide Book until the Early XIX Century', *JBAA*, 3, 1952
Berattino, G., G. Boaglio, A. Bongioanni, and A. Rolla (eds.), *In Egitto Prima di Napoleone: Viaggio della Palestina, Egitto e Sacro Monte Siinai fatto da' Pietro Lorenzo Pincia...1719, 1720, 1721*, Turin, Galleria del Libro, 1998
Braudel, F., *The Wheels of Commerce*, 2 vols, London, Collins, 1982
Breccia, E., *Alexandria ad Aegyptum*, Bergamo, 1922
Brejnik, C., and A. Brejnik (ed. and trans.), *Voyage en Egypt de Christophe Harant de Polzic et Bezdruzdic*, Cairo, IFAO, 1972
Breydenbach, B. von, *Perigrinatio in Terra Sanctum*, Mainz, Peter Schoffer for Erhard Renwich, facs. repr., 1986
Brock, E. van den, *The Myth of the Phoenix According to Classical and Early*

Christian Texts, Leiden, E.J. Brill, 1972

Bull, G. (ed. and trans.), *Vasari's Lives of the Artists*, Harmondsworth, Penguin, 1971

— *The Pilgrim: The Travels of Pietro della Valle*, London, Hutchinson, 1989

Burton, R., *Narrative of a Pilgrimage to El-Medinah and Meccah* (introd. J. Scott), Geneva, Heron Books, Edito Service

Burmester, O.H.K., *A Guide to the Ancient Coptic Churches of Cairo*, Cairo, Société d'Archéologie Copte, 1955

Bushnaq, I. (ed. and trans.), *Arab Folk Tales*, New York, Penguin, 1987

Butler, A.J., *Butler's Lives of the Saints*, Tunbridge Wells, Burns & Oates, 2000

— *The Ancient Coptic Churches of Egypt*, Oxford, Oxford University Press, 1970

Byron, E., *Genoese Shipping in the 12th and 13th Centuries*, New York, Medieval Academy of America, 1970

Cerulli, E., 'Eugenio IV egli Ethiopi al consiglio di Firenze del 1441', *Rende Accad. Lincei e di Sc. Morali*, 4.9, 1933, pp. 347–68

Colin, J., *Cyriaque d'Ancone: Le voyageur, le marchand, l'humaniste*, Paris, 1981

Colvin, S., *A Florentine Picture Chronicle*, London, Roxburghe Club, 1898

Cragg, F.A., *An Italian Portrait Gallery*, Boston, 1935

Crawford, O.G.S. (ed.), *Ethiopian Itineraries ca. 1400–1524*, Cambridge, Cambridge University Press and Hakluyt Society, 1956

— 'Some Medieval Theories About the Nile', *Geographical Journal*, 114, 1949, pp. 25–37

Creques, A., and J. Creques, *Carta nautico geografia de 1375 de los mallorquines, denominado Atlas Catalan, Servicio Geografico del Ejercto de Madrid*, in *Richardo Cerezo Martinex La Cartografia Nautico Espanola en los Siglos, XIV, XV, XVI*, Madrid, 1973

Cresswell, K., *A Brief History of the Mohammedan Monuments of Egypt to A.D. 1517*, Cairo, IFAO, 1919

Creswell, A.C., *The Muslim Architecture of Egypt*, 2 vols, Oxford, Clarendon Press, 1952, 1959

Cust, R.H.H., *The Pavement Masters of Siena 1369–1562*, London, Bell, 1901

Dannenfeldt, K., 'Egypt and Egyptian Antiquities in the Renaissance', *Studies in the Renaissance*, 6, 1959, pp. 12–24

Davies, H.W.M., *Bernhard von Breydenbach and his Journey to the Holy Land*, London, 1911

Dawood, N., *The Thousand and One Nights*, London, Penguin, 1955

Dawson, W.R., 'Refences to Mummification by Greek and Latin Authors', *Aegyptus*, 9, 1928, pp. 106–12

Day, J., *The Medieval Market Economy*, Oxford, Oxford University Press, 1987

Demus, O., *The Mosaics of San Marco Venice*, Chicago, Dumbarton Oaks, 1988

Denison Ross, E., 'Prester John and the Kingdom of Ethiopia', in A.P. Newton (ed.), *Travels and Travellers in the Middle Ages*, London, Kegan Paul, 1926, pp. 174–94

Description de l'Egypte, ed. G. Néret, Cologne, Benedikt Taschen, 1967 (facs. repr. of 1st edn, Paris, Imprimerie Impériale, 1809)

Dilke, O., and M. Dilke, 'Marin Sanudo – Was he a Great Mapmaker?', in *The Map Collector*, Vol. 39, Tring, Map Collector Publications, 1982, pp. 29–34

Dioxiadis, E., *The Mysterious Fayum Portraits: Faces from Ancient Egypt*, London, Thames and Hudson, 1995

Dopp, P.H. (ed.), *L'Egypte au commencement du quinzième siècle d'après le traité d'Emmanuel Piloti de Crete incipit 1420*, Cairo, University Fuad I, 1950

d'Onofrio, C., *Gli Obelischi di Roma*, 2nd edn, Rome, 1965

Dorigato, A., *Murano Glass Museum*, Milan, Electra, 1986

Edwards, A., *A Thousand Miles up the Nile*, London, Century Hutchinson, 1982

Edwards, I., *The Pyramids of Egypt*, Harmondsworth, Penguin, 1962

Empereur, J.-Y., *Alexandria Rediscovered*, London, British Museum Press, 1998

Encyclopedia of Islam, Leiden, E.J. Brill, 1993

Esposito, M. (ed.), *Itinerarium Symon Semeonis am Hibernia ad Terra Sanctum*, Scriptoris Latini Hyberniae, 4, Dublin, 1960

Evans, A. (ed.), *Francesco Pegolotti, La Practica della Mercatura*, Cambridge, MA, Harvard University Press, 1936

Fischel, W., 'The Spice Trade in Mamluk Egypt', *JESHO*, 1958, pp. 154–74

— *Jews in the Economic and Political Life of Medieval Islam*, London, Royal Asiatic Society, 1937

Fischel, W. (ed. and trans.), 'Ascensus Barcoch – A Latin Biography of the Mamluk Sultan Barquq of Egypt (d. 1399), written by B. de Mignanelli in 1416', *Arabica*, 6, 1959, pp. 57–74, 152–72

Forster, E.M., *Alexandria: A History and a Guide*, New York, Doubleday, 1961

— *Pharos and Pharillon*, London, Michael Haag, 1983

Fraser, P., *Ptolemaic Alexandria*, 3 vols, Oxford, Oxford University Press, 1972

Fulin, R., 'Il Canale di Suez e la Repubblica di Venezia', *Archivio Veneto*, 2, 1871, pp. 175–99

Gabra, G., and A. Alcock, *Cairo: The Coptic Museum and Old Churches*, Cairo, Egyptian International Publishing Co., 1993

Garcin, J.-C., 'The Regime of the Circassian Mamluks', in C. Petry (ed.), *Islamic Egypt (The Cambridge History of Egypt*, I), Cambridge, Cambridge University Press, 1998

Geramb, M.J., *Pélérinage à Jerusalem et au Mont Sinai*, 3 vols, Paris, 1839

Gibb, H.A.R. (ed.), *Ibn Battuta, Travels in Asia and Africa, 1325–1354*, London, Routledge and Kegan Paul, 1983

Gindici, P., *Niccolò di Poggibonsi, Viaggio in Terra santa, descritto da un anonimo trecentista*, Bologna, 1867

Giovio, P., *Catalogue for the 5th Century of his Birth 1433–1983*, Como, Fondi Archivistici Gioviani, 1983

Glubb, J., *Soldiers of Fortune: The Story of the Mamalukes*, New York, Stein and Day, 1973

Golubovich, G., *Biblioteca Bibliografica della Terra Santa e dell'oriente Francescano*, 5 vols, Tipografia di Collegio di S. Bonaventura, Quarachi, Florence, 1906–27 (vol. III 1300–1332, vol. IV 1338–1345, vol. V 1346–1400)

Haag, M., *Discovery Guide to Cairo*, London, Michael Haag, 1990

Hakluyt, R. (ed), Anon., 'A Description of the Yearley Voyage or Pilgrimage of the Mahomitans, Turks and Moores into Mecca in Arabia', in R. Hakluyt, *The Principal Navigations, Voyages, Trafiiques and Discoveries of the English Nation Made by Sea or Overland to the Remote and Furthest Distant Quarters of the World*, III, London, J.M. Dent, 1927, pp. 167–97

Harris, R., 'Medicine', in R. Harris (ed.), *The Legacy of Egypt*, 2nd edn, Oxford, Clarendon Press, 1971, pp. 130–37

Hattox, R., *Coffee and Coffee Houses: The Origins of a Social Beverage in the Medieval Near East*, Seattle, University of Washington Press, 1991

Heers, J., *Gênes au XVe Siècle*, Affaires et Gens d'Affaires, 24, Paris,1961

Heyd, W., *Histoire du Commerce du Levant au Moyen-Age*, trans. F. Reynaud, 2 vols, Leipzig, 1885–86 (repr. Amsterdam, 1967)

Hildebrand, C., *The Crusades: Islamic Perspectives*, Edinburgh, Edinburgh University Press, 1999

Holt, P.M., 'The Treaties of the Early Mamluk Sultans with the Frankish States', *BSOAS*, 43, 1980, pp. 67–76

— *The Age of the Crusades: The Near East from the Eleventh Century to 1517*, New York, Longman, 1986

Honey, W.B., *Glass: A Handbook for the Study of Glass Vessels of All Periods*, London, Victoria and Albert Museum, 1946

Hyde, J., 'Navigation in the Eastern Mediterranean According to Pilgrim's Books', *Papers in Italian Arch. 1, the Lancaster Seminar Part 1, BAR supplementary series 41*, 1, 1978, pp. 521–40

Inalci, R., *The Ottoman Empire: The Classical Age 1300–1600*, London, Phoenix, 1997

Irwin, R., *The Middle East in the Middle Ages: The Early Mamluk Sultanate 1250–1382*, London, Croom Helm, 1986

— *The Arabian Nights: A Companion*, London, Allen Lane, 1994

Iverson, E., 'The Hieroglyphic Tradition', in J. Harris (ed.), *The Legacy of Egypt*, Oxford, Oxford University Press, 2nd edn, 1971, pp. 170–97

Jacquet, J., 'Des couveuses artificiels au sixième siècle de notre era', in *Homages à Serge Sauneron*, II, Cairo, IFAO, 1979, pp. 165–74

Janssen, J., 'Athanase Kircher Egyptologue', *Chronique d'Egypte*, 36, 1943, pp. 240–41

Jones, M. (ed.), *The New Cambridge Medieval History*, VI, c.1300– c.1415, Cambridge, Cambridge University Press, 2000 (see especially Part 1, P. Spufford, 'Trade in Fourteenth-Century Europe', pp. 155–208)

Kamil, J., *The Monastery of Saint Catherine in Sinai*, Cairo, 1996

Kimble, G.H.T., *Memoirs on the Catalan World Map of the Royal Biblioteca Estense at Modena*, London, Royal Geographical Society, 1934

— *Geography in the Middle Ages*, New York, Russell and Russell, 1968

Lane, E.W., *The Modern Egyptians*, London, J.M. Dent, 1936

Lane, F.C., *Venetian Ships and Ship Builders of the Renaissance*, Baltimore, Johns Hopkins University Press, 1934

— *Andrea Barbarigo, Merchant of Venice, 1418–49*, Baltimore, Johns Hopkins

University Press, 1944

— *Fleets and Fairs: The Functions of the Venetian Muda*, Studi in honori di Armando Sapori, 2 vols, Milan, 1956

— *The Merchant Marine of the Venetian Republic in Venice and History*, Baltimore, Johns Hopkins University Press, 1966

Lapidus, I., *Muslim Cities in the Late Middle Ages*, Cambridge, MA, Harvard University Press, 1984

Latham, R. (trans.), *The Travels of Marco Polo*, Harmondsworth, Penguin, 1972

Leclerc, L., *Histoire de la Médecine Arabe*, 2 vols, Paris, 1876

Legrand, L., 'Relation du Pélérinage à Jerusalem de Nicolas de Martoni', *Revue de l'Orient Latin*, 3, 1895, pp. 566–669

Lehmann, P., *Cyriacus of Ancona's Egyptian Visit*, New York, 1977

Lepschy, A.L.M. (ed.), *Viaggio in Terrasanta di Santo Brasca 1480 con l'Itinerario di Gabriele Capodilista 1458*, I Cento Viaggi, 4, Milan, Longanesi, 1966

Lestringant, F. (ed. and introd.), *Voyages en Egypte des Années 1549–1552*, Cairo, IFAO, 1984 (contains André Thevet's *Cosmographie de Levant* and *Cosmogrophie Universelle*)

Letts, M., *Sir John Mandeville, the Man and his Book*, London, Batchworth, 1949

Letts, M. (ed.), *Mandeville's Travels*, London, Hakluyt, 1953

Letts, M. (ed. and trans.), *The Pilgrimage of Arnold von Harff from Cologne*, London, Hakluyt, 1946

Levanoni, A., *A Turning Point in Mamluk History: The Third Reign of al-Nasr Muhammad 1310–1341*, Leiden, E.J. Brill, 1995

Lewis, B., 'The Contribution to Islam', in J.R. Harris (ed.), *The Legacy of Egypt*, 2nd edn, Oxford, Oxford University Press, 1971, pp. 456–77

— *The Arabs in History*, Oxford, Oxford University Press, 1993

— *The Muslim Discovery of Europe*, London, Phoenix, 1994

— *The Middle East*, London, Weidenfeld and Nicolson, 1996

Lyster, W., *The Citadel of Cairo: A History and Guide*, 2nd edn, Cairo, The Palm Press, 1993

Maalouf, A., *The Crusades through Arab Eyes*, Cairo, Al Saqi Books, 1984

Mandowsky, E., and C. Mitchell, *Pirro Ligorio's Roman Antiquities*, London, Warburg Institute, 1963

Mansel, P., *Constantinople, City of the World's Desire, 1453–1924*, London, Penguin Books, 1997

Mayer, L.A., *Mamluk Costume: A Survey*, Geneva, Albert Kundig, 1952

Meinhardus, O., *Monks and Monasteries of the Egyptian Deserts*, Cairo, American University in Cairo Press, 1961

— 'An Examination of the Traditions Pertaining to the Relics of St Mark', *Orientalia Christiana Periodica*, 36, 1970, pp. 348–76

— *The Holy Family in Egypt*, Cairo, American University in Cairo Press, 1986

Mitchell, C., 'Ex Libris Kiriaci Anconitani', *Italia medievale e ummanistica*, 5, 1962, pp. 282–99

Mitchell, R., *The Spring Voyage*, London, John Murray, 1964

Monneret de Villard, U., 'La prima esplorazione archeologica dell'alto Egitto',

Bull. de la Société Royale de Géographie d'Egypte, 17, 1929, pp. 19–48

Morani, J. (ed.), *Del Viaggio in Terra Santa di Mariano di Sienna*, Florence, 1822

Morelli, J., *Dissertazione intorno ad alcuni viaggiatori eruditi veneziana poco noti*, Venice, 1803

Morris, J., *Venice*, London, Faber & Faber, 1961

— *The Venetian Empire*, London, Faber & Faber, 1980

Müntz, E., 'Le musée de portraits de Paul Jove', *Memoirs de l'Academie des inscriptions et belles-lettres*, 36.2, 1900–1901

Newett, M., *Pilgrimage of Canon Casola*, Manchester, Manchester University Press, 1907

Norwich, J., *A History of Venice*, London, Penguin, 1986

Origo, I., *The Merchant of Prato, Francesco di Marco Datini*, London, Penguin, 1986

Papaioannou, E., *The Monastery of St Catherine Sinai*, Cairo, Isis Press, 1980

Parlasca, K., *Mumienporträts und Verwandte Denkmäler*, Wiesbaden, F. Steiner Verlag, 1966

Peters, L., *The Hajj: The Muslim Pilgraimage to Mecca and the Holy Places*, Princeton, NJ, Princeton University Press, 1994

Petrie, W.F., *Pyramids and Temples of Gizeh*, London, 1893

Petry, C., *The Civilian Elite of Cairo in the Later Middle Ages*, Princeton, NJ, Princeton University Press, 1981

— 'Late Mamluk Military Institution and Innovation', in Petry (ed.), *Islamic Egypt*, pp. 464–85

Petry, C. (ed.), *Islamic Egypt* (*Cambridge History of Egypt*, I), Cambridge, Cambridge University Press, 1998

Pettigrew, T.D., *A History of Egyptian Mummies*, London, 1834

Pigafetta, F., 'Further Travels of Filippo Pigafetta with Anton Maria Ragone', in *Viaggio di Anton Maria Ragona in Francia, Inghiliterra e Spagna negli anni MDLXXXII*, Viaggi inediti, Bib. civ. Bertoliana Gonz. 5954, Vicenza, 1878

Popper, K., *Egypt and Syria under the Circassian Sultans 1382–1466 A.D.: Systematic Notes to Ibn Taghri Berdi's Chronicles of Egypt*, University of California Publications in Semitic Philology, 15, Berkeley, University of California, 1955

Prescot, H., *Jerusalem Journey*, London, Eyre and Spottiswoode, 1954

— *Once to Sinai*, Cambridge, Cambridge University Press, 1957

Quatremère, M. (trans.), *Al-Maqrizi: Histoire des Sultans Mamlouks d'Egypt*, 2 vols, Paris, 1837

Raymond, A., and G. Weit (ed. and trans.), *Les Marchés du Caire*, Textes Arabes et Etudes Islamiques, 14, Cairo, IFAO, 1979

Rey, C.L., *The Romance of the Portuguese in Abyssinia*, London, Witherby, 1929

Roberts, D., *A Journey in Egypt*, Florence, Casa Editrice Bonechi, 1994

Rodenbeck, M., *Cairo*, London, Picador, 1998

Röhricht, R., *Biblioteca Geografia Palestinae*, Berlin, 1890 (lists 570 narratives of pilgrims AD 300–1500)

Röhricht, R. (ed.), 'Liber Perigrinationis Fr. Jacobi de Verona 1335', *Revue de l'Orient Latin*, 3, 1895, pp. 155–230

Rovelli, L., *Paolo Giovio nella storia e nell' arte*, Como, 1952

Runciman, S., *A History of the Crusades*, 3 vols, Cambridge, Penguin, 1978

Russell, J.C., 'The Population of Medieval Egypt, *JARCE*, 5, 1966, pp. 69–82

Sandys, J., *A History of Classical Scholarship from the 6th Century to the End of the Middle Ages*, 3 vols, Cambridge, Cambridge University Press, 1921

Sauneron, J. (ed.), *Voyage en Egypte de Pierre Belon du Mans 1547*, Cairo, IFAO, 1970

— *Voyage en Egypte du Vénitien Anonyme 1589*, Cairo, IFAO, 1970

— *Voyage en Egypte de Jean Palerne Forestien 1581*, Cairo, IFAO, 1971

— *Voyages en Egypte Pendant les Années 1587–1588, S. Kiechel, H. Teufel*, Cairo, IFAO, 1972

Schio, A. da (introd.), *Filippo Pigafetta, Viaggio da Creta in Egitto ed al Sinai 1576–1577*, facs. ms. Malacarne, Vicenza, Biblioteca Civica Bertoliana di Vicenza, 1984

Seif, O., *Khan al-Khalili: A Comprehensive Mapped Guide to Cairo's Historic Bazaar*, Cairo, American University in Cairo Press, 1993

Seton Williams, M.V., and P. Stocks (eds), *Blue Guide Egypt*, 2nd edn, London, A. & C. Black, 1988

Shaw, M. (ed. and trans.) *Joinville and Villehardoun, Chronicles of the Crusades*, London. Penguin, 1963, pp. 201–64

Silliotti, A. (ed.), *Viaggiatori Veneti alla Scoperta dell' Egitto: Cataloga della Mostra da Rassegna Internazionale di Cinematografia Archeologica, Verone*, Venice, 1985

Simpson, W.K. (ed. and introd.), *The Literature of Ancient Egypt*, London, Yale University Press, 1973 (*The Shipwrecked Sailor*, pp. 50–56)

Smith, R. (ed.), *Medieval Muslim Horsemanship: A Fourteenth-Century Arab Cavalry Manual*, London, British Library, 1979

Spufford, P., *Power and Profit: The Merchant in Medieval Europe*, London, Thames & Hudson, 2002

Stevenson, E.L., 'Genoese World Map 1457', in *Stevenson and Fisher World Maps*, New York, Hispanic Society of America, 1912, p. 83

Stewart, A. (ed. and trans.), *The Book of Wanderings of Brother Felix Fabri c.AD 1480–1483*, London, Palestine Pilgrims' Text Society, 1893

— *Ludolphus de Suchen: Ludolph von Suchen's Description of the Holy Land*, London, Palestine Pilgrims' Text Society, 1895

— *Marino Sanuto's Secrets for True Crusaders*, Part XIV of Book III, London, Palestine Pilgrims' Text Society, 1896

Suys, E., 'Un Vénitien en Egypte et en Nubie au XVIième siècle', *Chronique d'Egypte*, 22, 1933, pp. 51–63

Thompson, D., *Mummy Portraits from the Paul Getty Museum*, Malibu, CA, Paul Getty Museum, 1982

Van Essen, C.C., 'Cyriaque d'Ancone en Egypte', *Mededelingen der Koninklijke Nederlanse Akademie van Wetenschappen, Afd Letterkunde* NR 21, 22, 1958.

van Gennep, A., 'Le Ducat Vénitien en Egypte', *Revue Numismatique*, Ser. 4, 1,

1897, pp. 373–81, 494–506

Varthema, L. di, *Travels in Egypt, Syria and Arabia* AD *1503–1508*, London, Hakluyt, 1863

Vecellio, C., *Vecellio's Renaissance Costume Book*, New York, Dover, 1977

Volkoff, O., 'À la Recherche de Manuscrits en Egypte', *Recherches d'Archéologie de Philologie et d'Histoire*, 30, 1970, pp. 45–47

Volkoff, O. (ed.), *Le voyage en Egypte de Johann Wild 1606–1610*, Cairo, IFAO, 1970

Voraigne, J. de, *The Golden Legend* (trans. W. Caxton), Cambridge, Cambridge University Press, 1914

Vyse, H., *The Pyramids of Gizeh*, 2 vols, London, 1840

Wansburgh, J., 'A Mamluk Ambassador to Venice in 913/1507', *BSOAS*, 26, 1963, pp.503–29

— 'Venice and Florence in the Mamluk Commercial Privileges', *BSOAS*, 28, 1965, pp. 483–95

Weit, G., 'Les marchands d'épices sous les sultans mamlouks', *Cahiers d'historie Égyptienne*, 7, 1955, pp. 69–82

Weit, G. (trans.), *Ibn Iyas, Histoire des Mamlouks circassien*, Cairo, 1945

Whitehouse, H., 'Egyptology and Forgery in the Seventeenth Century: The Case of the Bodleian Shabti', *Journal of the History of Collections*, 12, 1989, pp. 187–95

— 'Towards a Kind of Egyptology: The Graphic Documentation of Ancient Egypt, 1587–1666', in E. Cropper and G. Perrini (eds), *Documentary Culture: Florence and Rome from Grand Duke Ferdinand I to Pope Alexander VI*, Villa Spelman Colloquie, III, Bologna, Nuovo Alfa, 1992, pp. xxii–xxiii, 65–73

Wilson, C.W. (trans.), *Behâ Ed-Din (*AD *1137–1193): Life of Saladin*, London, Palestine Pilgrims' Text Society, 1897

Winter, M., *Egyptian Society under Ottoman Rule, 1517–1798*, Cambridge, MA, Harvard University Press, 1967

— 'Ottoman Occupation', in C. Petry (ed.), *Islamic Egypt*, pp. 493–506

Wolff, A., 'Two Pilgrims to St Catherine's Monastery, Niccolò di Poggibonsi and Christopher Harant', in J. Starkey and O. El-Daly (eds), *Desert Travellers: From Herodotus to T.E. Lawrence*, Durham, Astene, 2000, pp. 33–58

Wright, J.K., *Geographical Lore of the Time of the Crusades*, American Geographical Society Research Series, New York, American Geographical Society, 1925

Ziegler, P., *The Black Death*, London, Penguin, 1998

Zurla, P. (ed.), *Di Marco Polo e degli altri viaggiatori...*, 2 vols, Venice, 1818 (vol. II contains *Viaggi di Pietro della Valle il Pelegrino mandate in Napoliall all' erudito e fra piu cari* di molti *anni suo amico Mario Schapiro*, Rome, Vitale Mascardi, 1650)

Index

suspicious nature of 250
trade alliance with France 126,
246
women *131*

Padua University 69
medical school 69
Pagani, Zaccaria 94, 95, 155, 156–7,
160, 161, 162
Palestine 7, 8, 130, 204
Palladio (architect) 272
pallone (game) 54
panfano (long armed boat) 51
Paris 71
Pasqaligo, Francesco 153
Paul of Chaneto 281–2
Paul, St 44
Paulo the Greek 180
Pegolotti, Francesco Balducci 68, 80,
183
Pelagus, Cardinal 47
pepper 66, 246
Persians 107, 123
Peter, Abbot of Cluny 10
Peter Lusignan, King of Cyprus 67–8,
70
Pharaoh's rat *88, 89*
pharmacy 26
pharos, Alexandria 63–4
Philae, island of 268–9
phoenix 46–7
Piero, Alviso de 153
Pigafetta, Antonio 90
Pigafetta, Filippo 90–4, 99–100, 117–
19, 123, 134, 136, 142–3, 177–9,
183–4, 208–9, 215–16, 234, 236
Pigafetta, Matteo 90–1
pigeon post 81
'Pilgrims' Staircase' 221
pilgrims/pilgrimages (Christian) 49,
54, 56–60, 97–102, 104, 125, 126,
139–42, 149, 180, 282
as adventure 8
in Alexandria 71–4, 75–6, 79–80,
81–2

Classical knowledge of 63
equipment 57
finances 56–7, 80
of St Catherine's monastery 79, 97,
195–231
casualties 198
difficult conditions faced by
195–6
heat of 202–3
hygiene 196
journey times 208
merchant caravans 203–4, 229
the monastery 209–20
price for safe conduct 196, 197
provisions 197–8, 203
untrustworthy guides 206–7
water supplies 198, 204
wildlife 204–5
pilgrims/pilgrimages (Muslim), *hajj*
233–49
Piloti, Emanuel 17–19, 26, 31, 66,
70, 75, 83, 84–5, 100, 101, 114–15,
134, 135, 201
pirates 51–2
Pisa 7, 59
Pisani, Vettor 3
plague 52, 86, 114–15, 180, 247
Plato 45, 63
Pliny 9, 61, 103, 167, 170, 174
Plotinus 63
Poggibonsi, Niccolò di 49–51, 96,
141, 196, 197, 204–5, 207–8,
210, 212, 213–14, 216, 217, 220,
221–5
Pola (cog) 75–6, 79, 80, 81
polo 19, 20–4
Polo, Marco 9, 10, 46, 48
Pompey's Pillar 86–7, *87*
Ponte, Antonio da 272
Portugal 66–7, 272, 277, 280
postal service 6, 81
Potiphar 43
poultry rearing 100–1
Prester John (Ethiopian emperor) 76,
272, 273–4, 275–82, *276*, *279*